The **SSAT** Course Book

MIDDLE & UPPER LEVEL

VERBAL

SUMMIT
EDUCATIONAL
GROUP

Focusing on the Individual Student

Copyright Statement

The SSAT Course Book, along with all Summit Educational Group Course Materials, is protected by copyright. Under no circumstances may any Summit materials be reproduced, distributed, published, or licensed by any means.

Summit Educational Group reserves the right to refuse to sell materials to any individual, school, district, or organization that fails to comply with our copyright policies.

Third party materials used to supplement Summit Course Materials are subject to copyright protection vested in their respective publishers. These materials are likewise not reproducible under any circumstances.

Ownership of Trademarks

Summit Educational Group is the owner of the trademarks "Summit Educational Group" and the pictured Summit logo, as well as other marks that the Company may seek to use and protect from time to time in the ordinary course of business.

SSAT is a trademark of the Enrollment Management Association.

All other trademarks referenced are the property of their respective owners.

Copyright ©2018 Summit Educational Group, Inc.

ISBN: 978-0-692-13316-3

CONTENTS

TEST-TAKING FUNDAMENTALS

SYNONYMS

ANALOGIES

VOCABULARY

ANSWER KEY

Preface

Since 1988, when two Yale University graduates started Summit Educational Group, tens of thousands of students have benefited from Summit's innovative, comprehensive, and highly effective test preparation. You will too.

Successful test-takers not only possess the necessary academic skills but also understand how to take the SSAT. Through your SSAT program, you'll learn both. You'll review and develop the academic skills you need, and you'll learn practical, powerful and up-to-date test-taking strategies.

The *Summit SSAT Course Book* provides the skills, strategies, and practice necessary for success on the SSAT. The result of much research and revision, this book is the most effective, innovative and comprehensive preparation tool available.

The book is separated into chapters. The first chapter – Test-Taking Fundamentals – gives students a solid foundation of SSAT information and general test-taking strategies. Some of the more important topics covered include question difficulty, scoring, and avoiding attractors.

The next chapters correspond to the main strands of the SSAT Verbal content – Synonyms, Analogies, Reading, and Writing. Each chapter is divided into manageable topic modules. Modules consist of the skills, strategies, and common question types for particular topics, several *Try It Out* questions, and several *Put It Together* questions. The questions progress in order of difficulty. At the end of each chapter, homework questions provide additional practice.

We are confident that you will not find a more complete or effective SSAT program anywhere.

We value your feedback and are always striving to improve our materials. Please write to us with comments, questions, or suggestions for future editions at:

edits@mytutor.com

Your program will give you the skills, knowledge, and confidence you need to score your best.

Good luck, and have fun!

Chapter Summaries

We've reproduced the Chapter Summaries below to give you a preview of what you'll be covering. The Summaries are meant to serve as quick, condensed reference guides to the most important concepts. Obviously, you can't bring them into the test with you, but from now up until the night before the test, use them to preview and review the material covered in this book. Of course, Chapter Summaries also reside at the end of each chapter.

General Test-Taking Summary

❑ Your SSAT preparation will focus on learning strategies and strengthening core skills.

Your responsibilities include doing 1-2 hours of homework per session and learning as much vocabulary as you can.

Except for the Reading Comprehension, groups of questions progress from easy to difficult.

❑ Know your limits. Put your time and energy into the problems you are most capable of answering. If you struggle with difficult problems or with finishing sections in time, spend more of your time on the easy and medium problems and less time on the difficult problems.

❑ Never leave an easy problem blank. On an easy problem, an answer that instinctively seems right usually is.

❑ Avoid attractors. The test writers predict potential mistakes by students and include those mistakes as answer choices.

❑ If you can certainly eliminate at least two answers, you should guess from the remaining answer choices. The more answers you can eliminate, the greater advantage you have.

❑ On a multiple-choice test, the answer choices can provide you with further ammunition to solve the problem. Don't get stuck trying to find an answer with a certain method. If you can't solve the problem in the forward direction, try to solve in the reverse direction by using the answer choices.

Synonyms

❑ Format/Directions

Synonym questions make up the first 30 of the 60 Verbal questions on the SSAT. The questions go from easy to difficult.

❑ Before looking at the answer choices, define the stem word. If the stem word is familiar to you, try to come up with a definition of your own.

Choose the answer that most closely resembles your definition.

❑ Consider alternate meanings – Sometimes, your definition of the stem word won't fit the answer choices because a secondary definition (a less common meaning for the word) is being tested.

❑ Parts of speech are consistent – Knowing the stem word's part of speech will help you figure out what definition is called for. Since parts of speech will always be consistent between the stem word and the answer choices, you can look to the answers to help you figure out what part of speech is being used.

❑ Match the tone of words. Even if you can't define a word, you may have a sense of whether it's a positive or negative word.

Determine whether each answer choice is positive or negative and eliminate the ones that don't match the stem word. Put a "+" or a "–" next to the words to keep track. You can then guess from the remaining choices.

Keep in mind that some words are not necessarily positive or negative.

❑ Avoid answers that are related to the stem word but are not synonyms. Some questions, especially medium and difficult ones, will contain incorrect answer choices that are there to steer you away from the correct answer. We call these answer choices attractors because they "attract your attention."

❑ Use word roots to determine meaning. Sometimes, a stem word may look like a word you know; it may be a different form of the word, or a related word. Using your knowledge of word roots, you can sometimes figure out the meanings of unknown words.

Analogies

❑ Format/Directions

The verbal section of the SSAT has one set of 30 analogies. They appear after the 30 synonym questions. The questions go from easy to difficult.

❑ The key to solving an analogy is to determine what the relationship is between the paired words.

❑ Clearly state the relationship. Don't just look at the words and say "I know that these words are related." The more clearly you can state the relationship, the easier the analogy problem becomes.

❑ State the relationship as a complete sentence. Think of a short sentence that contains both of the stem words and defines one of the words in terms of the other. Consider how you would explain the connection between the stem words to a friend.

You can start the relationship with the first or second word. However, make sure you keep the same order when applying the stem relationship to the answers.

❑ Use the same relationship for each answer choice. Connect each pair of answer choices using the same relationship as you use to connect the stem words. Don't change the stem relationship to make it correspond to the relationship between a pair of answer choice words.

❑ Consider secondary definitions. If you cannot make sense of an analogy, check for alternate meanings of the stem words, such as when a words is used as a different part of speech.

Parts of speech are consistent in analogies. For example, if one of the first words in a pair is an adjective, all the other first words are also adjectives.

❑ Be specific. If the relationship you make yields two or more correct answers, make the relationship more specific or detailed. This should allow you to eliminate answer choices.

❑ Familiarize yourself with common analogy relationship types.

❑ Look out for different analogy structures. Occasionally, it will be the first and third words that are related, instead of the first two. We call these "First and Third" analogies. If you cannot determine a solid relationship between the first pair of words in an analogy, this is a good clue that it might be a "First and Third" analogy.

❑ Avoid answers that are related to the stem word but are not analogous.
Some analogies will contain answer choices that stand out because they contain words related to one or both of the stem words. Be careful not to choose these unless the answer choice has the same relationship as the stem.

Remember, you want to maintain the relationship between the two stem words.

❑ If you are stuck, eliminate answers. When you don't know the meaning of a stem word, you can still solve an analogy problem by eliminating answer choices. If you can eliminate at least two answer choices, make your best guess from the remaining choices!

❑ Answers must have clear relationships. Your first step when you are stumped by one of the stem words should be to look for the answer choice relationship(s) that are concise and clear. If you can't form a clear relationship, eliminate the answer choice.

❑ If you are stuck, apply the relationships in answer choices to stem words.
Take each answer choice and define one word in terms of the other. Test the relationship on the stem. Pick the answer choice whose relationship seems to work best.

Reading Comprehension

❏ Format/Directions

The SSAT contains one Reading Comprehension section. This section is 40 minutes and has 40 questions.

❏ Be an active reader. Never expect a passage to interest or entertain you. You have to get into it, on your own. Reading is not a passive experience. It's something you do actively. Don't wait to see what a passage says; go get it!

❏ Summarize and make connections. Restate phrases, sentences, and paragraphs in your own words. This will help you understand and remember what you have read.

❏ As you read, analyze the passage and ask questions:

What topic is the author writing about?

What type of passage is it?

What is the author's purpose?

What is the main idea of each paragraph?

What will come next?

❏ Underline or write down the main ideas of each paragraph. Marking the passage will force you to search actively for the important points, and it will also help keep your mind from wandering as you read.

❏ Don't try to retain every detail in the passage. Instead, try to develop a mental "picture" of the passage, so you'll know where to look to answer specific questions.

❏ Break the passage down into its parts. As you read, try to follow the path of the passage as it shifts from point to point. Pay attention to the first and last sentence in each paragraph as they will often announce the transition from one point to the next. Mark with a check in the margin where each shift takes place.

❏ Consider how parts of passage work together. After you finish a paragraph or supporting point, ask yourself how it fits into the overall main idea. For example, does that part of the passage introduce an idea, use examples to support an idea, compare things, are bring up a counterpoint?

❑ Don't waste too much time on a difficult sentence or word. There probably won't be a question on it. If you do get a question about the sentence or word, you can go back and figure it out then. You'll likely be more able to understand a difficult sentence or word when you go back with more knowledge of the passage.

❑ Before looking at the answer choices, try to think of the answer in your head.
Try not to look at the answer choices until you know what the answer should be. Then find the answer that most closely matches your anticipated one.

❑ Avoid "could be" answers. On many SSAT reading questions, there are multiple answer choices that could be correct, but there is only one best answer. If you try to test if you can prove the answer choices correct, you might get stuck with several answers that seem right. Instead, focus on finding your own best answer first.

❑ Eliminate answers which are too broad, too narrow, or simply incorrect. As you read through the possible answers, eliminate answer choices that:

- cover more than the passage does.

- talk only about a portion of the passage.

- have nothing to do with the discussed topic.

❑ For an answer choice to be correct, it must be entirely correct. Do not get stuck on answer choices that are only partly right.

❑ Answering the Questions

Main idea questions ask for the main idea or author's opinion. Anticipate the answer to main idea questions. Eliminate answers that are too broad, too narrow, or simply wrong.

Vocabulary questions ask you to define a word as it is used in context.

Defend your answer to detail questions with information from the passage.

Inference questions ask you to draw conclusions based on what is written. Do not expect the answer to be explicitly stated in the passage.

On except/least/not questions, find which answer choice doesn't fit with the others.

Use process of elimination to solve Roman numeral questions.

Writing

❑ Format/Directions

"Schools would like to get to know you better through an essay or story using one of the two topics below. Please select the topic you find most interesting and fill in the circle next to the topic you choose."

The writing sample is not scored, but is sent directly to admissions committees.

Typically, writing sample readers are checking that your writing is focused and well-organized. Make sure that you express your thoughts clearly.

The writing sample is an opportunity for you to show something about yourself.

❑ Creative or Formal?

The Middle Level SSAT will let you choose between two creative prompts.

The Upper Level SSAT will let you choose between a creative and a formal prompt.

❑ Preparing to Write

Plan before you begin writing. Create an outline to guide you through the writing and make sure you manage your time.

❑ Creative

The setup is used to introduce characters, describe settings, and establish situations. This usually comes first because it is needed in order to understand the rest of the story.

The confrontation is the main source of drama and tension in the story. Stories need some type of problem or conflict. This can be a personal desire, a disagreement, a difficult challenge, etc.

The resolution shows the outcome of the story. This is where the characters make important decisions, where relationships break apart or come together, where heroes succeed and problems are finally resolved.

❑ Formal

The introduction establishes the main idea and focus of your essay. It includes your thesis, which is your essay's central argument or point.

The body is used to explain your argument and describe how your examples support that argument.

The conclusion summarizes your essay and connects it back to your main idea.

Assessment and Objectives Worksheet

Complete this worksheet after the first session and refer back to it often. Amend it as necessary. It should act as a guide for how you and your tutor approach the program as a whole and how your sessions are structured.

Please be honest and open when answering the questions.

Student's Self-Assessment and Parent Assessment

- How do you feel about taking standardized tests? Consider your confidence and anxiety levels.

- Work through Table of Contents or Chapter Reviews. Are there particular areas that stand out as areas for development?

- Other Concerns

Diagnostic Test Assessment

- Pacing

  o Did you run out of time on any or all sections? Did you feel rushed? Look for skipped questions or wrong answers toward the end of sections.

  o How will the concept of Setting Your Goal help you?

- Carelessness

  o Do you feel that carelessness is an issue? Look for wrong answers on easy questions.

  o Why do you think you make careless mistakes? Rushing? Not checking? Not reading the question carefully? Knowing "why" will allow you to attack the problem.

- Are certain areas for development evident from the diagnostic? Work through the questions you got wrong to further identify areas that might require attention.

Program Objectives

Consider your assessment, and define your objectives. Make your objectives concrete and achievable.

Objective*	How to Achieve the Objective

*Sample Objectives

Objective	How to Achieve the Objective
Reduce carelessness by 75%.	Before starting to work on a question, repeat exactly what the question is asking.
Use Active Reading skills to avoid losing focus while reading passages.	Practice reading skills every day. Read novels or magazines at an appropriate reading level. Ask questions and engage the text while you read.
Reduce test anxiety.	Build confidence and create a detailed testing plan. Start with easier questions to build confidence and slowly build toward more challenging questions. Take pride in successes and continue to reach for goals. Try to relax.
Learn how to write a cohesive essay in a limited time.	Practice timed writing. Ensure I can effectively use paragraphs to structure my ideas.
Get excited about the test prep.	Stay positive. Know that score goals can be achieved. Learn tricks to beat the test. Make the test like a game. Focus on progress.

SUMMIT
EDUCATIONAL
GROUP

Test-Taking Fundamentals

About the SSAT

❑ The SSAT is used to determine acceptance into private or independent schools. The test is designed to measure students' academic potential and skills in relation to the rest of the private and independent school applicants. Because this group of test-takers is especially competitive and skilled, the test is designed to be highly challenging.

A student's performance on the SSAT is <u>not</u> designed to reflect the scores on typical school exams or grades.

The importance of this test is determined by each school's admission policies, so it is important to talk to your prospective schools as you plan your SSAT preparation.

❑ The SSAT is a "power" test, which means that its difficulty stems from how challenging its questions are rather than the challenge of a strict time constraint. Most students are able to move quickly enough to answer most of the questions on the SSAT, but the test has many tricks and traps to challenge them.

Over the course of this program, you are going to learn to recognize and overcome the SSAT's tricks and traps. You will master the SSAT by developing your test-taking abilities, working on fundamental SSAT skills, and practicing on real test questions.

❑ The SSAT is administered in two levels: the Middle Level and the Upper Level. Students who are currently in grades 5 through 7 take the Middle Level test, and students who are currently in grades 8 through 11 take the Upper Level test.

Your Responsibilities

❑ You will have about 1-2 hours of homework each session. You are expected to complete every assignment. Remember, your hard work will result in a higher score!

❑ Your scores on the verbal and reading portions of the test are determined in large part by your vocabulary and reading skill. Use flash cards, study the word groups, and read, read, read! The more you read and the more vocabulary you learn, the higher your score will be.

SSAT Structure

Writing Sample – 25 minutes

Quantitative – 30 minutes

												MATHEMATICS												
1	2	3	4	5	6	7	8	9	10	11	12	13	14	15	16	17	18	19	20	21	22	23	24	25
EASY						→						MEDIUM					→				DIFFICULT			

Reading Comprehension – 40 minutes

																READING PASSAGES																							
1	2	3	4	5	6	7	8	9	10	11	12	13	14	15	16	17	18	19	20	21	22	23	24	25	26	27	28	29	30	31	32	33	34	35	36	37	38	39	40
NOT IN ORDER OF DIFFICULTY																																							

Verbal – 30 minutes

														SYNONYMS															
1	2	3	4	5	6	7	8	9	10	11	12	13	14	15	16	17	18	19	20	21	22	23	24	25	26	27	28	29	30
EASY							→						MEDIUM						→					DIFFICULT				

														ANALOGIES															
31	32	33	34	35	36	37	38	39	40	41	42	43	44	45	46	47	48	49	50	51	52	53	54	55	56	57	58	59	60
EASY							→						MEDIUM						→					DIFFICULT				

Quantitative – 30 minutes

												MATHEMATICS												
1	2	3	4	5	6	7	8	9	10	11	12	13	14	15	16	17	18	19	20	21	22	23	24	25
EASY						→						MEDIUM					→				DIFFICULT			

❑ An official SSAT contains an additional section, not shown above, known as the "Experimental Section." This is used as a trial for new test questions, and your results are <u>not</u> used to calculate your score.

The Experimental Section contains 16 questions and is 15 minutes long. It can contain any type of question from the SSAT.

Scoring

❑ The SSAT scoring method is a complex system that is designed to best reflect each student's standing within the very competitive group of SSAT students.

❑ **Every question on the SSAT is worth one raw score point**. Therefore, the easiest question is worth just as much as the most difficult question. There are no points for skipped questions. Each incorrect answer results in a ¼ point deduction from the points that have been earned. **The total number of correct answers, minus the total penalty for incorrect answers, is the *raw score*.**

❑ Your raw score is converted to a *scaled score* for each section. **The raw score for each SSAT section is scaled to adjust for varying difficulty among the different editions of the test**. The SSAT is scaled on a bell curve so that the majority of students achieve middling scores.

For the Upper Level test, the scaled score for each section falls between 500 and 800. For the Middle Level test, the scaled score falls between 440 and 710. You will also receive a total scaled score, which is the sum of the section scores.

❑ You will receive percentile scores for each section that tell how you performed with respect to other students in your grade. For example, a score of 55 means you did as well as or better than 55% of students who also took the SSAT. Your percentile score ranks you among all students who have taken the test in your grade over the past three years. In general, your **percentile is the most important score**.

Your percentile might seem quite low because you are being compared to other students applying to independent schools, which is a very competitive and well-educated group. Within this group, achieving a high rank requires a great level of skill and preparation.

❑ Your writing sample is not scored, but is sent directly to the admissions committees of the schools to which you apply. Many schools consider your writing skills as a factor for admission and may want to see how well you write under test conditions.

Knowing Your Limits

❑ Put your time and energy into the problems you are most capable of answering. If you struggle with difficult problems or with finishing sections in time, spend more of your time on the easy and medium problems and less time on the difficult problems. Here's why:

- Because your percentile scores reflect your <u>grade level</u> performance, you may not need to answer every question to score well. If you are at the lower end of the grade spectrum, this means you may be able to omit several questions and still score well.

- You'll minimize mistakes on difficult questions, which often contain attractor or trap answers.

- You'll be less hurried, and you'll make fewer careless mistakes.

❑ Push your limits.

As you prepare for the SSAT, try to learn from the questions that give you trouble. Note your mistakes and make sure that you don't repeat them. Pay attention to the questions that are the most difficult and note what makes them so challenging and how to solve them.

As your skills improve, you will be able to answer more and more of the questions on the SSAT. You will learn to recognize tricks and traps and work with more speed and confidence.

Setting Your Verbal Goal

❑ Using your diagnostic results and previous test scores, set a realistic score goal.

❑ Unlike a school test where you might need to get 90% of the questions right to get a good score, you might need only 60% to reach your score goal on the SSAT.

❑ The following conversion tables are based on data for 8th grade students taking the Upper Level SSAT. Note that the scoring scale can vary significantly between different SSAT tests. Therefore, these conversion tables cannot always be accurate.

VERBAL SCORE CONVERSION		
Raw Score	Scaled Score	Percentile Rank
15	615	23
16	620	26
17	625	29
18	630	31
19	635	34
20	641	37
21	646	40
22	651	43
23	656	47
24	662	50
25	667	53
26	671	55
27	675	57
28	681	61
29	687	65
30	692	68
31	696	70
32	700	72
33	705	74
34	711	77
35	717	79
36	720	81
37	723	83
38	726	84
39	730	85
40	735	87
41	742	89
42	750	91
43	757	93
44	763	94
45	767	95

Setting Your Verbal Range

❑ Your range is the number of questions you need to attempt in order to achieve your goal.

For many students, answering every problem on the SSAT will prevent them from scoring to their potential. Attempting every question on the SSAT means you'll have to rush (which can lead to careless mistakes) and you'll make mistakes on difficult questions. Because of the penalty for incorrect answers, you should know your limits and stay within your range.

❑ Use the Goal and Range tables below to determine your approximate range for each section

VERBAL GOAL & RANGE			
Raw Goal	Questions to Attempt	Questions You Can Skip	Questions You Can Miss
20	37	23	14
25	41	19	13
30	45	15	12
35	49	11	11
40	52	8	10
45	55	5	8
50	57	3	6
55	59	1	3
60	60	0	0

MY VERBAL PLAN OF ATTACK

My Raw Score Goal: _____   Questions to Attempt: _____

Questions to Skip: _____   Missable Questions: _____

❑ Note you don't have to evenly split your skipped questions between Synonyms and Analogies. Take advantage of your strengths and minimize the impact of your weaknesses.

Setting Your Reading Goal

❑ Using your diagnostic results and previous test scores, set a realistic score goal.

❑ Unlike a school test where you might need to get 90% of the questions right to get a good score, you might need only 60% to reach your score goal on the SSAT.

❑ The following conversion tables are based on data for 8th grade students taking the Upper Level SSAT. Note that the scoring scale can vary significantly between different SSAT tests. Therefore, these conversion tables cannot always be accurate.

READING SCORE CONVERSION		
Raw Score	Scaled Score	Percentile Rank
15	619	26
16	623	29
17	628	32
18	635	37
19	643	42
20	651	47
21	657	51
22	662	56
23	667	59
24	672	63
25	681	68
26	685	72
27	690	76
28	700	81
29	706	85
30	711	87
31	716	90
32	721	92
33	730	95
34	737	97
35	745	97
36	751	98
37	757	98
38	761	99
39	781	99
40	800	99

Setting Your Reading Range

❑ Your range is the number of questions you need to attempt in order to achieve your goal.

For many students, answering every problem on the SSAT will prevent them from scoring to their potential. Attempting every question on the SSAT means you'll have to rush (which can lead to careless mistakes) and you'll make mistakes on difficult questions. Because of the penalty for incorrect answers, you should know your limits and stay within your range.

❑ Use the Goal and Range tables below to determine your approximate range for each section

READING GOAL & RANGE			
Raw Goal	Questions to Attempt	Questions You Can Skip	Questions You Can Miss
15	31	9	13
20	34	6	11
25	36	4	9
30	37	3	6
35	39	1	3
40	40	0	0

MY READING PLAN OF ATTACK

My Raw Score Goal: _____   Questions to Attempt: _____

Questions to Skip: _____   Missable Questions: _____

❑ Unlike in other SSAT sections, questions in the Reading section do not get progressively difficult. You may choose to skip the especially tough questions as you encounter them or skip an entire passage that is challenging and time-consuming.

Beating the SSAT

❑ Never leave an easy problem blank.

On an easy problem, an answer that instinctively seems right usually is. When the test writers construct a standardized test, they keep in mind the average student. They want the average student to answer the easy problems correctly and the difficult problems incorrectly.

Do not make the early problems harder than they really are. If all else fails, go with your hunch.

❑ Avoid attractors.

The test writers predict potential mistakes by students and include those mistakes as answer choices. In other words, they set traps for the unsuspecting student. We call these answer choices "attractors." Attractors show up most often on medium and difficult problems.

Try the following Synonym question, and look for attractors.

EXHAUSTIVE:

(A) tired
(B) polluted
(C) thorough
(D) extreme
(E) excessive

This is a difficult synonym. Notice how (A) and (B) attract your attention because both *tired* and *polluted* seem related to *EXHAUSTIVE*. It's easy to think of exhausted or exhaust, as in car exhaust. But *EXHAUSTIVE* has a different meaning: *thorough*. The correct answer is (C).

TRY IT OUT

Try to spot the attractor answer choices in the following problems.
Consider how a student might mistakenly choose each attractor answer.

1. Sword is to sheath as arrow is to

    (A) bull's eye
    (B) dart
    (C) gun
    (D) quiver
    (E) heart

Making Your Best Guess

❑ If you can certainly eliminate at least two answers, you should guess from the remaining answer choices. The more answers you can eliminate, the greater advantage you have.

Once you have eliminated an answer, cross it out in the test booklet. This prevents you from wasting time looking at eliminated answers over and over.

Note: Be careful using the guessing strategy on the difficult problems. When you eliminate an answer, be absolutely sure you have a legitimate reason for doing so. Once you've eliminated all the answers you can, guess from the remaining answer choices.

> Assume you don't know how to solve the following analogy problem.
> Which answer choices should you eliminate and why?
>
> Empathetic is to compassion as:
>
> (A) pitiful is to caring   _____
>
> (B) psychic is to energy   _____
>
> (C) insistent is to payment   _____
>
> (D) obsessive is to direction _____
>
> (E) contemptuous is to disdain _____

❑ To prove to yourself that eliminating answer choices and guessing helps your score, cover the answers at the bottom of the page and try the following exercise.

On the following 20 questions, assume you have correctly eliminated answer choices B and D. Try to guess the right answer for each question by filling in an oval for each.

1. Ⓐ ⊗ Ⓒ ⊗ Ⓔ
2. Ⓐ ⊗ Ⓒ ⊗ Ⓔ
3. Ⓐ ⊗ Ⓒ ⊗ Ⓔ
4. Ⓐ ⊗ Ⓒ ⊗ Ⓔ
5. Ⓐ ⊗ Ⓒ ⊗ Ⓔ
6. Ⓐ ⊗ Ⓒ ⊗ Ⓔ
7. Ⓐ ⊗ Ⓒ ⊗ Ⓔ
8. Ⓐ ⊗ Ⓒ ⊗ Ⓔ
9. Ⓐ ⊗ Ⓒ ⊗ Ⓔ
10. Ⓐ ⊗ Ⓒ ⊗ Ⓔ
11. Ⓐ ⊗ Ⓒ ⊗ Ⓔ
12. Ⓐ ⊗ Ⓒ ⊗ Ⓔ
13. Ⓐ ⊗ Ⓒ ⊗ Ⓔ
14. Ⓐ ⊗ Ⓒ ⊗ Ⓔ
15. Ⓐ ⊗ Ⓒ ⊗ Ⓔ
16. Ⓐ ⊗ Ⓒ ⊗ Ⓔ
17. Ⓐ ⊗ Ⓒ ⊗ Ⓔ
18. Ⓐ ⊗ Ⓒ ⊗ Ⓔ
19. Ⓐ ⊗ Ⓒ ⊗ Ⓔ
20. Ⓐ ⊗ Ⓒ ⊗ Ⓔ

\# RIGHT   _____

−¼ × (# WRONG)   _____

= RAW SCORE   _____

Unless you were extremely unlucky, you probably received a positive raw score (versus zero if you had chosen to leave these questions blank), and, of course, a higher raw score means a higher scaled score and percentile rank.

Answers to above exercise:

1. C   2. A   3. E   4. A   5. A   6. C   7. E   8. C   9. A   10. E

11. A   12. C   13. E   14. E   15. C   16. E   17. A   18. C   19. E   20. A

Using the Answer Choices

❑ On a multiple-choice test, the answer choices can provide you with further ammunition to solve the problem. Don't get stuck trying to find an answer with a certain method. If you can't solve the problem in the forward direction, try to solve in the reverse direction by using the answer choices.

> Ratify is to repeal as
>
> (A) inhabit is to repeat
> (B) decay is to depress
> (C) violate is to frighten
> (D) disperse is to reject
> (E) adore is to detest
>
> This might seem impossible if you don't know what ratify and repeal mean. If you use your answer choices, however, you can figure it out. Look at each answer choice, keeping in mind that any correct analogy pair must have a clearly defined relationship between the two words.
>
> Inhabit and repeat aren't connected at all. Eliminate (A).
>
> There's no relationship between these words. Eliminate (B).
>
> The words sound good together, but you can't define a relationship between them. It can't be (C).
>
> The words don't relate. Eliminate (D).
>
> Adore means not to detest. This is a good possibility.
> Pick (E). This word pair forms the most concise and clear relationship of all the answer choices. And as we'll see in the Analogies chapter, the correct word pair must always form a concise and clear relationship.

General Tactics

❑ Focus on one question at a time.

The SSAT is timed, so it's normal to feel pressure to rush. Resist the temptation to think about the 10 questions ahead of you or the question you did a minute ago. Relax and focus on one question at a time. Believe it or not, **patience** on the SSAT is what allows you to work more quickly and accurately.

❑ Carefully read and think about each question.

Before you jump to the answers, start scribbling things down, or do calculations, make sure you understand exactly what the question is asking.

❑ In SSAT problems, every bit of information is important and useful.

❑ Write in your test booklet.

When you're ready to solve the problem, use the space in your test booklet. Cross out incorrect answers, write down calculations to avoid careless errors, summarize reading passages, etc. Write down whatever will help you solve the problem.

❑ Memorize the format and instructions before you take the test. At test time, you can skip the instructions and focus on the problems.

Chapter Review

❑ General Test-Taking

Your SSAT preparation will focus on learning strategies and strengthening core skills.

Your responsibilities include doing 1-2 hours of homework per session and learning as much vocabulary as you can.

Except for the Reading Comprehension, groups of questions progress from easy to difficult.

❑ Know your limits. Put your time and energy into the problems you are most capable of answering. If you struggle with difficult problems or with finishing sections in time, spend more of your time on the easy and medium problems and less time on the difficult problems.

❑ Never leave an easy problem blank. On an easy problem, an answer that instinctively seems right usually is.

❑ Avoid attractors. The test writers predict potential mistakes by students and include those mistakes as answer choices.

❑ If you can certainly eliminate at least two answers, you should guess from the remaining answer choices. The more answers you can eliminate, the greater advantage you have.

❑ On a multiple-choice test, the answer choices can provide you with further ammunition to solve the problem. Don't get stuck trying to find an answer with a certain method. If you can't solve the problem in the forward direction, try to solve in the reverse direction by using the answer choices.

SUMMIT
EDUCATIONAL
GROUP

Synonyms

General Information

❑ Format/Directions

Synonym questions make up the first 30 of the 60 Verbal questions on the SSAT. The questions go from easy to difficult.

❑ Directions are as follows:

> Each of the following questions consists of one word followed by five words or phrases. You are to select the one word or phrase whose meaning is closest to the word in capital letters.
>
> Sample Question:
>
> FRAGILE:
>
> (A) delicate
> (B) useless
> (C) broken
> (D) moody
> (E) careless
>
>

SSAT Structure

Writing Sample – 25 minutes

Quantitative – 30 minutes

MATHEMATICS																								
1	2	3	4	5	6	7	8	9	10	11	12	13	14	15	16	17	18	19	20	21	22	23	24	25
EASY						→			MEDIUM					→			DIFFICULT							

Reading Comprehension – 40 minutes

READING PASSAGES																																							
1	2	3	4	5	6	7	8	9	10	11	12	13	14	15	16	17	18	19	20	21	22	23	24	25	26	27	28	29	30	31	32	33	34	35	36	37	38	39	40
NOT IN ORDER OF DIFFICULTY																																							

Verbal – 30 minutes

SYNONYMS																													
1	2	3	4	5	6	7	8	9	10	11	12	13	14	15	16	17	18	19	20	21	22	23	24	25	26	27	28	29	30
EASY					→				MEDIUM				→			DIFFICULT													

ANALOGIES																													
31	32	33	34	35	36	37	38	39	40	41	42	43	44	45	46	47	48	49	50	51	52	53	54	55	56	57	58	59	60
EASY					→				MEDIUM				→			DIFFICULT													

Quantitative – 30 minutes

MATHEMATICS																								
1	2	3	4	5	6	7	8	9	10	11	12	13	14	15	16	17	18	19	20	21	22	23	24	25
EASY						→			MEDIUM					→			DIFFICULT							

Anticipate the Answer

❑ **Before looking at the answer choices, define the stem word.** If the stem word is familiar to you, try to come up with a definition of your own.

Choose the answer that most closely resembles your definition.

OBNOXIOUS:

(A) clear
(B) slick
(C) offensive
(D) odorous
(E) athletic

> Before looking at the answers, try to define *OBNOXIOUS* in your own words.
> For instance, you might say *OBNOXIOUS* means "rude."
> *Offensive* (C) is the choice that most closely matches "rude."

PROFANITY :

(A) trouble
(B) fame
(C) prediction
(D) expletive
(E) popularity

❑ You do not need an exact synonym or definition to anticipate the answer. If you have a phrase or a general idea that helps you understand the stem word, this may be enough to find the correct answer.

TRY IT OUT

On the following synonym exercises, write your own definition of the stem word in the space provided, and then pick the answer choice that most closely matches your definition:

1. RELIABLE: _____

    (A) stable
    (B) creative
    (C) useful
    (D) variable
    (E) truthful

2. LIBERATE: _____

    (A) generate
    (B) enslave
    (C) argue
    (D) release
    (E) support

3. OBEDIENCE: _____

    (A) obscenity
    (B) debacle
    (C) defiance
    (D) conformity
    (E) royalty

Secondary Definitions

☐ **Consider alternate meanings** – Sometimes, your definition of the stem word won't fit the answer choices because a secondary definition (a less common meaning for the word) is being tested.

> Train
>> *Train* can mean a locomotive, a part of a dress, or to teach.
>
> Match
>> *Match* can mean a fire starter, a round of a game, or to group similar items.
>
> Minute
>> *Minute* can be used as a unit of time or as an adjective to mean very small or tiny.

BOW :

(A) wish
(B) hush
(C) praise
(D) respect
(E) curtsy

☐ **Parts of speech are consistent** – Knowing the stem word's part of speech will help you figure out what definition is called for. Since parts of speech will always be consistent between the stem word and the answer choices, you can look to the answers to help you figure out what part of speech is being used. For example, if you notice that all of the answer choices are verbs, then the stem word is also a verb.

TRY IT OUT

Think of at least two meanings for each of the following words:

set   _____

run   _____

stand   _____

trail   _____

pen   _____

champion   _____

moral   _____

spring   _____

hamper   _____

revolution _____

PUT IT TOGETHER

1. BRIDGE:

    (A) connect
    (B) suspend
    (C) elevate
    (D) fell
    (E) digest

2. PROMPT:

    (A) timely
    (B) expelled
    (C) lax
    (D) candid
    (E) improvised

3. UNIFORM:

    (A) authoritative
    (B) consistent
    (C) restrictive
    (D) unprepared
    (E) shapeless

4. SCREEN:

    (A) window
    (B) light
    (C) page
    (D) code
    (E) test

5. CONSTITUTION:

    (A) government
    (B) tradition
    (C) health
    (D) revolution
    (E) belief

6. BASE:

    (A) protected
    (B) dishonorable
    (C) victorious
    (D) important
    (E) related

Positive or Negative

☐ **Match the tone of words.** Even if you can't define a word, you may have a sense of whether it's a positive or negative word.

Determine whether each answer choice is positive or negative and eliminate the ones that don't match the stem word. Put a "+" or a "−" next to the words to keep track. You can then guess from the remaining choices.

Keep in mind that some words are not necessarily positive or negative.

> −   DESPICABLE:
>
> −   (A) disdainful
> \+   (B) admirable
> \+   (C) responsible
> ±   (D) animated
> −   (E) horrible
>
>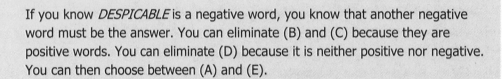
>
> If you know *DESPICABLE* is a negative word, you know that another negative word must be the answer. You can eliminate (B) and (C) because they are positive words. You can eliminate (D) because it is neither positive nor negative. You can then choose between (A) and (E).

☐ Checking whether words are positive or negative should NOT be your first strategy for synonyms questions. This is a backup strategy, and it should be used as a last resort when you cannot use other strategies because you don't know the meanings of the words.

TRY IT OUT

Put a + (for positive) or a – (for negative) next to each of the following words:

1. crass

2. caustic

3. beneficial

4. malice

5. squalor

6. paltry

7. vivacious

8. harmonious

9. ghastly

10. bountiful

PUT IT TOGETHER

1. BENEFICENT:

   (A) angry
   (B) sneaky
   (C) generous
   (D) attractive
   (E) majestic

2. NOXIOUS:

   (A) magnificent
   (B) religious
   (C) healthful
   (D) sinful
   (E) harmful

3. BANAL:

   (A) prolific
   (B) generous
   (C) eternal
   (D) soothing
   (E) bland

4. BENEVOLENT:

   (A) evil
   (B) veiled
   (C) sympathetic
   (D) anonymous
   (E) giving

5. DENOUNCE:

    (A) pronounce
    (B) defend
    (C) withstand
    (D) condemn
    (E) spur

6. MALICIOUS:

    (A) sadistic
    (B) upset
    (C) luscious
    (D) masterful
    (E) pathetic

Attractors

☐ **Avoid answers that are related to the stem word but are not synonyms.**
Some questions, especially medium and difficult ones, will contain incorrect answer choices that are there to steer you away from the correct answer. We call these answer choices attractors because they "attract your attention."

> BAZAAR:
>
> (A) oddity
> (B) market
> (C) publication
> (D) repository
> (E) deviation
>
> > (A) attracts your attention because *BAZAAR* looks and sounds like "bizarre," which means odd.
> > In fact, a *BAZAAR* is a market or marketplace, so (B) is correct.

> RENAISSANCE:
>
> (A) history
> (B) rebirth
> (C) festival
> (D) exploration
> (E) age
>
> > If you've studied the *RENAISSANCE* in history, or been to a *RENAISSANCE* fair, you might be tempted to pick (A), (C), or possibly (E).
> > (B) is the correct answer.

TRY IT OUT

Try to spot the attractors in the following synonym exercises. Why are they attractors?

1. FORTUNATE:

    (A) rich
    (B) golden
    (C) futuristic
    (D) lucky
    (E) protected

2. EXHAUSTIVE:

    (A) tired
    (B) thorough
    (C) polluted
    (D) mechanical
    (E) peculiar

3. BOMBASTIC:

    (A) explosive
    (B) destructive
    (C) pretentious
    (D) disastrous
    (E) ballistic

Roots

❑ **Use word roots to determine meaning.** Sometimes, a stem word may look like a word you know; it may be a different form of the word, or a related word. Using your knowledge of word roots, you can sometimes figure out the meanings of unknown words.

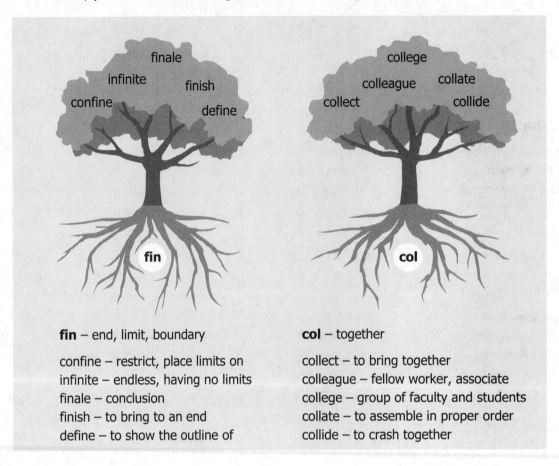

fin – end, limit, boundary

confine – restrict, place limits on
infinite – endless, having no limits
finale – conclusion
finish – to bring to an end
define – to show the outline of

col – together

collect – to bring together
colleague – fellow worker, associate
college – group of faculty and students
collate – to assemble in proper order
collide – to crash together

TRY IT OUT

For each of the following words, write a word of your own that seems related:

1. untimely   _____

2. alienate   _____

3. inexcusable   _____

4. vacuous   _____

5. malfunction   _____

6. detoxify   _____

7. inconsequential   _____

8. immovable   _____

9. beneficiary   _____

10. unobservant   _____

Now try to match the words to their definitions. Take your best guesses:

1) untimely		a)	unforgivable
2) alienate		b)	unimportant
3) inexcusable		c)	stationary
4) vacuous		d)	empty
5) malfunction		e)	inattentive
6) detoxify		f)	to remove poison
7) inconsequential		g)	failure
8) immovable		h)	to separate
9) beneficiary		i)	too early
10) unobservant		j)	person who receives profits or funds

PUT IT TOGETHER

1. EQUANIMITY:

    (A) nobility
    (B) level-headedness
    (C) sweetness
    (D) cowardice
    (E) imbalance

2. PREMATURE:

    (A) skillful
    (B) disorganized
    (C) hasty
    (D) backward
    (E) artificial

3. OPINIONATED:

    (A) clever
    (B) absurd
    (C) scarce
    (D) fierce
    (E) stubborn

4. POSTHUMOUS:

    (A) alongside
    (B) too late
    (C) appearing briefly
    (D) after death
    (E) with support

5. PREREQUISITE:
    (A) plan
    (B) equipment
    (C) estimation
    (D) necessity
    (E) glance

6. COLLOQUIAL:

    (A) conversational
    (B) organized
    (C) visiting
    (D) collected
    (E) friendly

Chapter Review

❏ Format/Directions

Synonym questions make up the first 30 of the 60 Verbal questions on the SSAT. The questions go from easy to difficult.

❏ **Before looking at the answer choices, define the stem word.** If the stem word is familiar to you, try to come up with a definition of your own.

Choose the answer that most closely resembles your definition.

❏ **Consider alternate meanings** – Sometimes, your definition of the stem word won't fit the answer choices because a secondary definition (a less common meaning for the word) is being tested.

❏ **Parts of speech are consistent** – Knowing the stem word's part of speech will help you figure out what definition is called for. Since parts of speech will always be consistent between the stem word and the answer choices, you can look to the answers to help you figure out what part of speech is being used.

❏ **Match the tone of words.** Even if you can't define a word, you may have a sense of whether it's a positive or negative word.

Determine whether each answer choice is positive or negative and eliminate the ones that don't match the stem word. Put a "+" or a "–" next to the words to keep track. You can then guess from the remaining choices.

Keep in mind that some words are not necessarily positive or negative.

❏ **Avoid answers that are related to the stem word but are not synonyms.**
Some questions, especially medium and difficult ones, will contain incorrect answer choices that are there to steer you away from the correct answer. We call these answer choices attractors because they "attract your attention."

❏ **Use word roots to determine meaning.** Sometimes, a stem word may look like a word you know; it may be a different form of the word, or a related word. Using your knowledge of word roots, you can sometimes figure out the meanings of unknown words.

Synonyms Practice – Middle Level

1. AUDIBLE:

   (A) capable of being eaten
   (B) capable of being taught
   (C) capable of being heard
   (D) capable of being seen
   (E) capable of being touched

2. DURATION:

   (A) short
   (B) survive
   (C) sneak
   (D) stand
   (E) span

3. TIRESOME:

   (A) exciting
   (B) absurd
   (C) tedious
   (D) useless
   (E) unruly

4. DEVOTED:

   (A) distant
   (B) fearful
   (C) patient
   (D) faithful
   (E) insane

5. TYPICAL:

   (A) beautiful
   (B) normal
   (C) tardy
   (D) dense
   (E) secure

6. HUMILIATE:

   (A) crash
   (B) verify
   (C) praise
   (D) trust
   (E) shame

7. EXPERT:

   (A) comedian
   (B) director
   (C) authority
   (D) inventor
   (E) sculptor

8. BENEFICIAL:

   (A) wicked
   (B) boring
   (C) observant
   (D) helpful
   (E) sensitive

9. FRANTIC:

   (A) massive
   (B) dejected
   (C) tepid
   (D) isolated
   (E) agitated

10. IMMENSE:

    (A) minute
    (B) pensive
    (C) antique
    (D) fictitious
    (E) colossal

11. COZY:

(A) cold
(B) easy
(C) snug
(D) careful
(E) shy

12. INTERIOR:

(A) entrance
(B) store
(C) inside
(D) terror
(E) paint

13. FLATTER:

(A) demolish
(B) praise
(C) mow
(D) insult
(E) desire

14. IDOLIZE:

(A) mimic
(B) adore
(C) uphold
(D) acquire
(E) survey

15. INTRICATE:

(A) harsh
(B) polite
(C) frustrating
(D) complicated
(E) perfect

16. MELODY:

(A) instrument
(B) spice
(C) weapon
(D) tune
(E) story

17. AUTHENTIC

(A) true
(B) desirable
(C) appropriate
(D) helpful
(E) copied

18. INCLEMENT:

(A) severe
(B) balmy
(C) leafy
(D) sadly
(E) graceful

19. SURLY:

(A) happy
(B) positive
(C) windy
(D) unfriendly
(E) soiled

20. NOVICE:

(A) secret
(B) ancient
(C) beginner
(D) thief
(E) expert

21. CULPRIT:

   (A) vessel
   (B) savage
   (C) felon
   (D) star
   (E) patron

22. PLACID:

   (A) serene
   (B) arrange
   (C) uneasy
   (D) location
   (E) ideal

23. AMBLE:

   (A) stroll
   (B) wager
   (C) desire
   (D) risk
   (E) disturb

24. CELEBRITY:

   (A) precision
   (B) scandal
   (C) haste
   (D) purity
   (E) renown

25. WRATH:

   (A) cover
   (B) twist
   (C) quiet
   (D) fury
   (E) folder

26. ELUDE:

   (A) mimic
   (B) support
   (C) avoid
   (D) fling
   (E) pursue

27. MUNDANE:

   (A) foolish
   (B) ordinary
   (C) cheerful
   (D) irate
   (E) promising

28. CONCEIT:

   (A) secret
   (B) modesty
   (C) honesty
   (D) ability
   (E) arrogance

29. RATTLE:

   (A) unnerve
   (B) brace
   (C) fasten
   (D) magnify
   (E) deliver

30. EXHIBIT:

   (A) deplete
   (B) inspect
   (C) vacate
   (D) feature
   (E) restrain

31. CATASTROPHE:

   (A) series
   (B) land
   (C) fever
   (D) animal
   (E) disaster

32. PECULIAR:

   (A) similar
   (B) unusual
   (C) particular
   (D) ready
   (E) angry

33. PROPEL:

   (A) tie down
   (B) push forward
   (C) hold up
   (D) leave out
   (E) fly away

34. SAVOR:

   (A) subtract
   (B) relish
   (C) prefer
   (D) maintain
   (E) assist

35. INSOLENT:

   (A) bankrupt
   (B) disrespectful
   (C) intelligent
   (D) rowdy
   (E) careless

36. HAMPER:

   (A) inquire
   (B) obstruct
   (C) resolve
   (D) imitate
   (E) persist

37. MANACLES:

   (A) staples
   (B) immigrants
   (C) relatives
   (D) tractors
   (E) fetters

38. LACKLUSTER:

   (A) clean
   (B) interesting
   (C) acceptable
   (D) dull
   (E) difficult

39. FEASIBLE:

   (A) relentless
   (B) possible
   (C) fraudulent
   (D) elaborate
   (E) measurable

40. INEVITABLE:

   (A) evasive
   (B) anxious
   (C) certain
   (D) hopeful
   (E) immaculate

41. PROFOUND:

   (A) close
   (B) intense
   (C) faint
   (D) pronounced
   (E) vanishing

42. CONFORM:

   (A) join
   (B) challenge
   (C) dictate
   (D) misuse
   (E) omit

43. GULLIBLE:

   (A) guilty
   (B) deceptive
   (C) blunt
   (D) tawdry
   (E) trusting

44. REFUTE:

   (A) attain
   (B) elevate
   (C) disclaim
   (D) jeer
   (E) recognize

45. AMBIGUOUS:

   (A) enlarged
   (B) ugly
   (C) sarcastic
   (D) vague
   (E) incomplete

46. EMULATE:

   (A) envy
   (B) copy
   (C) cast
   (D) transfer
   (E) mend

47. VULNERABLE:

   (A) visited
   (B) exposed
   (C) believable
   (D) dominated
   (E) portable

48. DISPERSE:

   (A) dismount
   (B) propel
   (C) spread
   (D) fasten
   (E) recoup

49. MONOTONY:

   (A) temperament
   (B) sameness
   (C) disbelief
   (D) concern
   (E) remorse

50. ECCENTRIC:

   (A) nonconformist
   (B) bitter
   (C) lofty
   (D) inhibited
   (E) casual

51. ELOQUENT:

   (A) uncertain
   (B) slippery
   (C) well-spoken
   (D) hesitant
   (E) confident

52. PETTY:

   (A) peevish
   (B) laughable
   (C) minor
   (D) stark
   (E) secret

53. ATTRIBUTE:

   (A) praise
   (B) attitude
   (C) fame
   (D) feature
   (E) remark

54. EXPEDITE:

   (A) travel
   (B) linger
   (C) hurry
   (D) stem
   (E) consent

55. HUMILITY:

   (A) embarrassment
   (B) humbleness
   (C) resourcefulness
   (D) sympathy
   (E) incompleteness

56. CANDID:

   (A) undone
   (B) forthcoming
   (C) unmerciful
   (D) unpleasant
   (E) unlikely

57. DEGENERATE:

   (A) support
   (B) designate
   (C) decay
   (D) bloom
   (E) beg

58. MEDIATE:

   (A) negotiate
   (B) measure
   (C) merit
   (D) blame
   (E) submerge

59. DETRIMENTAL:

   (A) injurious
   (B) compartmental
   (C) desperate
   (D) wholesome
   (E) influential

60. UNDERMINE:

   (A) tremble
   (B) dismay
   (C) corrode
   (D) repeal
   (E) explode

Synonyms Practice – Upper Level

1. INGENUITY:

    (A) denseness
    (B) happiness
    (C) stupidity
    (D) creativity
    (E) luck

2. PUNY:

    (A) jarring
    (B) ample
    (C) feeble
    (D) robust
    (E) odorous

3. BARBARIAN:

    (A) hairdresser
    (B) stranger
    (C) savage
    (D) inhabitant
    (E) spike

4. SOLITARY:

    (A) insulated
    (B) circular
    (C) intimate
    (D) isolated
    (E) sterile

5. INHABIT:

    (A) motivate
    (B) occupy
    (C) vanish
    (D) repress
    (E) drift

6. BELATED:

    (A) prompt
    (B) contented
    (C) tardy
    (D) gloomy
    (E) departed

7. TRANQUIL:

    (A) calm
    (B) noisy
    (C) striking
    (D) painful
    (E) lucky

8. RESIDENCE:

    (A) frame
    (B) dwelling
    (C) assembly
    (D) company
    (E) substance

9. JOVIAL:

    (A) argumentative
    (B) heavy
    (C) amiable
    (D) serious
    (E) melancholy

10. IRATE:

    (A) inspired
    (B) incensed
    (C) incisive
    (D) infatuated
    (E) insipid

11. TEDIOUS:

   (A) enthralling
   (B) hateful
   (C) monotonous
   (D) inferior
   (E) profound

12. UNIQUE:

   (A) systematic
   (B) singular
   (C) simple
   (D) stale
   (E) syrupy

13. VIRTUOUS:

   (A) essential
   (B) indecent
   (C) lethal
   (D) energetic
   (E) scrupulous

14. PROPEL:

   (A) sustain
   (B) hinder
   (C) consume
   (D) launch
   (E) annoy

15. LIABLE:

   (A) exempt
   (B) variable
   (C) favorable
   (D) responsible
   (E) considerate

16. AGITATE:

   (A) fluster
   (B) stabilize
   (C) hasten
   (D) inscribe
   (E) pacify

17. ARID:

   (A) extra
   (B) frigid
   (C) dry
   (D) visible
   (E) cautious

18. INTACT:

   (A) impaired
   (B) polished
   (C) skillful
   (D) tricky
   (E) whole

19. DEBRIS:

   (A) waste
   (B) injury
   (C) clothes
   (D) name
   (E) storm

20. WILY:

   (A) crafty
   (B) silly
   (C) scary
   (D) careful
   (E) dangerous

21. BOISTEROUS:

   (A) unruly
   (B) masculine
   (C) contaminated
   (D) irritating
   (E) tame

22. LUCID:

   (A) cloudy
   (B) novel
   (C) real
   (D) clear
   (E) intense

23. STATURE:

   (A) figure
   (B) standing
   (C) condition
   (D) structure
   (E) decree

24. CONTIGUOUS:

   (A) adjacent
   (B) proceed
   (C) include
   (D) regular
   (E) collect

25. VOLATILE:

   (A) disturb
   (B) preference
   (C) unstable
   (D) massive
   (E) steady

26. CHASM:

   (A) acquaintance
   (B) boundary
   (C) actuary
   (D) bough
   (E) abyss

27. CRONY:

   (A) witch
   (B) dowager
   (C) elevator
   (D) associate
   (E) traitor

28. RENOUNCE:

   (A) disavow
   (B) dispute
   (C) disclose
   (D) disappear
   (E) distress

29. REPLICA:

   (A) facsimile
   (B) substitute
   (C) response
   (D) democracy
   (E) original

30. ABHOR:

   (A) detest
   (B) cause
   (C) assemble
   (D) cherish
   (E) desist

31. REFUSE:

   (A) consent
   (B) evidence
   (C) beacon
   (D) neglect
   (E) debris

32. MOROSE:

   (A) dejected
   (B) detached
   (C) dependable
   (D) delighted
   (E) defective

33. MAR:

   (A) enhance
   (B) transport
   (C) orbit
   (D) erase
   (E) deface

34. PALATABLE:

   (A) tasty
   (B) polluted
   (C) ruined
   (D) insipid
   (E) sanitary

35. ABODE:

   (A) buttress
   (B) volume
   (C) stanza
   (D) residence
   (E) reception

36. RAVENOUS:

   (A) gratified
   (B) murky
   (C) putrid
   (D) famished
   (E) authentic

37. POSTERITY:

   (A) permanence
   (B) descendants
   (C) rear
   (D) attitude
   (E) ancestry

38. EXTOL:

   (A) expire
   (B) acclaim
   (C) admonish
   (D) include
   (E) entertain

39. OBSTINATE:

   (A) malleable
   (B) dogged
   (C) moderate
   (D) hesitant
   (E) animated

40. ASSIDUOUS:

   (A) critical
   (B) carefree
   (C) lax
   (D) industrious
   (E) excitable

41. OPULENT:

    (A) filthy
    (B) extravagant
    (C) mean
    (D) plausible
    (E) intimidating

42. CURTAIL:

    (A) distribute
    (B) cheat
    (C) decrease
    (D) wander
    (E) cheapen

43. REVERE:

    (A) model
    (B) exemplify
    (C) honor
    (D) revolt
    (E) humble

44. ZEALOUS:

    (A) stunned
    (B) anxious
    (C) prompt
    (D) blissful
    (E) passionate

45. DEBASE:

    (A) harden
    (B) devalue
    (C) detour
    (D) constrict
    (E) destroy

46. DESPONDENT:

    (A) hopeful
    (B) isolated
    (C) gloomy
    (D) absentminded
    (E) impatient

47. GREGARIOUS:

    (A) barren
    (B) solitary
    (C) outgoing
    (D) gorgeous
    (E) instinctive

48. PRECOCIOUS:

    (A) precious
    (B) gifted
    (C) childish
    (D) suspicious
    (E) unmanageable

49. AUSTERITY:

    (A) harshness
    (B) hospitality
    (C) concentration
    (D) wonder
    (E) irrationality

50. PRUDENT:

    (A) irrational
    (B) coordinated
    (C) doubtful
    (D) cautious
    (E) imposing

51. DISINCLINED:

   (A) resistant
   (B) disenchanted
   (C) glum
   (D) optimistic
   (E) minimal

52. SUPERFLUOUS:

   (A) flexible
   (B) seamless
   (C) excessive
   (D) minimal
   (E) flighty

53. EFFERVESCENT:

   (A) stunted
   (B) babbling
   (C) stagnant
   (D) high-spirited
   (E) crude

54. EMBELLISH:

   (A) take away
   (B) add to
   (C) reduce
   (D) explode
   (E) strain

55. IMPETUOUS:

   (A) steady
   (B) precise
   (C) sudden
   (D) monotonous
   (E) fragile

56. GARRULOUS:

   (A) gorgeous
   (B) long-winded
   (C) meek
   (D) svelte
   (E) flamboyant

57. DILATORY:

   (A) delegated
   (B) postponed
   (C) updated
   (D) transferred
   (E) canceled

58. SPURIOUS:

   (A) motivated
   (B) insecure
   (C) inauthentic
   (D) tricky
   (E) sincere

59. EXTRICATE:

   (A) skim
   (B) extinguish
   (C) liberate
   (D) erase
   (E) detain

60. FURTIVE:

   (A) nasty
   (B) sly
   (C) excessive
   (D) festive
   (E) disreputable

SUMMIT
EDUCATIONAL
GROUP

Analogies

General Information

❑ Format/Directions

The verbal section of the SSAT has one set of 30 analogies. They appear after the 30 synonym questions. The questions go from easy to difficult.

Directions are as follows:

> The following questions ask you to find relationships between words. For each question, select the answer choice that best completes the meaning of the sentence.
>
> Sample Question:
>
> > Cow is to bull as
> >
> > (A) rooster is to chicken
> > (B) goose is to gander
> > (C) pony is to horse
> > (D) frog is to toad
> > (E) dog is to cat
>
>
>
> Choice (B) is the best answer because a bull is a male cow just as a gander is a male goose. Of all the answer choices, (B) states a relationship that is most like the relationship between cow and bull.

❑ Some analogies will give you the first three words of the analogy in the question and one word in each answer choice.

> Marigold is to flower as piranha is to
>
> (A) Venus flytrap
> (B) tulip
> (C) shark
> (D) fish
> (E) ocean

SSAT Structure

Writing Sample – 25 minutes

Quantitative – 30 minutes

MATHEMATICS																								
1	2	3	4	5	6	7	8	9	10	11	12	13	14	15	16	17	18	19	20	21	22	23	24	25
EASY					→			MEDIUM				→			DIFFICULT									

Reading Comprehension – 40 minutes

READING PASSAGES																																							
1	2	3	4	5	6	7	8	9	10	11	12	13	14	15	16	17	18	19	20	21	22	23	24	25	26	27	28	29	30	31	32	33	34	35	36	37	38	39	40
NOT IN ORDER OF DIFFICULTY																																							

Verbal – 30 minutes

SYNONYMS																													
1	2	3	4	5	6	7	8	9	10	11	12	13	14	15	16	17	18	19	20	21	22	23	24	25	26	27	28	29	30
EASY					→			MEDIUM				→			DIFFICULT														

ANALOGIES																													
31	32	33	34	35	36	37	38	39	40	41	42	43	44	45	46	47	48	49	50	51	52	53	54	55	56	57	58	59	60
EASY					→			MEDIUM				→			DIFFICULT														

Quantitative – 30 minutes

MATHEMATICS																								
1	2	3	4	5	6	7	8	9	10	11	12	13	14	15	16	17	18	19	20	21	22	23	24	25
EASY					→			MEDIUM				→			DIFFICULT									

Defining the Relationship

❑ The key to solving an analogy is to determine what the relationship is between the paired words.

❑ **Clearly state the relationship.** Don't just look at the words and say "I know that these words are related." The more clearly you can state the relationship, the easier the analogy problem becomes.

> emerald is to gem
>> An *emerald* is a type of *gem*.

❑ **State the relationship as a complete sentence.** Think of a short sentence that contains both of the stem words and defines one of the words in terms of the other. Consider how you would explain the connection between the stem words to a friend.

You can start the relationship with the first or second word. However, make sure you keep the same order when applying the stem relationship to the answers.

> degree is to temperature
>> A *degree* is a unit of *temperature*.
>> *Temperature* is measured in *degrees*.

> joy is to ecstasy
>> *Ecstasy* means extreme *joy*.

> butterfly is to caterpillar

> What is the relationship? _____
>
> _____

TRY IT OUT

For each pair of words, state the relationship by defining one word in terms of the other. Make your relationships as clear and concise as possible.

1. Key is to padlock

   Key unlock

2. Pyramid is to triangle

   Pyramid extreme version 3D

3. Sculptor is to statue

   scolptor builds statue

4. Playwright is to script

   writer
   Playwright is to script

5. Reign is to king

   Reign is ecomy to kings Jcb

6. Cumulus is to cloud

   cumcles type of cloud

7. Melodious is to sound

   Nice Part
   Melodics is sings pert of sound

8. Pancake is to batter

   Pankate result

9. Sonnet is to poem

   sonnet type of poem
   Writer of poem

10. Neurologist is to physician

    Brain study of Physician

SUMMIT
EDUCATIONAL
GROUP

Applying the Relationship

❑ **Use the same relationship for each answer choice.** Connect each pair of answer choices using the same relationship as you use to connect the stem words. Don't change the stem relationship to make it correspond to the relationship between a pair of answer choice words.

Helmet is to head as	(A *helmet* is worn to protect the *head*)
(A) drug is to disease	(A *drug* is worn to protect a *disease*)
(B) lace is to shoe	(A *lace* is worn to protect a *shoe*)
(C) apron is to stain	(An *apron* is worn to protect a *stain*)
(D) field is to goal	(A *field* is worn to protect a *goal*)
(E) thimble is to finger	(A *thimble* is worn to protect a *finger*)

None of the choices make sense except for (E), the correct answer.

❑ **Consider secondary definitions.** If you cannot make sense of an analogy, check for alternate meanings of the stem words, such as when a words is used as a different part of speech.

Parts of speech are consistent in analogies. For example, if one of the first words in a pair is an adjective, all the other first words are also adjectives.

> Clown is to act as
>
> (A) understudy is to scene
> (B) chauffeur is to driveway
> (C) soloist is to recital
> (D) pitcher is to inning
> (E) editor is to column
>
> "Clown" and "act" can be both nouns and verbs. In order to make the proper relationship, it is important to determine how they are being used.
> Look to the answers. Because the first and second words of all the answer choices are nouns, "clown" and "act" must both be nouns. Now you can make the relationship: A clown performs an act, just as a soloist performs a recital. The correct answer is (C).

TRY IT OUT

State the relationship between the stem words and then apply that relationship to your answer choices:

1. Eye chart is to vision as   _Eye chart is to test vision_

   (A) map is to island   _Map is to test and more throw lt_

   (B) drill is to cavity   _Drill is to take away cavity_

   (C) stethoscope is to heartbeat   _To meas test heartbeat_

   (D) camera is to photograph   _camda is to test photo_

   (E) thermostat is to fuel   _____

2. Poem is to stanzas as   _____

   (A) novel is to contents   _____

   (B) sentence is to punctuation   _____

   (C) song is to verses   _____

   (D) question is to answers   _____

   (E) speech is to parts   _____

3. Apple is to fruit as wheat is to   _Apple type of fruit as wheat to grain_

   (A) field   _____

   (B) loaf   _____

   (C) grain   _____

   (D) rice   _____

   (E) vine   _____

4. Surprise is to start as   _____

   (A) ignore is to shrug   _____

   (B) finish is to commence   _____

   (C) bore is to yawn   _____

   (D) quit is to frustrate   _____

   (E) alarm is to sleep   _____

PUT IT TOGETHER

1. Minute is to size as

    (A) inconsequential is to vitality
    (B) superficial is to depth
    (C) shy is to personality
    (D) inclement is to weather
    (E) sparse is to weight

2. Tear is to rend as

    (A) temper is to aggravate
    (B) weep is to shed
    (C) wreck is to obliterate
    (D) own is to borrow
    (E) raze is to batter

3. Line is to insulate as

    (A) mend is to fabricate
    (B) hem is to fashion
    (C) circle is to encamp
    (D) fit is to upholster
    (E) oil is to lubricate

4. Deviate is to course as

    (A) travel is to country
    (B) deflect is to criticism
    (C) block is to attack
    (D) digress is to speech
    (E) shun is to doctrine

5.   Furlong is to distance as

   (A) mile is to speed
   (B) fathom is to depth
   (C) hourglass is to time
   (D) heft is to weight
   (E) knot is to height

6.   Fledgling is to experience as

   (A) hermit is to seclusion
   (B) student is to discipline
   (C) philanthropist is to benevolence
   (D) philosopher is to rationality
   (E) boor is to sensitivity

Refining the Relationship

❑ **Be specific.** If the relationship you make yields two or more correct answers, make the relationship more specific or detailed. This should allow you to eliminate answer choices.

Trunk is to automobile as

(A) limb is to tree
(B) closet is to bedroom
(C) page is to manual
(D) grass is to lawn
(E) toe is to body

First relationship: A *trunk* is part of an *automobile*.

If you apply this relationship, almost all of the answer choices work:

(A) a limb is part of a tree
(B) a closet is part of a bedroom
(C) a page is part of a manual
(D) grass is part of a lawn
(E) a toe is part of a body

More specific: A *trunk* is the part of an *automobile* in which one stores things. Only one pair of words, choice (B), fits that relationship.

TRY IT OUT

State the relationship in the following analogies:

1. Judge is to courthouse as

    (A) cashier is to store
    (B) teacher is to school
    (C) secretary is to office
    (D) salesman is to car
    (E) captain is to ship

Relationship: _____

2. Goggles are to welders as

    (A) chisels are to sculptors
    (B) armor is to knights
    (C) microscopes are to scientists
    (D) authors are to publishers
    (E) scripts are to actors

Relationship: _____

3. Rhinoceros is to horn as

    (A) weed is to root
    (B) vine is to leaf
    (C) tree is to bark
    (D) rose is to thorn
    (E) flower is to petal

Relationship: _____

PUT IT TOGETHER

1. Sole is to shoe as

   (A) brim is to hat
   (B) husk is to corn
   (C) base is to statue
   (D) shelf is to book
   (E) basement is to floor

2. Façade is to building as

   (A) cover is to book
   (B) beard is to face
   (C) vegetation is to landscape
   (D) runway is to airstrip
   (E) constellation is to galaxy

3. Stalk is to leopard as

   (A) molt is to crab
   (B) breach is to whale
   (C) lick is to anteater
   (D) vault is to roebuck
   (E) circle is to hawk

4. Babble is to speak as

   (A) garble is to hear
   (B) dawdle is to hurry
   (C) doodle is to draw
   (D) quibble is to laugh
   (E) sniffle is to cry

5. Balcony is to theater as

    (A) banister is to landing
    (B) portico is to library
    (C) threshold is to house
    (D) freighter is to bridge
    (E) loft is to barn

6. Cradle is to baby as

    (A) nest is to hatchling
    (B) rattle is to infant
    (C) lily pad is to frog
    (D) bed is to rocker
    (E) toy is to child

7. Prelude is to performance as

    (A) preface is to summary
    (B) foreword is to novel
    (C) intermission is to drama
    (D) introduction is to conclusion
    (E) epilogue is to essay

SUMMIT
EDUCATIONAL
GROUP

Common Analogy Relationships

❏ Familiarize yourself with the following analogy relationship types.

Synonym

bold is to courageous   (bold means being courageous)
frenetic is to energetic   (frenetic means energetic)

Antonyms

offhand is to forethought   (offhand means without forethought)
impudent is to respectful   (impudent is the opposite of respectful)

Function or Use

bridge is to river   (a bridge is used for passage over a river)
aviary is to birds   (an aviary houses birds)

Person/Activity

spectator is to watch   (a spectator is someone who watches)
teacher is to instruct   (a teacher is someone who instructs)

Person/Tool

policeman is to handcuffs   (handcuffs are a tool of a policeman)
painter is to brush   (a brush is a tool of a painter)

Person/Creation

playwright is to script   (a playwright writes/creates scripts)
cobbler is to shoe   (a cobbler makes/creates shoes)

Action/Result

insult is to offended   (an insult will make someone offended)
assault is to injured   (an assault will make someone injured)

Characteristic

sphere is to round   (a sphere is round)
menace is to threatening   (a menace is threatening)

Type

fly is to insect   (a fly is a type of insect)

Part/Whole

flower is to bouquet   (a bouquet is an arrangement of flowers)
novel is to chapter   (a chapter is a part of a novel)

Degree of Intensity

hill is to mountain   (a mountain is a large hill)
cold is to frigid   (frigid means extremely cold)

TRY IT OUT

For each pair of stem words, identify the type of relationship (e.g., function, part/whole, etc.) and state the relationship between the words:

1. Carpenter is to hammer

    _____   _____
              type   relationship

2. Globe is to spherical

    _____   _____
              type   relationship

3. Sculptor is to statue

    _____   _____
              type   relationship

4. Atlas is to maps

    _____   _____
              type   relationship

5. Mask is to face

    _____   _____
              type   relationship

6. Stress is to agitated

    _____   _____
              type   relationship

7. Rodent is to mouse

    _____   _____
              type   relationship

8. Ripple is to tidal wave

    _____   _____
              type   relationship

9. Angry is to furious

    _____   _____
              type   relationship

10. Scalpel is to dissect

    _____   _____
              type   relationship

PUT IT TOGETHER

1. Colander is to drain as

    (A) screen is to brighten
    (B) axe is to split
    (C) drawer is to open
    (D) spatula is to slice
    (E) grill is to grate

2. Accountant is to audit as

    (A) reviewer is to literature
    (B) professor is to quiz
    (C) lawyer is to docket
    (D) doctor is to physical
    (E) witness is to hearing

3. Bolster is to reinforce as

    (A) dissent is to object
    (B) listen is to sermonize
    (C) apprehend is to flee
    (D) topple is to support
    (E) tamper is to mend

4. Ream is to paper as

    (A) page is to book
    (B) deck is to cards
    (C) column is to magazine
    (D) package is to gift
    (E) jar is to honey

5. Paragraph is to chapter as

    (A) tributary is to river
    (B) house is to block
    (C) brick is to mortar
    (D) station is to train
    (E) peak is to mountain

6. Late is to prompt as

    (A) incorrect is to flawless
    (B) early is to punctual
    (C) fast is to urgent
    (D) clean is to quick
    (E) tired is to restless

First and Third Analogies

❑ **Look out for different analogy structures.** Occasionally, the first and third words are related, instead of the first two. We call these "First and Third" analogies. If you cannot determine a solid relationship between the first pair of words in an analogy, this is a good clue that it might be a "First and Third" analogy.

Dalmatian is to Siamese as dog is to

(A) Labrador
(B) Persian
(C) cat
(D) puppy
(E) pet

Just as a *Dalmatian* is a type of *dog*, a *Siamese* is a type of *cat*.
(C) is the correct answer.

PUT IT TOGETHER

1. Hand is to foot as arm is to

   (A) knee
   (B) leg
   (C) wrist
   (D) body
   (E) hip

2. Brush is to chisel as painter is to

   (A) sculptor
   (B) palette
   (C) clay
   (D) art
   (E) gallery

3. Album is to atlas as pictures is to

   (A) journeys
   (B) states
   (C) maps
   (D) chapters
   (E) globes

Attractors

❑ **Avoid answers that are related to the stem word but do not fit the analogy.**
Some analogies will contain answer choices that stand out because they contain words related to one or both of the stem words. Be careful not to choose these unless the answer choice has the same relationship as the stem.

Remember, you want to maintain the relationship between the two stem words.

> Shelter is to storm as
>
> (A) violation is to intrusion
> (B) downpour is to flood
> (C) inoculation is to disease
> (D) home is to protection
> (E) winter is to cold
>
> Notice how the words in choices (B) and (D) attract your attention because they are related to the words in the stem pair.
> For example, *downpour* and *flood* in choice (B) relate to *storm*.
> Also, *home* and *protection* in choice (D) relate to *shelter*.
> These are attractors because they try to attract your attention and make you choose the wrong answer.
>
> The correct answer is (C) because the relationship in (C) is the same as the relationship in the stem.
> A *shelter* protects you from a *storm* just as an *inoculation* protects you from a *disease*.

TRY IT OUT

Circle the attractors in the following analogy and find the correct answer.

1. Land is to acre as

    (A) farm is to soil
    (B) currency is to money
    (C) earth is to circumference
    (D) ground is to property
    (E) sound is to decibel

2. Jungle is to tree as

    (A) swamp is to water
    (B) forest is to clearing
    (C) blade is to grass
    (D) swarm is to bee
    (E) pack is to herd

3. Rifle is to trigger as

    (A) blade is to sheath
    (B) center is to target
    (C) car is to ignition
    (D) bullet is to shell
    (E) lightning is to thunder

Eliminating Answer Choices

☐ **If you are stuck, eliminate answers.** When you don't know the meaning of a stem word, you can still solve an analogy problem by eliminating answer choices. If you can eliminate at least two answer choices, make your best guess from the remaining choices!

☐ **Answers must have clear relationships.** Your first step when you are stumped by one of the stem words should be to look for the answer choice relationship(s) that are concise and clear. If you can't form a clear relationship, eliminate the answer choice.

> deserted is to inhabitants
>
> > *Deserted* means to have no *inhabitants* – a concise, clear relationship.
>
> furniture is to wood
>
> > *Furniture* can be made of *wood*, but it doesn't have to be, so this is not a strong relationship.
>
> posture is to improve
>
> > There is not a clear relationship between *posture* and *improve*. One's *posture* may or may not need to *improve*.
>
> smile is to awe
>
> > *Smile* is not related to *awe* at all.
>
> oil is to lubricant
>
> > *Oil*, by definition, is a type of *lubricant*.

TRY IT OUT

Determine if each pair of words is related. If the words relate, state the relationship in the space provided.

1. champion is to speed _____

2. storm is to hurricane _____

3. editor is to personality _____

4. success is to expect _____

5. goggles is to eyes _____

6. arrogant is to silly _____

7. quartz is to rock _____

8. ticket is to admission _____

9. shoe is to leather _____

10. nightmare is to dream _____

11. radio is to television _____

12. class is to practice _____

13. common is to rare _____

14. cage is to endangered _____

15. wheat is to flour _____

PUT IT TOGETHER

1. Carroter is to fur as

    (A) lawyer is to document
    (B) architect is to office
    (C) potter is to clay
    (D) painter is to audience
    (E) gardener is to vine

2. Piquant is to bland as

    (A) level is to flat
    (B) brisk is to plodding
    (C) alert is to indistinct
    (D) spicy is to delectable
    (E) engaging is to theatrical

3. Effulgent is to bright as

    (A) shining is to impressive
    (B) gnarled is to torturous
    (C) apparent is to popular
    (D) serial is to sporadic
    (E) quixotic is to idealistic

4. Nod is to acquiescence as

    (A) salute is to solitude
    (B) jog is to memory
    (C) stumble is to interruption
    (D) shake is to compliance
    (E) blink is to insincerity

5. Mendacious is to liar as

   (A) dull is to lecturer
   (B) parsimonious is to skinflint
   (C) generous is to doctor
   (D) rebellious is to youth
   (E) appreciative is to subordinate

6. Laud is to castigate as

   (A) extreme is to moderate
   (B) unanimous is to elected
   (C) superlative is to good
   (D) simultaneous is to timed
   (E) inconsiderate is to immoral

Solving Backwards

❏ **If you are stuck, apply the relationships in answer choices to stem words.**
Take each answer choice and define one word in terms of the other. Test the relationship on the stem. Pick the answer choice whose relationship seems to work best.

> ????? is to wealth as
>
> (A) bleached is to texture
> (B) energetic is to uncaring
> (C) friendly is to hostility
> (D) eager is to anxiety
> (E) melodious is to sound
>
>
> Assume you don't know what the first stem word means.
> Use the answer choices to "solve backwards."
>
>
> (A) There is no relationship at all between these two words.
> (B) Having energy has nothing to do with caring.
> (C) *Friendly* means lacking *hostility*. A definite possibility.
> (D) No clear relationship. An *eager* person may have *anxiety*, but also may not.
> (E) *Melodious* means having a nice *sound*. A definite possibility.
>
>
> You've now narrowed your choices down to (C) and (E).

> Now, solve backwards by applying the relationships to the stem words:
> Could the first word mean lacking *wealth*, just as *friendly* means lacking *hostility*?
> That could work!
> Could it mean having a nice *wealth*, just as melodious means to have a nice sound?
> Probably not.
> Therefore, you pick (C) as your answer.

TRY IT OUT

Solve backwards to answer the following analogies:

1. Eardrum is to ????? as

    (A) air is to nostril
    (B) blood is to vein
    (C) retina is to eye
    (D) virus is to illness
    (E) scalp is to hair

2. ????? is to foresight as

    (A) talkative is to conversation
    (B) logical is to idea
    (C) cloudy is to sight
    (D) hopeful is to peace
    (E) perfect is to flaw

3. Literature is to ????? as

    (A) sprint is to marathon
    (B) history is to historian
    (C) collection is to porcelain
    (D) museum is to gallery
    (E) flowers is to bouquet

PUT IT TOGETHER

1. Augmentative is to large as

   (A) extreme is to moderate
   (B) unanimous is to elected
   (C) infuriating is to angry
   (D) superlative is to good
   (E) simultaneous is to timed

2. Jejune is to maturity as

   (A) eager is to anxiety
   (B) exhausted is to energy
   (C) hostile is to invitation
   (D) partial is to bias
   (E) empathy is to understanding

3. Support is to exponent as

   (A) avoid is to outcast
   (B) fear is to criminal
   (C) advise is to counselor
   (D) applaud is to performer
   (E) hurt is to doctor

4. Bold is to pusillanimous as

   (A) wise is to thoughtful
   (B) trusting is to gullible
   (C) astounding is to revolting
   (D) creative is to childlike
   (E) arrogant is to humble

SUMMIT
EDUCATIONAL
GROUP

5. Tyro is to experience as

(A) hermit is to seclusion
(B) student is to school
(C) philanthropist is to benevolence
(D) philosopher is to memory
(E) boor is to sophistication

6. Kinesiology is to motion as

(A) astrology is to progress
(B) biology is to life
(C) harmonies is to energy
(D) history is to habitat
(E) physics is to healing

Chapter Review

❑ Format/Directions

The verbal section of the SSAT has one set of 30 analogies. They appear after the 30 synonym questions. The questions go from easy to difficult.

❑ The key to solving an analogy is to determine what the relationship is between the paired words.

❑ **Clearly state the relationship.** Don't just look at the words and say "I know that these words are related." The more clearly you can state the relationship, the easier the analogy problem becomes.

❑ **State the relationship as a complete sentence.** Think of a short sentence that contains both of the stem words and defines one of the words in terms of the other. Consider how you would explain the connection between the stem words to a friend.

You can start the relationship with the first or second word. However, make sure you keep the same order when applying the stem relationship to the answers.

❑ **Use the same relationship for each answer choice.** Connect each pair of answer choices using the same relationship as you use to connect the stem words. Don't change the stem relationship to make it correspond to the relationship between a pair of answer choice words.

❑ **Consider secondary definitions.** If you cannot make sense of an analogy, check for alternate meanings of the stem words, such as when a words is used as a different part of speech.

Parts of speech are consistent in analogies. For example, if one of the first words in a pair is an adjective, all the other first words are also adjectives.

❑ **Be specific.** If the relationship you make yields two or more correct answers, make the relationship more specific or detailed. This should allow you to eliminate answer choices.

❑ Familiarize yourself with common analogy relationship types.

❑ **Look out for different analogy structures.** Occasionally, it will be the first and third words that are related, instead of the first two. We call these "First and Third" analogies. If you cannot determine a solid relationship between the first pair of words in an analogy, this is a good clue that it might be a "First and Third" analogy.

❑ **Avoid answers that are related to the stem word but do not fit the analogy.** Some analogies will contain answer choices that stand out because they contain words related to one or both of the stem words. Be careful not to choose these unless the answer choice has the same relationship as the stem.

Remember, you want to maintain the relationship between the two stem words.

❑ **If you are stuck, eliminate answers.** When you don't know the meaning of a stem word, you can still solve an analogy problem by eliminating answer choices. If you can eliminate at least two answer choices, make your best guess from the remaining choices!

❑ **Answers must have clear relationships.** Your first step when you are stumped by one of the stem words should be to look for the answer choice relationship(s) that are concise and clear. If you can't form a clear relationship, eliminate the answer choice.

❑ **If you are stuck, apply the relationships in answer choices to stem words.** Take each answer choice and define one word in terms of the other. Test the relationship on the stem. Pick the answer choice whose relationship seems to work best.

Analogies Practice – Middle Level

1. Hungry is to eat as

    (A) thirsty is to pour
    (B) tired is to sleep
    (C) happy is to cry
    (D) itchy is to bite
    (E) cold is to huddle

2. Car is to land as

    (A) train is to track
    (B) bicycle is to wheel
    (C) skate is to board
    (D) tire is to engine
    (E) boat is to water

3. Sick is to healthy as poor is to

    (A) lazy
    (B) destitute
    (C) wealthy
    (D) unfortunate
    (E) joyous

4. Cow is to calf as

    (A) ram is to lamb
    (B) duck is to duckling
    (C) colt is to pony
    (D) fox is to coyote
    (E) puppy is to kitten

5. Tooth is to dentist as

    (A) leg is to doctor
    (B) car is to mechanic
    (C) house is to architect
    (D) scalpel is to surgeon
    (E) trial is to lawyer

6. Water is to ice as

    (A) rain is to hail
    (B) blood is to vein
    (C) juice is to fruit
    (D) milk is to cream
    (E) cola is to soda

7. Airplane is to bird as submarine is to

    (A) boat
    (B) snorkel
    (C) animal
    (D) water
    (E) fish

8. Duck is to quack as

    (A) dog is to purr
    (B) bird is to beak
    (C) cow is to milk
    (D) cat is to meow
    (E) goose is to gander

9. Hammer is to wrench as carpenter is to

    (A) builder
    (B) architect
    (C) plumber
    (D) chauffeur
    (E) piper

10. Cotton is to plant as silk is to

    (A) worm
    (B) tree
    (C) cloth
    (D) factory
    (E) satin

11. Half-time is to game as

    (A) inning is to baseball
    (B) scene is to opera
    (C) intermission is to play
    (D) foul is to penalty
    (E) pause is to video

12. Book is to film as publisher is to

    (A) writer
    (B) producer
    (C) audience
    (D) actor
    (E) editor

13. Furious is to angry as ravenous is to

    (A) flighty
    (B) calm
    (C) hungry
    (D) tired
    (E) shy

14. Opera is to music as

    (A) vegetable is to fruit
    (B) heart is to body
    (C) song is to singer
    (D) flower is to petal
    (E) dog is to animal

15. Inch is to centimeter as yard is to

    (A) meter
    (B) kilogram
    (C) foot
    (D) mile
    (E) quart

16. Fish is to school as

    (A) cow is to ranch
    (B) sock is to dresser
    (C) soldier is to battle
    (D) pupil is to bus
    (E) bird is to flock

17. Guitar is to strum as flute is to

    (A) listen
    (B) press
    (C) blow
    (D) beat
    (E) buzz

18. Teacher is to school as surgeon is to

    (A) college
    (B) stadium
    (C) study
    (D) courtroom
    (E) hospital

19. Book is to chapter as

    (A) play is to act
    (B) word is to line
    (C) magazine is to journal
    (D) poem is to anthology
    (E) scene is to stage

20. Ruler is to thermometer as length is to

    (A) depth
    (B) strength
    (C) season
    (D) temperature
    (E) wind

21. Start is to begin as

 (A) finish is to launch
 (B) stop is to cease
 (C) end is to repeat
 (D) lead is to follow
 (E) move is to dance

22. Hut is to house as

 (A) flower is to stem
 (B) roof is to floor
 (C) dress is to skirt
 (D) raft is to boat
 (E) wall is to building

23. Telephone is to talking as letter is to

 (A) writing
 (B) recording
 (C) hearing
 (D) sending
 (E) seeing

24. Medicine is to pharmacist as meat is to

 (A) farmer
 (B) vendor
 (C) butcher
 (D) baker
 (E) grocer

25. Arm is to body as

 (A) husk is to corn
 (B) fur is to bear
 (C) wheel is to car
 (D) branch is to tree
 (E) pearl is to oyster

26. Drum is to percussion as

 (A) clarinet is to music
 (B) oboe is to woodwind
 (C) violin is to bow
 (D) cymbals is to crash
 (E) trumpet is to trombone

27. Orange is to rind as

 (A) slice is to loaf
 (B) milk is to butter
 (C) egg is to yolk
 (D) walnut is to shell
 (E) cherry is to stem

28. Painter is to brush as

 (A) cook is to egg
 (B) conductor is to violin
 (C) writer is to newspaper
 (D) sculptor is to chisel
 (E) teacher is to student

29. Circle is to sphere as

 (A) line is to point
 (B) triangle is to pyramid
 (C) hexagon is to cone
 (D) square is to rectangle
 (E) trapezoid is to cylinder

30. Visible is to seeing as

 (A) edible is to hearing
 (B) optical is to sensing
 (C) audible is to smelling
 (D) amiable is to speaking
 (E) tangible is to touching

31. Pipe is to plumber as acrylics are to

    (A) tailor
    (B) painter
    (C) carpenter
    (D) mechanic
    (E) critic

32. Doorbell is to chime as

    (A) telephone is to ring
    (B) sound is to sight
    (C) drum is to cymbal
    (D) book is to announcement
    (E) lamp is to light

33. Boundary is to border as

    (A) center is to nucleus
    (B) edge is to middle
    (C) library is to book
    (D) side is to front
    (E) fence is to neighbor

34. Greenhouse is to plants as incubator is to

    (A) animals
    (B) eggs
    (C) tomatoes
    (D) sunshine
    (E) weeds

35. Sculptor is to clay as

    (A) author is to board
    (B) gambler is to challenge
    (C) printer is to plastic
    (D) weaver is to yarn
    (E) manager is to desk

36. Cradle is to baby as

    (A) nest is to hatchling
    (B) toy is to child
    (C) rattle is to infant
    (D) bed is to rocker
    (E) lily pad is to frog

37. Adept is to unable as

    (A) predicted is to rainy
    (B) preferred is to choosy
    (C) precise is to careless
    (D) previewed is to ugly
    (E) prepared is to arranged

38. Leopard is to spots as

    (A) camel is to desert
    (B) robin is to speck
    (C) butterfly is to moth
    (D) cricket is to music
    (E) zebra is to stripes

39. Fly is to airplane as operate is to

    (A) surgeon
    (B) machinery
    (C) exploration
    (D) land
    (E) opening

40. Blue is to sadness as

    (A) yellow is to sky
    (B) purple is to tears
    (C) red is to paper
    (D) orange is to banana
    (E) green is to envy

41. Ewe is to lamb as

   (A) buck is to deer
   (B) puppy is to dog
   (C) goose is to gander
   (D) cow is to bull
   (E) doe is to fawn

42. Step is to staircase as rung is to

   (A) hallway
   (B) telephone
   (C) ladder
   (D) rooftop
   (E) railing

43. Milk is to cow as egg is to

   (A) rooster
   (B) pig
   (C) horse
   (D) hen
   (E) sheep

44. Soda is to beverage as

   (A) cereal is to sugar
   (B) milk is to water
   (C) rye is to bread
   (D) juice is to fruit
   (E) candy is to chocolate

45. Waiter is to waitress as

   (A) calf is to cow
   (B) cat is to lioness
   (C) sheep is to ewe
   (D) chicken is to egg
   (E) duck is to duckling

46. Flute is to woodwind as

   (A) violin is to music
   (B) sound is to instrument
   (C) trumpet is to brass
   (D) stick is to drum
   (E) percussion is to viola

47. Kilometer is to mile as

   (A) foot is to inch
   (B) gram is to pound
   (C) millimeter is to centimeter
   (D) speed is to distance
   (E) one thousand is to one hundred

48. Paragraph is to prose as

   (A) letter is to salutation
   (B) essay is to writing
   (C) story is to sentence
   (D) song is to chorus
   (E) stanza is to poetry

49. Drama is to tragedy as

   (A) book is to reading
   (B) poem is to anthology
   (C) performance is to stage
   (D) poem is to sonnet
   (E) biography is to nonfiction

50. Affable is to friendly as

   (A) amiable is to perfect
   (B) sullen is to dirty
   (C) irritable is to easygoing
   (D) insolent is to rude
   (E) tasteful is to fancy

51. Coal is to mine as

    (A) silt is to meadow
    (B) textile is to forest
    (C) fire is to grill
    (D) nylon is to cave
    (E) marble is to quarry

52. Nursery is to tree as

    (A) orchard is to leaf
    (B) canyon is to river
    (C) hatchery is to fish
    (D) greenhouse is to light
    (E) pasture is to cow

53. Dim is to light as

    (A) audible is to din
    (B) rough is to touch
    (C) vacant is to emptiness
    (D) faint is to noise
    (E) flashy is to brilliance

54. Itinerary is to trip as

    (A) biography is to fate
    (B) accommodations is to destination
    (C) outline is to essay
    (D) instructions is to lecture
    (E) detour is to arrival

55. Fish is to school as

    (A) cattle is to ranch
    (B) clothes is to dresser
    (C) soldiers is to platoon
    (D) pupils is to bus
    (E) flock is to birds

56. Ticket is to admission as

    (A) program is to playhouse
    (B) concession is to event
    (C) stub is to refreshment
    (D) receipt is to sale
    (E) coupon is to discount

57. Lullaby is to sleep as

    (A) limerick is to melancholy
    (B) refrain is to ecstasy
    (C) serenade is to love
    (D) poem is to rhyme
    (E) maxim is to honesty

58. Filter is to impurity as

    (A) fumigate is to pest
    (B) resolve is to integrity
    (C) confess is to indiscretion
    (D) erase is to foible
    (E) cultivate is to soil

59. Commitment is to dedication as

    (A) hesitation is to tentativeness
    (B) zeal is to implementation
    (C) bent is to resolution
    (D) rationale is to causation
    (E) determination is to ambivalence

60. Contestant is to compete as

    (A) entrant is to vanquish
    (B) dictator is to concur
    (C) arbitrator is to decide
    (D) teammate is to rival
    (E) onlooker is to participate

Analogies Practice – Upper Level

1. Poverty is to money as

   (A) happiness is to whistle
   (B) pride is to danger
   (C) relief is to laughter
   (D) confidence is to faith
   (E) ignorance is to education

2. Ream is to paper as

   (A) page is to book
   (B) deck is to cards
   (C) column is to magazine
   (D) package is to gift
   (E) jar is to honey

3. Aquarium is to fish as

   (A) terrarium is to plants
   (B) library is to lawn
   (C) garage is to sale
   (D) planetarium is to aliens
   (E) museum is to history

4. Picnic is to ants as

   (A) swim is to jellyfish
   (B) hunt is to deer
   (C) hike is to trail
   (D) badminton is to tennis
   (E) lunch is to eat

5. Altitude is to mountain as

   (A) width is to candle
   (B) temperature is to valley
   (C) depth is to ocean
   (D) weight is to river
   (E) length is to paper

6. Wealthy is to impoverished as vigorous is to

   (A) growing
   (B) worried
   (C) loud
   (D) poor
   (E) lethargic

7. Dime is to nickel as

   (A) change is to silver
   (B) penny is to dollar
   (C) whole is to half
   (D) money is to wallet
   (E) part is to quarter

8. Pride is to lions as

   (A) honor is to person
   (B) gaggle is to geese
   (C) herd is to music
   (D) hump is to camel
   (E) bull is to frog

9. Valiant is to cowardly as

   (A) victorious is to glorious
   (B) frank is to dishonest
   (C) fearful is to miserable
   (D) cautious is to careful
   (E) controllable is to manageable

10. Cross is to grumpy as cheerful is to

    (A) sad
    (B) buoyant
    (C) manic
    (D) religious
    (E) clairvoyant

11. Glacier is to ice as

   (A) river is to ocean
   (B) jungle is to sand
   (C) sun is to frost
   (D) reef is to coral
   (E) grass is to lawn

12. Dwell is to domain as

   (A) walk is to library
   (B) dine is to bistro
   (C) stroll is to bazaar
   (D) read is to spectacles
   (E) print is to gallery

13. Fertilizer is to nourish is as

   (A) poison is to destroy
   (B) weed is to garden
   (C) insect is to burrow
   (D) wall is to border
   (E) blanket is to knit

14. Hot is to tepid as

   (A) spicy is to zesty
   (B) freezing is to cool
   (C) strong is to forceful
   (D) sweet is to tasty
   (E) loving is to childish

15. Century is to years as

   (A) book is to pages
   (B) poem is to verses
   (C) dollar is to pennies
   (D) hour is to minutes
   (E) year is to days

16. Bed is to cot as

   (A) couch is to chair
   (B) room is to house
   (C) house is to mansion
   (D) lake is to fish
   (E) sleep is to dream

17. Abhor is to detest as

   (A) love is to hate
   (B) mope is to merriment
   (C) admire is to disgust
   (D) adore is to revere
   (E) attack is to exalt

18. Goose is to geese as

   (A) abode is to adobe
   (B) mouse is to mice
   (C) choose is to piece
   (D) moose is to antler
   (E) spouse is to spice

19. Permit is to allow as

   (A) forbid is to prohibit
   (B) license is to drive
   (C) ventilate is to irritate
   (D) repair is to realize
   (E) divert is to recognize

20. Battery is to power as

   (A) acid is to base
   (B) jigsaw is to piece
   (C) carburetor is to car
   (D) fuel is to energy
   (E) string is to kite

21. Hurdle is to jump as

    (A) obstacle is to course
    (B) wing is to fly
    (C) blender is to mix
    (D) vehicle is to stall
    (E) discus is to throw

22. Poet is to words as

    (A) choreographer is to movement
    (B) cinematographer is to editing
    (C) calligrapher is to pictures
    (D) graphic designer is to public relations
    (E) singer is to accompanist

23. Cage is to bird as hutch is to

    (A) dog
    (B) pigeon
    (C) chicken
    (D) rabbit
    (E) cow

24. Counselor is to guidance as

    (A) master is to deliberation
    (B) teacher is to verification
    (C) minister is to obligation
    (D) decorator is to ramification
    (E) overseer is to supervision

25. Sentry is to fortress as

    (A) warden is to prison
    (B) goalie is to soccer
    (C) chief is to engine
    (D) witch is to mirror
    (E) inmate is to asylum

26. Bluebird is to happiness as

    (A) pigeon is to nuisance
    (B) swallow is to consumption
    (C) dove is to peace
    (D) robin is to tint
    (E) turkey is to celebration

27. Ignite is to fire as incite is to

    (A) riot
    (B) notation
    (C) perception
    (D) flames
    (E) job

28. Sunset is to daybreak as

    (A) region is to vicinity
    (B) dusk is to dawn
    (C) morning is to sunrise
    (D) crisis is to conclusion
    (E) afternoon is to recess

29. Crocus is to spring as

    (A) rain is to summer
    (B) frog is to pond
    (C) frost is to winter
    (D) summer is to autumn
    (E) garden is to harvest

30. Joy is to agony as

    (A) hope is to happiness
    (B) delight is to detail
    (C) sad is to heartache
    (D) nasty is to nervous
    (E) pleasure is to pain

31. Rectangle is to box as

    (A) triangle is to staple
    (B) square is to pyramid
    (C) ellipse is to circle
    (D) circle is to tube
    (E) hexagon is to traffic

32. Doe is to buck as

    (A) cow is to bull
    (B) puppy is to kitten
    (C) frog is to tadpole
    (D) minnow is to bait
    (E) caterpillar is to cricket

33. Prevail is to defeat as

    (A) persuade is to convince
    (B) detain is to gloat
    (C) salvage is to isolate
    (D) saunter is to soothe
    (E) protect is to incarcerate

34. Seasoned is to unskilled as mature is to

    (A) old
    (B) impractical
    (C) green
    (D) unable
    (E) senior

35. Sweet is to sugar as aromatic is to

    (A) mechanical
    (B) dynamic
    (C) passion
    (D) sound
    (E) fragrance

36. Lofty is to humble as

    (A) fancy is to ornate
    (B) flowery is to plain
    (C) simple is to poor
    (D) windy is to breezy
    (E) hard is to tough

37. Pick is to bow as

    (A) flute is to piccolo
    (B) guitar is to violin
    (C) banjo is to cymbal
    (D) tuba is to trombone
    (E) piano is to cello

38. Virtuoso is to neophyte as

    (A) sophisticated is to naive
    (B) virulent is to lucid
    (C) sanguine is to inebriated
    (D) palatable is to delectable
    (E) realistic is to nihilistic

39. Pristine is to spotless as

    (A) unkempt is to sloppy
    (B) sterile is to miserable
    (C) serene is to distraught
    (D) affluent is to effective
    (E) chaste is to promiscuous

40. Prudent is to careless as stingy is to

    (A) careful
    (B) generous
    (C) mean
    (D) playful
    (E) jealous

41. Indifferent is to emotion as

   (A) immediate is to feedback
   (B) impassive is to reaction
   (C) insincere is to lie
   (D) immature is to behavior
   (E) insecure is to worry

42. Chaos is to order as

   (A) disorder is to disaster
   (B) peace is to harmony
   (C) disarray is to organization
   (D) confusion is to corruption
   (E) neatness is to cleanliness

43. Visibility is to seeing as mobility is to

   (A) moving
   (B) looking
   (C) writing
   (D) listening
   (E) acting

44. Land is to sound as acre is to

   (A) speedometer
   (B) decibel
   (C) money
   (D) scale
   (E) calendar

45. Eloquent is to writing as

   (A) expensive is to money
   (B) graceful is to movement
   (C) wealthy is to demeanor
   (D) fanciful is to whimsy
   (E) acceptable is to risk

46. Avaricious is to greed as

   (A) entitled is to ignorance
   (B) stable is to equality
   (C) deceptive is to honor
   (D) disgruntled is to faith
   (E) altruistic is to generosity

47. Anonymous is to name as

   (A) incognito is to identity
   (B) recognizable is to face
   (C) clandestine is to affair
   (D) enormous is to pressure
   (E) curious is to knowledge

48. Proud is to arrogant as talkative is to

   (A) specious
   (B) meticulous
   (C) mutinous
   (D) garrulous
   (E) ponderous

49. Clean is to immaculate as thrifty is to

   (A) obdurate
   (B) meticulous
   (C) parsimonious
   (D) intrepid
   (E) illustrious

50. Saccharine is to sweet as

   (A) artificial is to synthetic
   (B) processed is to pure
   (C) fawning is to respectful
   (D) forged is to genuine
   (E) acrid is to salty

51. Opacity is to transparence as

    (A) bravura is to heroism
    (B) sincerity is to integrity
    (C) disinclination is to aversion
    (D) pretension is to disingenuousness
    (E) fanaticism is to apathy

52. Inquire is to interrogate as

    (A) bequeath is to beseech
    (B) decorate is to desecrate
    (C) tantalize is to attract
    (D) disarm is to manipulate
    (E) suggest is to dictate

53. Preordained is to random as

    (A) allotted is to sufficient
    (B) moderate is to excessive
    (C) skewed is to global
    (D) amassed is to cumulative
    (E) contrived is to persuasive

54. Enlighten is to obfuscate as

    (A) entertain is to distract
    (B) elucidate is to clarify
    (C) inspire is to discourage
    (D) repeal is to prohibit
    (E) espouse is to conjugate

55. Cursory is to scrutinize as

    (A) sprightly is to plod
    (B) disobedient is to tyrannize
    (C) articulate is to speak
    (D) guilty is to suspect
    (E) curt is to abrupt

56. Dilapidated is to building as

    (A) renovated is to apartment
    (B) energized is to jogger
    (C) delinquent is to rent
    (D) antiquated is to cottage
    (E) threadbare is to clothing

57. Vivacity is to lethargic as

    (A) secrecy is to stealthy
    (B) zeal is to apathetic
    (C) inferno is to external
    (D) ire is to furious
    (E) adroitness is to mediocre

58. Unabridged is to dictionary as

    (A) fused is to metal
    (B) comparative is to thesaurus
    (C) inconclusive is to theory
    (D) uncut is to movie
    (E) rudimentary is to lexicon

59. Extol is to complimentary as

    (A) rebuke is to disapproving
    (B) criticize is to instructive
    (C) applaud is to theatrical
    (D) confess is to criminal
    (E) complain is to painful

60. Gaze is to glance as

    (A) sink is to skip
    (B) stroke is to sweep
    (C) dash is to creep
    (D) ponder is to decide
    (E) stroll is to dash

SUMMIT
EDUCATIONAL
GROUP

Reading Comprehension

General Information

❏ Format/Directions

The SSAT contains one Reading Comprehension section. This section is 40 minutes and has 40 questions.

❏ Directions are as follows:

> Read each passage carefully and then answer the questions about it. For each question, decide on the basis of the passage which one of the choices best answers the question.

❏ There are four basic types of passages on the SSAT.

In **fact** passages, the author describes something using details and objective information. Examples might include a description of the way a volcano erupts, an explanation of the digestive system, or a biography of Florence Nightingale.

In **opinion** passages, the author offers and explains his or her opinion on a topic. Examples might include an argument that drinking water should contain fluoride or that economic factors, not slavery, caused the Civil War.

In **prose** passages, the author tells a story. This can be a story from the author's own experiences or a fictional story. Examples might include a musician's memories of how she learned to play an instrument, a father describing his child's first steps, or a story of a fight between a girl and her best friend.

In **poetry** passages, the author tells a story or describes an imagined scene. Examples might include a poem about the ocean, the emotion of love, or a woman's life.

❏ The passages are taken out of context, and may have been edited to fit the questions and the length required for the test. As a result, you may find that the passages are boring or confusing, especially if they are on unfamiliar topics. Don't worry; this is normal.

SSAT Structure

Writing Sample – 25 minutes

Quantitative – 30 minutes

MATHEMATICS																								
1	2	3	4	5	6	7	8	9	10	11	12	13	14	15	16	17	18	19	20	21	22	23	24	25
EASY				→			MEDIUM			→			DIFFICULT											

Reading Comprehension – 40 minutes

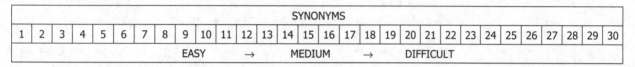

READING PASSAGES																																							
1	2	3	4	5	6	7	8	9	10	11	12	13	14	15	16	17	18	19	20	21	22	23	24	25	26	27	28	29	30	31	32	33	34	35	36	37	38	39	40
NOT IN ORDER OF DIFFICULTY																																							

Verbal – 30 minutes

SYNONYMS																													
1	2	3	4	5	6	7	8	9	10	11	12	13	14	15	16	17	18	19	20	21	22	23	24	25	26	27	28	29	30
EASY				→			MEDIUM			→			DIFFICULT																

ANALOGIES																													
31	32	33	34	35	36	37	38	39	40	41	42	43	44	45	46	47	48	49	50	51	52	53	54	55	56	57	58	59	60
EASY				→			MEDIUM			→			DIFFICULT																

Quantitative – 30 minutes

MATHEMATICS																								
1	2	3	4	5	6	7	8	9	10	11	12	13	14	15	16	17	18	19	20	21	22	23	24	25
EASY				→			MEDIUM			→			DIFFICULT											

Active Reading

❑ Because there are many passages on the test, you may feel tempted to rush through them. However, if you read too quickly, you may miss important information in the passage. The key to reading comprehension is to read swiftly but carefully.

❑ We do **not** recommend reading the questions first. It is difficult enough to understand a passage without having to keep so many questions in your head as well.

❑ **Be an active reader.** Never expect a passage to interest or entertain you. You have to get into it, on your own. Reading is not a passive experience. It's something you do **actively**. Don't wait to see what a passage says; go get it!

❑ **Summarize and make connections.** Restate phrases, sentences, and paragraphs in your own words. This will help you understand and remember what you have read.

Pay attention to how different parts of a passage are related. Information and details might be used to explain, support, contrast, describe, etc.

❑ **As you read, analyze the passage and ask questions:**

What topic is the author writing about?

What type of passage is it?

What is the author's purpose?

What is the main idea of each paragraph?

What will come next?

❑ **Underline or write down the main ideas of each paragraph.** Marking the passage will force you to search actively for the important points, and it will also help keep your mind from wandering as you read.

TRY IT OUT

Read the following passage actively and be prepared to answer the "active reading" questions that follow:

The Hopi people of northeastern Arizona are known for the Kachina dolls. The Kachinas are known to be divine spirits who represent natural forces, elements, animals, or ancestors. People in the tribe carve figures of the Kachinas from cottonwood. These figures are given as gifts and symbolize different types of Kachina. Early Kachina dolls were carved from single pieces of cottonwood root and were painted with basic pigments. Over the last century, the dolls have become more intricate, with exquisite details, multiple pieces, and high-quality paints. The creation of these dolls has evolved from a traditional practice to a profitable art, with individual dolls selling for thousands of dollars.

The Kachina dolls are an important part of Hopi culture, which the Hopi have struggled to protect throughout the last several centuries. When the first European settlers came to America, many tribesmen gave up their traditional Hopi culture in exchange for European beliefs and customs. Today, the Hopi are surrounded by different cultures. Due to the Dawes Allotment Act of 1887, the Hopi have retained only a small patch of their land in the Arizona desert, and this territory is in the middle of the much larger Navajo Reservation. Because the U.S. government granted them so little land, the Hopi were not able to maintain the type of farming that had been so important to their culture and prosperity. The Hopi have had to find other resources in order to survive. For the modern Hopi tribe, Kachina dolls are not only a cherished tradition but also a necessary form of income for many Hopi artists.

1. What do Kachina dolls represent for the Hopi?

2. How have Kachina dolls changed over time?

3. What two reasons does the author give for the importance of Kachina dolls?

TRY IT OUT

Read the following passage actively and be prepared to answer the "active reading" questions that follow:

The photography bug bit me when I was young. The first time I rode a bike, and when I learned to juggle, and on my earliest birthdays: my mother was always there with her Polaroid. Within seconds of her snapping a shot, a picture came crawling out from the slot on the front of the camera. The image would be black at first, but within a few minutes, the photo would materialize, as if a dark fog was clearing. It is hard to describe the joy I felt as I watched the images form in these Polaroid photographs. There was an *inexplicable* excitement in waiting to see what would develop in the little square frame of the picture. It was a feeling like nothing else, and it is linked to many of my favorite memories of growing up. That anticipation is why I am a photographer today.

In modern photography, film is being replaced by digital technologies. Pictures no longer develop; they appear instantly on digital displays and are stored as data. Despite these advancements, I stubbornly continue to use my old cameras. Whenever I can, I use actual film in creating my photos because I don't want immediate, predictable results. For me, the joy of photography lies in a childlike sense of wonder and excited expectation.

1. What does the author mean by "The photography bug bit me"?

2. Do you know the meaning of "inexplicable"? If not, what do you think it means?

3. Why did the author decide to become a photographer?

4. What is the author comparing in the second paragraph?

5. How does the author feel about digital photography? How does this relate to his passion for photography?

PUT IT TOGETHER

Astray: A Tale of a Country Town, is a very serious volume. It has taken four people to write it, and even to read it requires assistance. Its dullness is premeditated and deliberate and comes from a laudable desire to rescue fiction from flippancy. It is, in fact, tedious from the noblest motives and wearisome through its good intentions. Yet the story itself is not an uninteresting one. Quite the contrary. It deals with the attempt of a young doctor to build up a noble manhood on the ruins of a wasted youth. Burton King, while little more than a reckless lad, forges the name of a dying man, is arrested and sent to penal servitude for seven years. On his discharge he comes to live with his sisters in a little country town and finds that his real punishment begins when he is free, for prison has made him a pariah. Still, through the nobility and self-sacrifice of his life, he gradually wins himself a position, and ultimately marries the prettiest girl in the book. His character is, on the whole, well drawn, and the authors have almost succeeded in making him good without making him priggish. The method, however, by which the story is told is extremely tiresome. It consists of an interminable series of long letters by different people and of extracts from various diaries. The book consequently is piecemeal and unsatisfactory. It fails in producing any unity of effect. It contains the rough material for a story, but is not a completed work of art. It is, in fact, more of a notebook than a novel. We fear that too many collaborators are like too many cooks and spoil the dinner. Still, in this tale of a country town there are certain solid qualities, and it is a book that one can with perfect safety recommend to other people.

1. The primary purpose of this passage is to

    (A) consider the use of letters and diaries in the telling of a story
    (B) judge the strengths and weaknesses of a particular book
    (C) summarize the events of a story
    (D) argue against the opinions of a group of authors
    (E) demonstrate the effectiveness of collaborating in writing

2. The author implies that *Astray: A Tale of a Country Town* is a novel that

    (A) is entirely composed of literary essays
    (B) does not effectively describe its characters
    (C) narrates a series of difficulties and hardships
    (D) is based on traditional folk tales
    (E) succeeds in creating a cohesive, exciting story

3. According to the passage, *Astray: A Tale of a Country Town* is organized in a form that resembles

    (A) an archive of personal writings
    (B) a newspaper
    (C) a popular magazine
    (D) a comedic play
    (E) an encyclopedia article

4. The author criticizes *Astray: A Tale of a Country Town* by commenting that the novel

    (A) does not have an interesting story
    (B) is too fragmented, due to its many authors
    (C) tells a story that is too simple and obvious
    (D) is not believable
    (E) is too short for such an ambitious story

Mapping the Passage

☐ **Break the passage down into parts.** As you read, try to follow the path of the passage as it shifts from point to point. Pay attention to the first and last sentence in each paragraph as they will often announce the transition from one point to the next. Mark with a check in the margin where each shift takes place.

Sometimes a shift can take place mid-paragraph. Be on the lookout for words like: *but, nevertheless, however, despite, on the other hand.*

☐ **Consider how parts of a passage work together.** After you finish a paragraph or supporting point, ask yourself how it fits into the overall main idea. For example, does that part of the passage introduce an idea, use examples to support an idea, compare things, or bring up a counterpoint?

☐ Don't try to retain every detail in the passage. Instead, try to develop a mental "picture" of the passage, so you'll know where to look to answer specific questions.

☐ Don't waste too much time on a difficult sentence or word. There probably won't be a question on it. If you do get a question about the sentence or word, you can go back and figure it out then. You'll likely be more able to understand a difficult sentence or word when you go back with more knowledge of the passage.

TRY IT OUT

Read the following passage actively and be prepared to answer the "active reading" questions that follow:

Slash-and-burn agriculture was practiced for thousands of years in the tropical rain forests of South America with little effect on the environment. It is a primitive agricultural system in which sections of forest are repeatedly cleared, cultivated, and allowed to regrow over a period of many years. Small groups practicing slash-and-burn agriculture generally clear one or two new plots a year, working a few areas at various stages of cultivation at a time. As the nutrients are used up and the land produces less, a plot cleared for slash-and-burn agriculture is rarely abandoned; species such as fruit trees are still cultivated as the forest begins to reclaim the open spaces.

Although it is relatively harmless when practiced on a small scale, this system of agriculture can cause considerable destruction when practiced by too many people. The pressures exerted by a rapidly growing population in South America have made slash-and-burn agriculture much more harmful. As the population grows, more and more peasants do not own their own land; they have been forced to move into the forests, where they support themselves by practicing slash-and-burn agriculture. More of these forests are being destroyed and some species have already been forced into extinction. If we fail to respond to this crisis in time, the loss of these forests will have permanently damaged the planet for us and for future generations.

1. What topic is the passage about?

2. What type of passage is it?

3. What is the main idea of paragraph 1?

4. What is the main idea of paragraph 2?

5. What is the author's main idea?

6. Why did the author write the passage?

Checkpoint Review

The cuckoo solves housekeeping difficulties by leaving its eggs to the tender mercy of other species. The mother cuckoo watches other birds as they build their nests, and as soon as the chosen nest contains a few eggs, the cuckoo deposits her egg in the stranger's nest, throwing out at the same time a few of the rightful eggs. If two cuckoo's eggs are found in the same nest, they are almost surely the produce of two different birds. Cuckoos do not

5   tend to put more than one of their eggs in a given nest. Having deposited her eggs, the mother cuckoo takes no further interest in her chicks. Instead, she continues to lead a life of leisure until early in August, when she and her mate leave us for their southern winter-quarters.

The eggs of this species are extremely variable, but as a rule are of a pale bluish or greenish ground color, with reddish spots and mottlings. Sometimes they agree so closely with the eggs of their foster-parents as to be almost

10   indistinguishable, but such cases are exceptional. When the young cuckoo has been hatched about twenty-four hours, he sets to work to eject the other nestlings by getting them on his back, in which there is a hollow, and pushing them over the side of the nest. He is most forceful in his demands for food, and continues to be a burden on the foster-parents long after he is able to feed himself. However, once he is fledged, he wings his way southwards and we see him no more, till he returns the following spring to gladden us with his cheering "cuckoo!"

1.   In line 3, what is the meaning of the phrase "rightful eggs"?

2.   How would you describe the author's tone in this passage?

3.   Why does the passage say that the female cuckoo leads "a life of leisure" (line 6)?

4.   What are examples of ways that a cuckoo nestling is a burden, or problem, for its "foster parents"?

Checkpoint Review

In 1879, Thomas Edison's incandescent light bulbs first illuminated a New York street, and the modern era of electric lighting began. Since then, the world has become awash in electric light. Powerful lamps light up streets, yards, parking lots, and billboards. Sports facilities blaze with light that is visible for tens of miles. Business and office building windows glow throughout the night. According to the Tucson, Arizona–based International Dark-
5 Sky Association (IDA), the sky glow of Los Angeles is visible from an airplane 200 miles away. In most of the world's large urban centers, stargazing is something that happens at a planetarium. Indeed, when a 1994 earthquake knocked out the power in Los Angeles, many anxious residents called local emergency centers to report seeing a strange "giant, silvery cloud" in the dark sky. What they were really seeing—for the first time—was the Milky Way, long obliterated by the urban sky glow.
10 None of this is to say that electric lights are inherently bad. Artificial light has benefited society by, for instance, extending the length of the productive day, offering more time not just for working but also for recreational activities that require light. But when artificial outdoor lighting becomes inefficient, annoying, and unnecessary, it is known as light pollution. Many environmentalists, naturalists, and medical researchers consider light pollution to be one of the fastest growing and most pervasive forms of environmental pollution. And a growing body of scientific
15 research suggests that light pollution can have lasting adverse effects on both human and wildlife health.

1. What is the most likely reason why the author included lines 2-4? What vocabulary choices in those sentences help to make the author's point?

2. According to the passage, why did the inhabitants of Los Angeles call emergency centers after the 1994 earthquake?

3. Based on the passage, how would you describe the author's views on artificial lighting?

4. Imagine that the author decided to write a new paragraph. What topic would be logical to cover next? Why?

Anticipate the Answer

❑ **Before looking at the answer choices, try to think of the answer in your head.**
Try not to look at the answer choices until you know what the answer should be. Then find the answer that most closely matches your anticipated one.

❑ **Avoid "could be" answers.** On many SSAT reading questions, there are multiple answer choices that could be correct, but there is only one best answer. If you try to test if you can prove the answer choices correct, you might get stuck with several answers that seem right. Instead, focus on finding your own best answer first.

> Surprisingly, the history of flea circuses begins with watchmaking. In a display of their incredibly precise metal-working skills, watchmakers created tiny props for fleas. This led to the first flea circuses. Fleas were used as the performers because of their strength and availability. At the time, before effective pest control, fleas were a common part of everyday life.
>
> According to the passage, flea circuses were created in order to
>
> (A) pass the time while watchmakers were not busy working
> (B) promote the need for pest control to eliminate fleas
> (C) test the capabilities of different metals and metal-working tools
> (D) demonstrate the talents of watchmakers
> (E) exhibit the incredible skill of fleas
>
> This might be a challenging question, because several answer choices could be correct.
>
> (A) could be right, because making flea circuses could have been a hobby to pass the time.
> (C) could be right, because the watchmakers could test new materials and methods by creating the tiny props.
> (E) could be right, because the circuses would show the strength of fleas.
>
> If you ignore the answer choices and just consider the question, it is clear from the information in the passage that flea circuses were made to display watchmakers' skills. (D) is the answer that best matches this idea.

❑ Anticipating the answer will save you time on the Reading Comprehension section. Instead of seeing if you can prove each answer choice right, you only need to find the correct answer once.

TRY IT OUT

Many organisms have developed incredible adaptations for the environments in which they live. The most impressive examples are classified as "extremophiles," which are organisms that can thrive in conditions that are too harsh for most forms of life. One of the most well-known and unique extremophiles is the tardigrade, also known as the "water bear" or "moss piglet." This microscopic animal looks like a cross between a grub and a gummy bear.
5   Tardigrades can survive in environments that would be lethal to any other animal. They can live in temperatures colder than -400 degrees and hotter than 300 degrees Fahrenheit. They can also survive without water for nearly a decade. This is necessary because tardigrades commonly live in puddles and moss, which often dry out. They can reduce their metabolism to less than one-thousandth of their normal rate, and will return from this dormant state when they have a supply of water. Tardigrades have been found in many of the harshest environments on earth, such
10   as boiling hotsprings and arctic ice. They can even survive the vacuum of space! These amazing creatures show the surprising resilience of life. Research on extremophiles has led to new discoveries that allow scientists to work in conditions that would be too severe for our own bodies.

1. The author mentions "boiling hotsprings" (line 10) as an example of

    _____

    _____

    _____

2. As used in line 8, "state" means which of the following?

    _____

    _____

    _____

3. It can be inferred from the passage that the tardigrade can survive dehydration by

    _____

    _____

    _____

4. This passage is primarily about

    _____

    _____

    _____

SUMMIT
EDUCATIONAL
GROUP

PUT IT TOGETHER

Many organisms have developed incredible adaptations for the environments in which they live. The most impressive examples are classified as "extremophiles," which are organisms that can thrive in conditions that are too harsh for most forms of life. One of the most well-known and unique extremophiles is the tardigrade, also known as the "water bear" or "moss piglet." This microscopic animal looks like a cross between a grub and a gummy bear.

5 Tardigrades can survive in environments that would be lethal to any other animal. They can live in temperatures colder than -400 degrees and hotter than 300 degrees Fahrenheit. They can also survive without water for nearly a decade. This is necessary because tardigrades commonly live in puddles and moss, which often dry out. They can reduce their metabolism to less than one-thousandth of their normal rate, and will return from this dormant state when they have a supply of water. Tardigrades have been found in many of the harshest environments on earth, such

10 as boiling hotsprings and arctic ice. They can even survive the vacuum of space! These amazing creatures show the surprising resilience of life. Research on extremophiles has led to new discoveries that allow scientists to work in conditions that would be too severe for our own bodies.

1. The author mentions "boiling hotsprings" (line 10) as an example of

(A) new scientific discoveries
(B) a source of water for dehydrated tardigrades
(C) the most common habitat for extremophiles
(D) how organisms affect their environment
(E) an extreme environment in which most organisms cannot survive

2. As used in line 8, "state" means which of the following?

(A) area
(B) declare
(C) condition
(D) public
(E) structure

3. It can be inferred from the passage that the tardigrade can survive dehydration by

(A) shrinking its size
(B) slowing its bodily processes
(C) living on moss
(D) burrowing underground
(E) melting ice

4. This passage is primarily about

(A) the hardiness and adaptability of organisms
(B) why tardigrades do not need water
(C) the world's smallest living animal
(D) the tardigrade's ability to survive in extreme temperatures
(E) the benefits of biological research

Process of Elimination

❑ **Eliminate answers which are too broad, too narrow, or simply incorrect.**

As you read through the possible answers, eliminate answer choices that:

- cover more than the passage does.

- talk only about a portion of the passage.

- have nothing to do with the discussed topic.

❑ Process of elimination is extremely effective on Reading Comprehension since you will usually have at least some understanding of the passage. Eliminate wrong answers and then make an educated guess.

> What better way to show the values of a society than through its folklore? America is known for its rugged individuality, work ethic, and national pride. In its frontier legends, with heroes such as Paul Bunyan, Davy Crockett, and Pecos Bill, this American spirit shines brightly.
>
> The passage is primarily concerned with
>
> (A) describing American traditions
> (B) evaluating the connection between myth and reality
> (C) explaining how folklore is a source for symbols of cultural values
> (D) summarizing the author's favorite stories
> (E) examining how national pride is represented in stories
>
> With this question, it might be hard to anticipate the answer before looking at the answer choices, so it is best to use Process of Elimination.
>
> (A) is not correct, because the passage is focused on folklore, not all American traditions: **too broad**.
>
> (B) is not correct, because the passage is concerned with folklore and social values. "Myth and reality" is **too broad**.
>
> (D) is not correct, because there is no mention of "favorite stories": **incorrect**.
>
> (E) is not correct, because the passage is concerned with all social values, not only "national pride." This answer is **too narrow**.
>
> Through the Process of Elimination, we can reason that (C) is the best answer.

❑ For an answer choice to be correct, it must be **entirely** correct. Do not get stuck on answer choices that are only partly right.

TRY IT OUT

Give reasons for eliminating answer choices (e.g. too broad, too narrow, incorrect) and find the correct answers.

When groups of people live together, massive amounts of waste are produced. Some of the waste, such as paper, food scraps, and other natural materials, is biodegradable. Biodegradable materials can break down in a short time, degrading into useful nutrients and resources. However, some waste materials, like plastics, are not biodegradable. These can remain in their original form in the environment for hundreds of years. Scientists are working to replace many of the non-biodegradable materials with biodegradable ones, such as plastics made from potato starch. Also, scientists have discovered a fungus from the Amazon that is capable of breaking down and consuming plastic. This research could dramatically reduce the amount of non-biodegradable waste. However, this will not entirely solve the problem of waste, and the amount of available space where waste can be deposited is diminishing rapidly. Earth may soon become little more than a garbage dump, unless even more imaginative methods of dealing with waste materials are developed in the near future.

1. The purpose of the passage is to

    (A) persuade readers to invest in research on   (A) _____
        plastics.
                                                               _____

    (B) show the connection between the   (B) _____
        environment and human civilization.
                                                               _____

    (C) describe the processes of biodegradation of   (C) _____
        different materials.
                                                               _____

    (D) demonstrate that even the most troubling   (D) _____
        problems can have simple solutions.
                                                               _____

    (E) present the problem of waste disposal and   (E) _____
        describe potential scientific solutions.
                                                               _____

2. Which of the following questions is fully
    answered by the passage?

    (A) What type of waste is the most   (A) _____
        biodegradable?
                                                               _____

    (B) What are the consequences and effects of   (B) _____
        modern human society?
                                                               _____

    (C) Why is plastic less biodegradable than other   (C) _____
        materials?
                                                               _____

    (D) What are some solutions to the problem of   (D) _____
        non-biodegradable waste?
                                                               _____

    (E) How much waste is biodegradable?   (E) _____

                                                               _____

TRY IT OUT

The widespread popularity of TV dinners began in the 1950s, with the Swanson company. After Thanksgiving one year, Swanson had a large surplus of turkeys. Trying to figure out what to do with the leftover holiday turkey is a common concern for many families, but Swanson was faced with over 200 tons of extra turkey! Fortunately, one of the company's executives had an idea. While on an airplane trip, he noticed that the flight service offered meals that had been pre-cooked and packaged. The flight attendants only had to reheat the meals, and they were quickly ready to serve. The executive imagined that meals at home could be prepared in a similar fashion, which would be a convenience for busy families as well as a solution to Swanson's surplus turkey problem.

Although they are convenient, TV dinners are usually less healthy than freshly prepared meals: the freezing process degrades the taste of the food, and so extra fat and salt are often added. Because of this, TV dinners are not as popular today as they were decades ago. Even so, the TV dinner remains in the iconic image of the 1950s American family, pioneers of convenience, gathered around their television set and dining from dinner trays.

3. On the airplane, the Swanson executive realized

   (A) many families value the convenience of modern technologies.   (A) _____

   (B) families often gather around their television set to enjoy meals together.   (B) _____

   (C) the company needed a way to sell their large amount of extra turkey.   (C) _____

   (D) the company could sell prepared meals in order to utilize its extra turkey.   (D) _____

   (E) frozen meals are often not as healthy as fresh foods.   (E) _____

4. It can be inferred from the passage that modern American families are

   (A) more concerned with the health of meals than earlier generations were.   (A) _____

   (B) less interested in watching television together than earlier generations were.   (B) _____

   (C) unaware of the traditions of earlier generations.   (C) _____

   (D) more capable of utilizing leftover foods than earlier generations were.   (D) _____

   (E) often enjoying meals on airplanes.   (E) _____

Checkpoint Review

An attentive watch of the sky on almost any clear, moonless night will show one or more so-called "shooting stars." They are little flashes of light which have the appearance of a star darting across the sky and disappearing. Instead of being actual stars, which are great bodies like our sun, they are, as a matter of fact, tiny masses so small that a person could hold one in his hand. Under certain circumstances of motion and position, they dash into the earth's atmosphere at a speed of from 10 to 40 miles per second, and the heat generated by the friction with the upper air vaporizes or burns them. The products of the combustion and pulverization slowly fall to the earth if they are solid, or are added to the atmosphere if they are gaseous. Since it is misleading to call them "shooting stars," they will always be called "meteors" hereafter.

If a person scans the sky for an hour or so and finds that he can see only a few meteors, he is tempted to draw the conclusion that the number of them which strike the earth's atmosphere daily is not very large. He bases his conclusion mostly on the fact that half of the celestial sphere is within his range of vision, but a diagram representing the earth and its atmosphere to scale will show him that he can see by no means half the meteors which strike the earth's atmosphere. As a matter of fact, he can see the atmosphere over only a few square miles of the earth's surface.

From many counts of the number of meteors which can be seen from a single place during a given time, it has been computed that between 10 and 20 millions of them strike into the earth's atmosphere daily. There are probably several times this number which are so small that they escape observation. Often when astronomers are working with telescopes they see faint meteors dart across the field of vision which would be quite invisible with the unaided eye.

1. This passage is mainly about the

   (A) latest discoveries about shooting stars
   (B) difference between shooting stars and meteors
   (C) features and common misconceptions of meteors
   (D) ways to find shooting stars without a telescope
   (E) number of meteors that hit the earth daily

2. According to the passage, which of the following statements is NOT true?

   (A) "Shooting stars" and "meteors" are the same thing.
   (B) By simply looking at the sky, humans can see half of the meteors that fall to Earth.
   (C) Meteors can travel at speeds from 10 to 40 miles per second.
   (D) Some meteors are so small that they go unnoticed by astronomers.
   (E) Every day, millions of meteors enter the Earth's atmosphere.

3. The main purpose of paragraph 2 is most likely to

   (A) show how the author does his research
   (B) illustrate an example of how an average person might count meteors
   (C) provide a reason why telescopes may not be necessary to see meteors
   (D) call into question the use of technology in astronomy
   (E) discuss the future of space imaging

4. According to the passage, once a meteor passes into earth's atmosphere, the products of combustion and pulverization may be

   (A) solid only
   (B) gas only
   (C) liquid only
   (D) solids or gases
   (E) solids or liquids

Checkpoint Review

If a populous hive is examined on a warm Summer day, a considerable number of bees will be found standing on the alighting board, with their heads turned towards the entrance, the extremity of their bodies slightly elevated, and their wings in such rapid motion that they are almost as indistinct as the spokes of a wheel, in swift rotation on its axis. A brisk current of air may be felt proceeding from the hive, and if a small piece of down be suspended by a
5   thread, it will be blown out from one part of the entrance, and drawn in at another. What are these bees expecting to accomplish, that they appear so deeply absorbed in their fanning occupation, while busy numbers are constantly crowding in and out of the hive? And what is the meaning of this double current of air?

To Huber, we owe the first satisfactory explanation of these curious phenomena. These bees, plying their rapid wings in such a singular attitude, are performing the important business of *ventilating* the hive; and this double
10   current is composed of pure air rushing in at one part, to supply the place of the foul air forced out at another. By a series of the most careful and beautiful experiments, Huber ascertained that the air of a crowded hive is almost, if not quite, as pure as the atmosphere by which it is surrounded. Now, as the entrance to such a hive is often, more especially in a state of nature, very small, the interior air cannot be renewed without resort to some artificial means. If a lamp is put into a close vessel with only one small orifice, it will soon exhaust all the oxygen, and go out. If
15   another small orifice is made, the same result will follow; but if by some device a current of air is drawn out from one, an equal current will force its way into the other, and the lamp will burn until the oil is exhausted.

1. This passage is mainly about

    (A) atmospheric pollution
    (B) experiments performed on beehives
    (C) the many responsibilities of worker bees
    (D) measuring oxygen levels in beehives
    (E) how and why bees ventilate the hive

2. In line 8, the word "curious" most nearly means

    (A) questioning
    (B) peculiar
    (C) inquisitive
    (D) medicinal
    (E) apathetic

3. If the bees did not perform the fanning activity described in the passage, it can be inferred that

    (A) the inside of the hive would get too cold
    (B) the bees may suffocate from lack of oxygen
    (C) the entrances to the hive would become more crowded
    (D) the air inside the hive would be purer than the air outside
    (E) the bees would not have enough work to do

4. Which of the following best describes the relationship between the first and second paragraphs of the passage?

    (A) Paragraph 1 introduces a behavior of bees and Paragraph 2 explains that behavior
    (B) Paragraph 1 describes the beehive and Paragraph 2 focuses on bees' movements
    (C) Paragraph 1 is written from the perspective of the bees, while Paragraph 2 is written from the perspective of the beekeeper
    (D) Paragraph 1 explains why bees create air currents and Paragraph 2 describes how they create those currents
    (E) Paragraph 1 discusses bee behavior in spring, while Paragraph 2 focuses on their behavior in winter

5. The author included questions at the end of Paragraph 1 of this passage in order to

    (A) show the reader that he is not an expert in bee behavior
    (B) transition the reader to a paragraph that explains the answers to those questions
    (C) show the reader that bees are more complicated than one might expect
    (D) establish a scholarly tone
    (E) describe phenomena that baffle beekeepers

Passage Types

❑ Learn to recognize passage types.

Different types of passages may require different approaches.

❑ Adapt the focus of your reading depending on the type of passage.

In **fact** passages, pay attention to details and information. Look for explanations and reasons why things occurred.

In **opinion** passages, understand the author's argument and the logic that supports it. Look for information that the author uses to support the argument. Try to distinguish between what is fact and what is opinion.

In **prose** passages, understand the major events of the story and the emotions of the characters. Read dialogue carefully. Characters may use metaphors or mean more than the literal words they say.

In **poetry** passages, pay careful attention to descriptions and metaphors. Most poems have a deeper meaning. Try to determine if the poem is referring to something more than its literal meaning. Note strong words, because these may be used to create a certain tone.

Answering the Questions

❑ Learn to recognize question types.

Unlike the rest of the test, Reading Comprehension questions do not progress from easy to difficult. It may help to do the passages out of order, but try to complete all of the questions relating to a passage before you move on to the next passage.

Both easy and hard questions are worth one point, so learn to spot the easy questions and do them first. In general, questions break down as follows:

Easier: Detail, Main Idea, Vocabulary

Harder: Tone, Inference, Application

There are more inference questions on the Upper Level SSAT than there are on the Middle Level SSAT.

❑ Do one question at a time.

You may feel pressed for time during the reading. Relax! Rushing or jumping from one question to the next will only lessen your effectiveness. Work methodically.

❑ Use process of elimination. Even on difficult questions, you will likely be able to eliminate a couple answer choices and make a good guess.

Main Idea Questions

❑ Main idea questions ask you to identify the "primary purpose" or "focus" of the passage. In order to answer these questions correctly, you must be able to identify the main point of the passage and those ideas that support this point.

❑ Common main idea questions:

- Which of the following most accurately states the main idea of the passage?
- The primary purpose of the passage is to…
- The passage is primarily concerned with which of the following?
- The author of this passage is primarily concerned with…
- The main point made by the passage is…

Main Idea questions will often contain these words: *main*, *primary*, *overall*, *purpose*.

❑ The main idea of a passage is not simply the topic that the passage is about. Instead, the main idea is an idea, opinion, or feeling about the passage's topic.

❑ As you read, ask "What is the author's purpose?"

For *fact passages* ask: What is the author trying to explain to me?

For *opinion passages* ask: What is the author trying to convince me of?

For *prose passages* ask: What is the author sharing with me? What does the story show about the characters?

For *poetry passages* ask: What is the author trying to evoke? What thoughts or feelings is the author trying to share?

TRY IT OUT

In African cultures, as elsewhere, art has served both religious and practical purposes. A bronze figure of a king is a symbol of the ruler's divine nature. It is also a decorative work. Beautifully carved masks also have a dual purpose. A dancer wears a mask to represent a spirit in a religious ceremony. According to traditional beliefs, the mask gives the dancer the powers of that spirit.

African artists are probably best known for their fine sculpture. In forested areas, artists carved green wood into human figures, masks, and everyday objects. Other African sculptors created excellent works in bronze. Ancient craftsmen from the African nation of Benin are renowned for their many incredible casts of bronze heads and wall plaques that showed important events in history. These bronze figures can be appreciated for both their aesthetic and their instructive value.

1. The main idea of the passage is that

   _____

   _____

2. The passage is mostly about the

   (A) cost of different types of art
   (B) evolution of artistic styles in Africa
   (C) reasons why art gains popularity
   (D) materials used in African art
   (E) different ways in which African art
       functions

3. According to the passage, African sculptors are

   (A) wealthy nobles
   (B) incredibly talented
   (C) underappreciated
   (D) highly religious
   (E) researchers of history

4. The most appropriate title of the passage would be

   (A) Africa: The Land of Bronze
   (B) Africa: A King's Wealth
   (C) The Multiple Roles of African Art
   (D) The Great Expense of African Sculpture
   (E) The History of Great Art

5. The author's main purpose in the passage is to

   (A) describe the skill of African artists and the different purposes of their art
   (B) point out the differences between African and European art
   (C) amuse and entertain the reader by ridiculing the absurd price of sculpture materials
   (D) discredit the inefficiency of certain sculpting methods
   (E) illustrate the cultural influences on African artistic styles

Detail / Supporting Idea Questions

❑ Detail questions ask for specific facts from the passage.

Most of the questions that fit into this category could be called "find the fact" as they ask you to find a specific piece of information, often contained in two or three sentences. Unlike main idea questions, which are more broad, these questions refer to a specific idea.

❑ Common detail / supporting idea questions:

- According to the passage, which of the following is true of _____?
- According to the passage, if _____ occurs then...
- The passage states that _____ occurs because...
- The author believes...
- On line 10, the author compares pollution to...

Detail questions will often contain these words: *states*, *mentions*, *specific*, *example*.

❑ The answers to detail questions can be found in specific parts of the passage. For most detail questions, you won't remember the answer from the first reading. However, if you map the passage, you may remember where the detail appears in the passage. Go to the appropriate place in the passage and search for the answer.

❑ You should be able to support your answer with material in the passage. Practice defending your answer choices by showing the evidence for your answer.

❑ Read above and below any line-numbers cited in the question to get the full context of the sentence. Line numbers point to the general area where the answer is found. You will usually need the context around those lines to get the right answer.

TRY IT OUT

Plato, it seems, was the first person to define the characteristics of the soul. Plato considered the soul to be divided into three distinct energies that are at the core of all human behavior. His reason for this view was based on the conflicting desires people often have; people are often attracted to and averse to something at the same time, such as when someone both wants to commit a crime and is reluctant to do it. Plato believe there must be multiple
5   parts of the soul that control these contradictory motivations. According to Plato, the soul consists of three parts: Reason, Emotion, and Appetite. Plato compared these, metaphorically, to the brain, the heart, and the stomach. He believed that each of these parts of the soul was essential and that they must work in balance in order to live in peace. He gave Reason the greatest value, arguing that a person who is virtuous and wise will use reason to control their passions and desires and that this is the only way to achieve true happiness. He believed so strongly in this idea
10 of the soul that he designed social systems based on it, believing that the harmony of the soul could serve as a model for harmony in the operation of an entire civilization.

1. According to the passage, Plato based his social design on his concept of the soul because

    _____

    _____

2. According to the passage, Plato believed that the most influential part of the soul should be

    (A) the heart
    (B) the stomach
    (C) Emotion
    (D) Reason
    (E) Appetite

3. The author mentions parts of the body (line 6) as an example of

    (A) Plato's knowledge of anatomy
    (B) the different energies of the soul as
         theorized by Plato
    (C) factors that contribute to criminal behavior
    (D) opposing theories of the characteristics of
         the soul
    (E) the modern understanding of biology

Vocabulary Questions

❑ Vocabulary questions ask you to define a word in the context in which it is used. The word may be unfamiliar to you, or the word may normally be used in another context.

❑ Common vocabulary questions:

- In line 6, the word "appreciate" most nearly means...

- Which of the following best captures the meaning of the word "compensate" in line 2?

Vocabulary questions will often contain these words: *the word, meaning, definition, in context.*

❑ Anticipate the answer on vocabulary questions.

Pretend the word in question is a blank. Without looking at the choices, try to fill in the blank with your own word(s). Look for the answer choice that most nearly matches your anticipated answer.

Similar to with Synonyms, you do not need an exact definition to anticipate the answer on vocabulary questions. If you have a phrase or a general idea that helps you understand the word, this may be enough to find the correct answer.

❑ Watch for attractor answers.

Often, vocabulary questions ask you to define words that have more than one meaning. Usually, the most common definition of the word is not the right answer. Be sure to look back at the sentence in which the word appears. The right answer should make sense when you plug it into the sentence.

TRY IT OUT

The geography of Southeast Asia has contributed to ethnic and cultural diversity. The mountains cut groups of people off from one another. In many countries, a majority ethnic group controls the rich river valleys as well as the government. For example, Laos is the home to Lao, Tai, Hmong, Mon, and Khmer peoples, as well as to many Chinese and Vietnamese. The Lao make up 48% of the population and occupy the valleys of the Mekong River and
5   its tributaries. They control the government, determine the official language, and set education policies.

Ethnic minorities often live in the rugged highlands of the main land. Since the poor soil can support only a sparse population, highlanders tend to live in smaller groups. Cut off from other people, these minorities have preserved their own languages and customs. Many feel little kinship to the lowlanders or loyalty to the central government.

1.   What is the meaning of "kinship" as used in line 8?

_____

_____

2.   As used in line 2, "rich" means which of the following?

(A) fertile
(B) heavy
(C) wealthy
(D) settled
(E) lowland

3.   When the author mentions "tributaries" in line 5, he is referring to

(A) donations
(B) testimonials
(C) small rivers
(D) highlands
(E) wishes

4.   Which of the following can best be substituted for the phrase "Cut off" (line 7) without changing the author's meaning?

(A) Disfigured
(B) Attacked
(C) Separated
(D) Plucked
(E) Ruined

Tone / Attitude Questions

❑ Tone questions ask you to identify the author's tone, or the mood of the passage. Look for descriptive words to help you identify the author's opinions or feeling about the topic of the passage.

❑ Common tone / attitude questions:

- The author's tone can best be described as...

- Which of the following best describes the author's attitude?

Tone questions will often contain these words: *tone, attitude, mood, feel, opinion*.

❑ When determining the tone of a passage, look for words that convey emotion or judgment.

> Dark house, by which once more I stand
> Here in the long unlovely street,
> Doors, where my heart was used to beat
> So quickly, waiting for a hand,
> A hand that can be clasped no more--
> Behold me, for I cannot sleep,
> And like a guilty thing I creep
> At earliest morning to the door.
> He is not here; but far away
> The noise of life begins again,
> And ghastly through the drizzling rain
> On the bald street breaks the blank day.

> The tone of this poem is gloomy and sad. The somber mood is clearly seen in words such as "dark," "guilty," and "ghastly." A sense of loss is felt in the images of a heart that "used to beat so quickly" and "a hand that can be clasped no more."
> Even if you struggle to understand what the poem is about, it is easy to see that it is not a happy subject.

TRY IT OUT

One of the greatest testaments to the ingenuity and perseverance of modern man is the success of the desert cities of the American Southwest. In the middle of a vast, harsh land, great cities have grown and thrived. The success of our desert cities is especially remarkable because of the many challenges presented by the desert environment. With most rain falling in the hills and mountains of California, very little moisture comes as far as
5   Utah, Arizona, or New Mexico. With no access to oceans and few rivers, these areas rely on man-made canals and reservoirs for their necessary water. The city of Phoenix receives only a few inches of rain per year; however, the average inhabitant uses 150 gallons of water per day. In order to bring water to the city, an impressive 300-mile system of pumps, pipes, and aqueducts was built to bring water from Lake Havasu across the desert to the residents of Arizona's largest city. 20 years in the making, this project is an amazing achievement of engineering and
10   determination. This is a sign of the great abundance and productiveness of the whole United States. These desert cities show that we can succeed in even the harshest and most unproductive land because of our hard work and many resources.

There are some critics who would argue that the cities of the American Southwest are a drain on our country and that there is no compelling reason for so many people to live in such a remote, unproductive area. However,
15   while it is true that the modern cities of the Southwest are dependent on the resources they can bring from other areas, these desert cities also provide valuable resources to other regions. The Southwest is a major source of American copper, gold, silver, and uranium. While these deserts may be harsh, they contain a wealth of resources.

1.   The tone of this passage is best described as

   (A) delighted
   (B) skeptical
   (C) critical
   (D) admiring
   (E) mocking

2.   The style of this passage is most like what would be found in

   (A) an author's diary
   (B) a geography textbook
   (C) a dramatic novel
   (D) a short story
   (E) a letter sent to a friend

3.   The attitude expressed by "some critics" (line 13) can best be described as

   (A) sarcastic
   (B) humorous
   (C) negative
   (D) sympathetic
   (E) curious

Inference Questions

❑ Inference questions ask you to draw logical conclusions based on what is written in the passage.

❑ Common inference questions:

- The author talks about _____ primarily to illustrate...

- The author's conclusion is supported most directly by...

- The author assumes all of the following except...

- It can be inferred from the passage that

- The passage suggests which of the following about _____?

Inference questions will often contain these words: *assumes, illustrates, infers, implies, suggests.*

❑ Answers to inference questions are never directly stated in the passage, but are defendable with information from the passage.

Inference questions ask you to interpret the information in the passage, or to apply the ideas from the passage to something new. Even though the answer isn't directly stated in the passage, you should still be able to find evidence to support your answer.

TRY IT OUT

The contestants stand side by side, shuffling tentatively on a crumpling asphalt track. All around them are weeds that climb the chain-link fence and muscle up through cracks in the soft, hot asphalt. You get so used to seeing weeds in this neighborhood, you don't even notice them after a while. They are just there, like the drugs and the tragedy, blending into the wounded landscape. On the other side of the playground is deserted Condon Middle School, gloomy and massive, vulnerable to thieves who circle the building in trucks, then move in and peck away like buzzards. Before they gathered at the starting line, there was talk about a guy named Johnson. His street name was Bang, and he considered himself pretty fast. He had planned on being there for the event. But Bang was gunned down the night before. He was twenty-five.

1. What sport are the contestants probably doing? How do you know?

2. Is the neighborhood in a city, the country, or the suburbs? How do you know?

3. About how old are the contestants? How do you know?

4. What sort of mood is the author trying to create? How do you know?

5. Why does the author point out the growing weeds?

TRY IT OUT

9 July 1825

Dear Mama,

Tomorrow will be the most important day of my 11 years. The lawyers will read Miss Margaret's will at the court house. I know that I was her favorite, and all my friends think that she will set me free. Freedom! The word tastes like Christmas when I say it out loud. Like a juicy orange or a cup of sweetened milk.

Grandma has always been a hopeful person like you, Mama. But she says she cannot let hope in the door. You're worth too much money, she tells me. She recalls that Mark was worth one hundred dollars when he was only a boy of twelve, and now he's a grown man of 25.

I am not afraid to hope. I know Miss Margaret has remembered you, her childhood friend, and the promise she made the night you died. Besides, she taught me these words: Love thy neighbor as thyself.

Tomorrow I will taste freedom.

You loving daughter,

–Harriet Ann.

1. How old is the author? How do you know?

2. What does she hope for? How do you know?

3. Who is Miss Margaret? How do you know?

4. What does the author mean when she says "the word tastes like Christmas. . . a juicy orange or a cup of sweetened milk"?

PUT IT TOGETHER

At the age of six, Amos Alcott already recognized the risk of his ambitions. As a young boy, he witnessed a total solar eclipse and, bewildered by the phenomenon, he and his friends threw stones up toward the moon. Amos was too excited and not careful enough; he fell and dislocated his shoulder. Over sixty years later, he judged that this boyhood accident represented much of the rest of his life, because he often pursued grand ideals that led to trouble and failure.

As an adult, Alcott was plagued with disappointments. His books were ridiculed for being too dense and abstract. His Fruitlands experiment, an attempt to create a perfect agricultural community, failed disastrously. His progressive educational ideas were underappreciated and misunderstood. He often had to borrow money, because his ethics were more important than his income. Amos Alcott was perhaps too ambitious and idealistic, but despite his criticisms and failures he has left a positive legacy. His thoughts on education have been particularly influential in promoting the interaction, self-expression, and critical thinking seen in modern classrooms. Thanks to the ideas of Alcott, school instruction has shifted away from repetition and memorization and toward discussion, reflection, and problem-solving. He is remembered for his determination, his innovation, and his bold defense of equality and creativity, which pioneered many changes seen in modern education.

1. It can be inferred from the passage that Amos Alcott would agree with which of the following statements?

   (A) The most effective education is achieved by memorizing a large number of facts.
   (B) Students learn the most when they are allowed to think and express themselves creatively.
   (C) More classes should focus on research on astronomical phenomena.
   (D) The easiest plans are always the best.
   (E) All accidents are the result of poor planning.

2. The author suggests that Amos Alcott

   (A) never recognized that he failed in so many of his endeavors
   (B) would have been more successful if he had pursued grander goals
   (C) was given more praise than he deserved
   (D) was a profoundly different person as an adult than he was as a child
   (E) was ultimately successful

3. The passage implies that Alcott was very concerned about

   (A) avoiding risk and disappointment
   (B) making his ideas easy to understand
   (C) earning as much money as possible
   (D) putting grand ideas into action
   (E) correcting the mistakes he made as a child

Application Questions

❑ Application questions ask you to take information and conclusions in the passage and connect them to similar situations or ideas. The key to this question type is the ability to identify the core of an argument or idea in the passage.

❑ Common application questions:

- The author of the passage would be most likely to agree with which of the following?

- Which of the following statements would provide the most logical continuation of the final paragraph?

Application questions will often contain these words: *most likely, probably*.

TRY IT OUT

The birth of modern computer development is often considered to be around the year 1890. To prepare for the population census of the United States that year, Herman Hollerith developed a machine that used electromagnetism to "read" information encoded in cards punched with holes. The holes in the cards allowed small electrical currents to pass through, which activated counters. By employing this system, Hollerith completed the 1890 census in one quarter of the time it had taken for the 1880 census! The invention of the punch card system symbolizes the dawn of the computer age.

In 1946, the United States military developed the first general purpose computer. Dubbed ENIAC, or the Electronic Numerical Integrator and Calculator, the massive computer consisted of thousands of vacuum tubes and filled an entire warehouse. It broke down often, costing millions of dollars to repair. In addition, ENIAC used enormous amounts of energy, generated great amounts of heat, and was costly to maintain. Compared to computers today, ENIAC was ploddingly slow, completing only about 6,000 calculations per second.

Computers became available to the public through advances in technology and reduction in size and cost, which were driven by increased demand. Interest in computer technology encouraged research and development of faster, cheaper, and smaller transistors and the invention of integrated circuits. These advances made computers more efficient, more useful, and more affordable, bringing computers within the reach of small businesses and home users.

Intense research and development in computer technology has led to great progress since the development of the ENIAC. Integrated circuits called microprocessors have been developed to provide processing capability in tiny chips. Also, large groups of computers have been connected to form supercomputers to provide huge amounts of processing. Whether smaller and more efficient or interconnected and more powerful, computer technology continues to advance far beyond the punch cards Herman Hollerith created.

1. Which of the following is the author most likely to discuss next?

    _____

    _____

2. From the information in the passage, how would one expect modern computer technology to continue advancing?

    _____

    _____

3. Which of the following would the author probably believe best represents the advancement of computer technology since the earliest computers?

    (A) increased reliability and decreased cost
    (B) increased size and decreased energy usage
    (C) increased speed and decreased efficiency
    (D) increased cost and decreased reliability
    (E) increased efficiency and decreased speed

4. As described by the author, when the ENIAC was first created it was most like

    (A) a sports car used for recreational driving
    (B) an enormous, costly vehicle used to haul large amounts of material
    (C) an old train that is still used because a newer model would be too expensive
    (D) an appliance that is used for something other than its intended function
    (E) a modern laptop computer used for creative projects

Except/Least/Not Questions

❑ Except/least/not questions twist questions around by asking you to identify an answer choice that is not supported by the passage.

These questions may take longer to solve, because you cannot anticipate the answer; instead, you have to carefully test each answer choice.

❑ Common except/least/not questions:

- The author would probably agree with all of the following EXCEPT. . .

- Which is the LEAST likely to be. . .

- Which of the following is NOT a characteristic of _____. . .

❑ Find which answer choice doesn't fit with the others.

You can use process of elimination by crossing out the four answers that are supported by the passage, leaving the correct answer.

Roman Numeral Questions

❑ Roman numeral questions present multiple true/false options. These questions also take longer to solve, because each option must be tested.

❑ Common Roman numeral questions:

- It can be inferred that the author would agree with which of the following?

- The _____ includes which of the following?

TRY IT OUT

Most people can appreciate the pleasing effects of music. When your head is bobbing, your feet are tapping, or when you feel a sense of calmness or invigoration, music clearly has a unique and distinctive power. So it is no surprise that therapists are able to use music to great advantage in many forms of treatment.

For millennia, music has been used as a method of healing. Hippocrates, the "Father of Medicine," used music as a treatment for mental illness. Aristotle also described the importance of music, writing, "Music is able to produce a certain effect on the character of the soul." Many therapists today recognize the deep effects that music can have and continue to use it to manage emotional and behavioral disorders. Music therapy comes in many forms: playing instruments, listening, composing, and following rhythms are all activities used in modern treatment.

What makes music so therapeutic? For some people, music is a way to express ideas and emotions. Another benefit is that, in its very nature, music harmonizes. By attuning oneself to the rhythms of a musical composition, one's mind and body can find a sense of regularity. According to studies, this bond with music begins in the womb, where the fetus experiences the mother's heartbeat. Our relationships with music are universal and widespread. The effects of music can be felt by everyone, and in this way it serves to unify us and can help ease troubled minds.

Most people have their own particular songs, musicians, and composers that bring them joy. Also, most people have particular pieces of music that help them through sad or stressful times, as well as music that calms or excites them. In these ways, we use our favorite music as a form of self-treatment, because we recognize the force it has on us.

1. The author mentions all of the following as an effect of music EXCEPT

    (A) calming
    (B) pleasing
    (C) exciting
    (D) stressing
    (E) energizing

2. According to the passage, which of the following is NOT a reason why music can be therapeutic?

    (A) It allows people to bond.
    (B) It promotes stability and consistency.
    (C) It can influence emotions.
    (D) It is used in one standardized form.
    (E) It allows people to express themselves.

3. According to the passage, music therapy involves which of the following practices?

    I.   creating new musical compositions
    II. reading books about music history
    III. listening to favorite pieces of music

    (A) I only
    (B) I and II only
    (C) I and III only
    (D) II and III only
    (E) I, II, and III

Checkpoint Review

As soon as we had reached the rock, my uncle, the Professor, took the compass, placed it horizontally before him, and looked keenly at the needle.

As he had at first shaken it to give it vivacity, it oscillated considerably, and then slowly assumed its right position under the influence of the magnetic power.

5   The Professor bent his eyes curiously over the wondrous instrument. A violent start immediately showed the extent of his emotion.

He closed his eyes, rubbed them, and took another and a keener survey.

Then he turned slowly round to me, stupefaction depicted on his countenance.

"What is the matter?" said I, beginning to be alarmed.

10   He could not speak. He was too overwhelmed for words. He simply pointed to the instrument.

I examined it eagerly according to his mute directions, and a loud cry of surprise escaped my lips. The needle of the compass pointed due north—in the direction we expected was the south!

It pointed to the shore instead of to the high seas.

I shook the compass; I examined it with a curious and anxious eye. It was in a state of perfection. No blemish in

15   any way explained the phenomenon. Whatever position we forced the needle into, it returned invariably to the same unexpected point.

It was useless attempting to conceal from ourselves the fatal truth.

There could be no doubt about it, unwelcome as was the fact, that during the tempest, there had been a sudden slant of wind, of which we had been unable to take any account, and thus the raft had carried us back to the shores

20   we had left, apparently forever, so many days before!

---

1.   The tone of this passage is best described as

(A) shock and amusement
(B) informative and enthusiastic
(C) bewildered and dismayed
(D) betrayal and hostility
(E) critical and awkward

2.   In the context of the passage, the term "countenance" (line 8) most nearly means

(A) numbers
(B) voice
(C) face
(D) compass
(E) map

3.   It is most reasonable to infer from the passage that

(A) the compass was malfunctioning
(B) the characters are experienced sailors
(C) the Professor had expected to return to the island
(D) the characters had been lost at sea for days
(E) the characters are being chased

4.   The passage is written from the viewpoint of which of the following?

(A) an omniscient narrator
(B) the Professor
(C) a crew member
(D) the captain of a ship
(E) the Professor's relative

Checkpoint Review

There are primal things which move us. Fire has the character of a free companion that has travelled with us from the first exile; only to see a fire, whether he need it or no, comforts every man. Again, to hear two voices outside at night after a silence, even in crowded cities, transforms the mind. A Roof also, large and mothering, satisfies us here in the north much more than modern necessity can explain; so we built in beginning: the only way
5 to carry off our rains and to bear the weight of our winter snows. A Tower far off arrests a man's eye always: it is more than a break in the sky-line; it is an enemy's watch or the rallying of a defense to whose aid we are summoned. Nor are these emotions a memory or a reversion only as one crude theory might pretend; we craved these things— the camp, the refuge, the sentinels in the dark, the hearth—before we made them; they are part of our human manner, and when this civilization has perished they will reappear.

10 Of these primal things the least obvious but the most important is The Road. It does not strike the sense as do those others I have mentioned; we are slow to feel its influence. We take it so much for granted that its original meaning escapes us. Men, indeed, whose pleasure it is perpetually to explore even their own country on foot, and to whom its every phase of climate is delightful, receive, somewhat tardily, the spirit of The Road. They feel a meaning in it; it grows to suggest the towns upon it, it explains its own vagaries, and it gives a unity to all that has arisen
15 along its way. But for the mass The Road is silent; it is the humblest and the most subtle, but, as I have said, the greatest and the most original of the spells which we inherit from the earliest pioneers of our race. It was the most imperative and the first of our necessities. It is older than building and than wells; before we were quite men we knew it, for the animals still have it to-day; they seek their food and their drinking-places, and, as I believe, their assemblies, by known tracks which they have made.

1. In the context of the passage, the word "arrests" (line 5) most nearly means

   (A) jails
   (B) captures
   (C) relaxes
   (D) punishes
   (E) fights

2. The main point made by the passage is that

   (A) The Road is the humblest of all the primal things
   (B) certain physical things hold special meaning for mankind as a whole
   (C) Fire, Towers, Roofs, and Roads would reappear even if civilization perished
   (D) animals and humans have The Road in common
   (E) the symbols discussed protect humans from nature

3. According to the passage, which of the following statements is true?

   (A) Man always needs Fire to survive.
   (B) Towers always represent protection.
   (C) The Road is the most important and most obvious of the primal things.
   (D) Mankind feels the influence of The Road before all other primal things.
   (E) The Road represents exploration and unity.

4. The tone of the author is best described as

   (A) argumentative
   (B) disappointed
   (C) indifferent
   (D) amused
   (E) contemplative

Chapter Review

❑   Format/Directions

The SSAT contains one Reading Comprehension section. This section is 40 minutes and has 40 questions.

❑   **Be an active reader.** Never expect a passage to interest or entertain you. You have to get into it, on your own. Reading is not a passive experience. It's something you do **actively**. Don't wait to see what a passage says; go get it!

❑   **Summarize and make connections.** Restate phrases, sentences, and paragraphs in your own words. This will help you understand and remember what you have read.

❑   **As you read, analyze the passage and ask questions:**

What topic is the author writing about?

What type of passage is it?

What is the author's purpose?

What is the main idea of each paragraph?

What will come next?

❑   **Underline or write down the main ideas of each paragraph.** Marking the passage will force you to search actively for the important points, and it will also help keep your mind from wandering as you read.

❑   Don't try to retain every detail in the passage. Instead, try to develop a mental "picture" of the passage, so you'll know where to look to answer specific questions.

❑   **Break the passage down into parts.** As you read, try to follow the path of the passage as it shifts from point to point. Pay attention to the first and last sentence in each paragraph as they will often announce the transition from one point to the next. Mark with a check in the margin where each shift takes place.

❑   **Consider how parts of a passage work together.** After you finish a paragraph or supporting point, ask yourself how it fits into the overall main idea. For example, does that part of the passage introduce an idea, use examples to support an idea, compare things, or bring up a counterpoint?

❑ Don't waste too much time on a difficult sentence or word. There probably won't be a question on it. If you do get a question about the sentence or word, you can go back and figure it out then. You'll likely be more able to understand a difficult sentence or word when you go back with more knowledge of the passage.

❑ **Before looking at the answer choices, try to think of the answer in your head.** Try not to look at the answer choices until you know what the answer should be. Then find the answer that most closely matches your anticipated one.

❑ **Avoid "could be" answers.** On many SSAT reading questions, there are multiple answer choices that could be correct, but there is only one best answer. If you try to test if you can prove the answer choices correct, you might get stuck with several answers that seem right. Instead, focus on finding your own best answer first.

❑ **Eliminate answers which are too broad, too narrow, or simply incorrect.** As you read through the possible answers, eliminate answer choices that:

- cover more than the passage does.
- talk only about a portion of the passage.
- have nothing to do with the discussed topic.

❑ For an answer choice to be correct, it must be **entirely** correct. Do not get stuck on answer choices that are only partly right.

❑ Answering the Questions

Main idea questions ask for the main idea or author's opinion. Anticipate the answer to main idea questions. Eliminate answers that are too broad, too narrow, or simply wrong.

Vocabulary questions ask you to define a word as it is used in context.

Defend your answer to detail questions with information from the passage.

Inference questions ask you to draw conclusions based on what is written. Do not expect the answer to be explicitly stated in the passage.

On except/least/not questions, find which answer choice doesn't fit with the others.

Use process of elimination to solve Roman numeral questions.

Reading Practice – Middle Level

More than 200 resorts and spas in the United States offer their guests the use of hot springs for bathing, swimming, or therapy. Geothermal waters have been used recreationally for a very long time, even before the word "spa," derived from a Belgium hot spring called "Espa," found its way into the English language during the 1300s. The U.S. National Park Service estimates that humans have bathed in the Arkansas hot springs for at least 10,000

5   years. Native American tribes revered the hot springs area—which they called the "Valley of Vapors"— as a sacred place where the Great Spirit lived and brought forth Mother Earth's healing warmth. The tribes established these hot springs, like many others throughout the New World, as neutral ground. Tribal warriors could rest and bathe at the springs, taking refuge from their battles, without the threat of attack.

When Europeans began to settle in the New World, many Native Americans tried to keep the existence of hot

10   springs a secret. But these early settlers eventually discovered them. And by the 1800s, some settlers realized the commercial potential of the hot springs and began to develop them into spas and resorts, which were very popular in Europe at the time. Currently, The Hot Springs Resort in Glenwood Springs, Colorado, features the world's largest, outdoor geothermal swimming pool.

1. What is the main idea of the first paragraph?

2. Why do you think that ancient Native American tribes considered the Arkansas hot springs to be a "sacred place" (lines 5-6)?

3. In line 7, what does it mean that the hot springs were considered "neutral ground"?

4. What is the purpose of the last paragraph of this passage?

5. Based on clues in the passage, what is the meaning of the term "geothermal"?

Opened in 1915, Teatro La Paz was an early 20th century cultural center that screened Mexican films and hosted visiting entertainers, scholars, and politicians. It is located in the city of Mission, Texas, which is known for its production of ruby red grapefruit.

Teatro La Paz was an integral part of the culture of the region until the Depression of the 1930s, when the
5   building was used in relief efforts to assist the poorest in the community.

In 1945, a new owner, Enrique Flores, refurbished the theater to show Spanish language films and host live entertainment, and changed the name to the Rio Theater. It continued to serve the Spanish-speaking community until it closed in 1969. In 1976, the building was revived by Flores' son, Enrique Jr., as the Xochil Art and Culture Center, one of the earliest Chicano art centers in Texas. The art center served as a lively exhibition and theater space
10   for Chicano and Latino artists during the 1970s and 1980s.

6.   In what sort of book or publication would you expect to find a passage like this?

7.   As it is used in line 4, what is the meaning of the word "integral"?

8.   Over the years, the building of Teatro La Paz was used for many different purposes. What are all of the different uses mentioned in the passage?

9.   Imagine that you were asked to give this passage a title that would help readers understand the main idea. What title would you give this piece?

Ruby always remembers the day that Jack came to the station.

It is the twenty-sixth day of December, the day after Christmas, and Ruby, having busied herself about the house most of the morning, in her usual small way, has gone down to the creek to do Fanny and Bluebell's washing.

There is no reason in the world why those young ladies' washing should not be undertaken in the privacy of the
5   kitchen, save that Jenny, in an inadvertent moment, has enlightened her young mistress as to the primitive Highland way of doing washing, and has, moreover, shown her a tiny wood-cut of the same, carefully preserved in her large-print Bible.

It is no matter to Ruby that the custom is now almost obsolete. The main thing is that it is Scottish, and Scottish in every respect Ruby has quite determined to be.

10   Fanny and Bluebell sit in upright waxen and wooden silence against a stone, wrapped each in a morsel of calico, as most of their garments are now immersed in water. Bluebell is a brunette of the wooden-jointed species, warranted to outlive the hardest usage at the hands of her young owner. She has lost the roses from her cheeks, the painted wig from her head, one leg, and half an arm, in the struggle for existence; but Bluebell is still good for a few years more wear. The painted wig Ruby has restored from one of old Hans' paint-pots when he renewed the station
15   outbuildings last summer; but the complexion and the limbs are beyond her power. And what is the use of giving red cheeks to a doll whose face is liable to be washed at least once a day?

Fanny, the waxen blonde, has fared but little better. Like Bluebell, she is one-legged, and possesses a nose from which any pretensions to wax have long been worn away by too diligent use of soap and water. Her flaxen head of hair is her own, and so are her arms, albeit those latter limbs are devoid of hands. Dolls have no easier a time of it in
20   the Australian bush than anywhere else.

10. Why does Ruby decide to go down to the creek?

11. Who are Fanny and Bluebell?

12. In what country does this story take place? How do you know?

13. Who is the narrator of this story?

14. Why are Ruby's dolls in such poor condition?

Through the fields of nodding clover
Comes a dainty little rover;
On from bud to blossom hasting,
Not the smallest moment wasting.
5   Ever gay and uncomplaining,
Nature's honeyed chalice draining;
Merry little worker bee,
Ev'ry day a jubilee.

Past the "red-cap's" fragrant bower
10   To a modest sister flower,
In whose tender heart reposes
All the sweets of all the roses;
Then with golden trophies laden
Homeward hums this busy maiden;
15   Merry little worker bee,
Ev'ry day a jubilee.

15. What technique does the author use to describe the clover?

16. What is a word that could be substituted for "hasting" (line 3)?

17. In your own words, what is the meaning of lines 9-12?

18. What are some ways that the poet plays upon the reader's senses?

19. Why might the poet have decided to use repetition at the end of each stanza?

20. How would you describe the main idea of the poem?

During the Viking period (about 800 AD to 1050 AD), Scandinavian navigational practices may have been the most skillful in Europe. True, the Viking sailor may have been no better than others while traveling coastal waters. Knowing the location of sandbars and other hazards and the tendencies of tides, coastal winds, and currents was part of any sailor's stock-in-trade since at least the time of the ancient Greeks. What distinguished the Viking as a

5   navigator were his methods of crossing wide and open seas during the traditional sailing season from April to October.

As is often the case with the history of early navigation, direct contemporary evidence for Viking navigation is lacking; the Viking navigator passed along only orally what he learned for himself and what he had learned from previous generations. We are forced to gather what we can about his practices from mostly casual references in

10   sagas and other accounts of his time that were written considerably afterward, usually by men who themselves were inexperienced at sea. Inadequate as it is, this evidence reveals at least the Viking's most important navigational methods.

Faced with the dangers of sudden shifts of wind or lack of it altogether, blanketing fog, and other perils of the harsh North Atlantic, the Viking who crossed the vast ocean was always an intrepid adventurer. That the mishaps he

15   had, as recounted in sagas and other sources, are the exception rather than the rule owes much to his navigational skill.

21. The primary purpose(s) of this passage is (are) to

   (A) criticize today's sailors for failing to learn from the Vikings
   (B) give a historical overview of Viking culture and describe its influence on America
   (C) familiarize readers with weather patterns in the North Atlantic
   (D) describe the skill of Viking navigators and explain how we came to learn about it
   (E) depict the dangers of sailing in the Atlantic

22. According to the passage, Viking sailors differed from other sailors mainly through their

   (A) advanced methods of ship construction
   (B) skill in reading the compass
   (C) method of sailing in the open seas
   (D) willingness to sail in cold weather
   (E) ability to recognize hazards

23. Which of the following best describes the author's attitude toward Viking navigators?

   (A) Angry
   (B) Admiring
   (C) Envious
   (D) Indifferent
   (E) Encouraging

24. The author suggests that our knowledge of Viking navigation methods comes from what source?

   (A) Written accounts by later authors
   (B) Written accounts by the Vikings themselves
   (C) Careful study of Viking ships
   (D) Ancient Greek written accounts
   (E) Logical assumptions by modern sailors

25. The author implies that our knowledge of Viking navigation methods is

   (A) incomplete
   (B) comprehensive
   (C) likely to improve in the near future
   (D) fundamentally wrong
   (E) unfortunately biased

26. The last paragraph suggests that

   (A) the Vikings are the discoverers of America
   (B) sailing the North Atlantic posed no problems to the Vikings
   (C) the Vikings occasionally encountered problems, despite their skill
   (D) the author questions the courage of certain Viking sailors
   (E) only the Vikings could sail in the Atlantic

To see the earth as it truly is, small and blue and beautiful in that eternal silence where it floats, is to see ourselves as riders on the earth together, brothers on that bright loveliness in the eternal cold – brothers who know now they are truly brothers.

We are astronauts – all of us. We ride a spaceship called Earth on its endless journey around the sun. This ship
5 of ours is blessed with life-support systems so ingenious that they are self-renewing, so massive that they can supply the needs of billions.

But for centuries we have taken them for granted, considering their capacity limitless. At last we have begun to monitor the systems, and the findings are deeply disturbing.

Scientists and government officials of the United States and other countries agree that we are in trouble. Unless
10 we stop abusing our vital life-support systems, they will fail. We must maintain them, or pay the penalty. The penalty is death.

27. The main purpose of this passage is to

    (A) persuade
    (B) entertain
    (C) relive
    (D) discriminate
    (E) dictate

28. In the 2ⁿᵈ paragraph, the author uses the word "astronauts" as

    (A) a satirical commentary
    (B) an alliteration
    (C) a truism
    (D) an analogy
    (E) a criticism

29. With which of the following statements would the author most likely agree?

    (A) It is impossible to get a clear understanding of the way the planet survives.
    (B) Natural resources are unlimited.
    (C) Earth is dying and there is nothing people can do about it.
    (D) Unless humanity takes better care of the planet, there will be dire consequences.
    (E) Ecology and conservation are only to be understood by scientists.

30. The author compares the earth to a spaceship in order to

    (A) explain his interest in science fiction
    (B) illustrate the interdependent structure of systems on earth
    (C) explain the rotation of the planets
    (D) give a reason for government officials to perform studies
    (E) describe unexplained occurrences

Martin Gray, a survivor of the Warsaw Ghetto and the Holocaust, writes of his life in a book called *For Those I Loved.* He tells how, after the hardships of the Holocaust, he rebuilt his life, became successful, married, and raised a family. Life seemed good after the horrors of the concentration camp. Then one day, his wife and children were killed when a forest fire ravaged their home in the South of France. Gray was distraught, pushed almost to the
5   breaking point by this added tragedy. People urged him to demand an inquiry into what caused the fire, but instead he chose to put his resources into a movement to protect nature from future fires. He explained that an inquiry, an investigation, would focus only on the past, on issues of pain and sorrow and blame. He wanted to focus on the future instead. An inquiry would set him against other people – "Was someone negligent? Whose fault was it?" – and being against other people, setting out to find a villain, accusing other people of being responsible for your
10   misery, only makes a lonely person lonelier. Life, he concluded, has to be lived for something, not just against something.

31. The word "distraught" in line 4 means

    (A) peaceful
    (B) troubled
    (C) accusatory
    (D) alert
    (E) shattered

32. Martin Gray is most likely

    (A) an example of how to handle suffering
    (B) a fictional character
    (C) not very inquisitive
    (D) an infamous writer
    (E) shy and passive

33. The author would likely agree that

    (A) people always get what they deserve
    (B) success leads to loneliness
    (C) tragedy ruins people's lives forever
    (D) a positive attitude helps people to cope with troubles
    (E) mysteries are meant to be solved

34. What does the author mean when he says that "life… has to be lived for something, not just against something" (lines 10-11)?

    (A) People should never question circumstances.
    (B) It is better to do something positive than to concentrate on negative things.
    (C) Dreams don't always come true.
    (D) Happiness is fleeting.
    (E) The best way to understand something is to recognize its opposite.

In a society impregnated with racism, even the most secure and respectable black home cannot shelter a child from the ugly realities which daily ravage his or her life and those of millions. Martin got his first lesson in "race relations" when he was six. Among his playmates from the time he was very little were two white boys, the neighborhood grocer's sons. When Martin entered first grade, they were not among his classmates – they attended

5   another school for whites only. Martin attached little importance to this at first, but whenever he ran across the street to see them, their mother found some excuse to send him away. Finally she told Martin what she had already told her sons: "We're white and you're colored, and you can't play together anymore."

Bewildered and hurt, Martin burst into tears and ran home to his mother. As best she could, she told the boy how their ancestors had been abducted and enslaved, brought to America generations ago and used like animals,

10   sometimes kindly, often brutally, but always under the control of the white man. Negroes deserved to be free, they supposedly had been for over seventy years. But white people remained afraid, and so there was a whole system of Jim Crow laws and practices and attitudes. But for every question Mrs. King could answer, there arose others which the child would carry with him into adolescence and adulthood. "So I'm colored," the boy thought. "Why is that? What does it really mean? Why should things be the way they are?" His mother could not satisfactorily deal with

15   such questions. So she brought him back to his rejection by the grocer's wife. "Don't let this thing impress you," she said. "Don't let it make you feel you are not as good as white people. You are just as good as anyone else, and don't you forget it."

35. "Impregnated" in line 1 most closely means

    (A) untouched by
    (B) filled with
    (C) immune to
    (D) ashamed of
    (E) free from

36. Which of the following would be the best title for the passage?

    (A) The History Of Slavery
    (B) The Cruelty Of Children
    (C) A Lesson In Injustice
    (D) Believe In Yourself
    (E) Friends for Life

37. How would the author describe the young Martin?

    (A) emotionally unstable
    (B) unpopular
    (C) inquisitive
    (D) hot-tempered
    (E) jealous

38. The author suggests that Martin's mother was

    (A) insensitive and unable to answer simple questions
    (B) uneducated and illiterate
    (C) loving and overprotective
    (D) wise and nurturing
    (E) strong and harsh

39. The author suggests all of the following reasons for poor "race relations" EXCEPT

    (A) white people's fear
    (B) the biological difference between colored people and whites
    (C) the legacy of slavery
    (D) Jim Crow laws
    (E) an ongoing culture of racist behavior

The Federal judicial system of the United States is made by the Constitution independent both of the Legislature and of the Executive. It consists of the Supreme Court, the circuit courts, and the district courts.

The Supreme Court is created and authorized by the Constitution, and consists of nine judges, who are nominated by the President and confirmed by the Senate. They hold office during "good behavior," that is, they are
5   removable only by impeachment, thus having a tenure more secure than that of English judges. The court sits in Washington from October to July in every year. A rule requiring the presence of six judges to pronounce a decision prevents the division of the court into two or more benches; and while this secures a thorough consideration of every case, it also slows down the dispatch of business.

The jurisdiction of the Federal courts extends only to those cases in which the Constitution makes Federal law
10   applicable. All other cases are left to the state courts, unless where some specific point arises which is affected by the Federal Constitution or a Federal law.

40. The Supreme Court gets its authority from

(A) the President
(B) the House of Representatives
(C) the Senate
(D) the Constitution
(E) the circuit courts

41. The passage implies that once appointed,
Supreme Court justices can remain in office

(A) for life
(B) as long as the President says
(C) from October to July
(D) four years
(E) until they are voted out of office

42. To which of the following are the Supreme Court
Justices compared in the passage?

(A) Circuit court judges
(B) District court judges
(C) The President
(D) Senators
(E) English judges

43. It can be inferred that the author would be most
critical of

(A) the size of the Supreme Court
(B) the circuit courts
(C) the speed of the Supreme Court
(D) the rules of impeachment
(E) English judges

44. Which of the following is NOT true of the
Federal Supreme Court?

(A) It has authority to decide questions of
Federal law.
(B) It meets every year.
(C) Six or more judges are needed to pronounce
a decision.
(D) Its justices cannot be removed.
(E) It has authority only in matters of Federal
law or the Federal Constitution.

I was six when my mother taught me the art of invisible strength. It was a strategy for winning arguments, respect from others, and eventually, though neither of us knew it at the time, chess games.

"Bite back your tongue," scolded my mother when I cried loudly, yanking her hand toward the store that sold bags of salted plums. At home, she said, "Wise man, he not go against wind. In Chinese we say, Come from South, blow with wind – poom! – North will follow. Strongest wind cannot be seen."

5

The next week I bit back my tongue as we entered the store with the forbidden candies. When my mother finished her shopping, she quietly plucked a small bag of plums from the rack and put it on the counter with the rest of the items.

45. The narrator's mother would most likely agree with which of the following statements?

  (A) The strongest people are those who fight for what they want.
  (B) Self-control can be a powerful source of strength.
  (C) Strong people do not talk.
  (D) Chinese people are naturally stronger than other people.
  (E) Eating salted plums keeps you from being strong.

46. "Strategy" (line 1) most nearly means

  (A) game
  (B) battle
  (C) conspiracy
  (D) level
  (E) technique

47. According to the passage, the narrator's mother

  (A) did not want her daughter to eat salted plums
  (B) bought her daughter whatever she wanted
  (C) wanted her daughter to express herself more openly
  (D) used the plums to teach her daughter a lesson
  (E) only bought the things she absolutely needed

48. The passage implies that the mother bought the plums at the end because

  (A) she was convinced by her daughter's arguments
  (B) she wanted some for herself
  (C) they were on sale
  (D) she wanted to reward her daughter for controlling herself
  (E) she accidentally mixed them in with her other groceries

It wasn't until the twentieth century that the intimate life of the duckbill platypus came to be known. It is an aquatic animal, living in Australian fresh water at a wide variety of temperatures – from tropical streams at sea level to cold lakes at an elevation of a mile.

The duckbill is well adapted to aquatic life, with its dense fur, its flat tail, and its webbed feet. Its bill has
5   nothing really in common with that of the duck, however. The nostrils are differently located and the platypus bill is different in structure, rubbery rather than duckishly horned. It serves the same function as the duck's bill, however, so it has been shaped similarly by the pressures of natural selection.

The water in which the duckbill lives is invariably muddy at the bottom and it is in this mud that the duckbill roots for its food supply. The duckbill's large bill, ridged with horny plates, is used as a sieve, dredging about
10   sensitively in the deep mud, filtering out the shrimps, earthworms, tadpoles and other small creatures that serve as its food.

49. It can be inferred from the passage that in the nineteenth century

(A) scientists did not fully understand the duckbill's lifestyle
(B) duckbills were considered strange and dangerous
(C) duckbills did not yet exist
(D) platypuses were too common to arouse much interest
(E) science had a better understanding of duckbills than we do today

50. According to the passage, the duckbill is equipped for aquatic life in all of the following ways EXCEPT:

(A) thick fur
(B) ability to adapt to large range of water temperatures
(C) webbed feet
(D) fish-like gills
(E) flat tail

51. As used in line 9, "roots" means

(A) anchors itself
(B) supports
(C) fights
(D) travels
(E) rummages

52. The passage states that the duckbill platypus's bill differs from the duck's in which of the following ways?

(A) It serves a different function.
(B) It has no nostrils.
(C) Natural selection has shaped it differently.
(D) It has a different structure.
(E) It is not used for finding food.

53. This passage is primarily about

(A) the history of the duckbill platypus
(B) the duckbill platypus's aquatic lifestyle
(C) twentieth-century zoological discoveries
(D) the difficulties of classifying aquatic animals
(E) the uses of a platypus's bill

Reading Practice – Upper Level

Japanese immigrants first arrived in America between 1868 and 1869 when a group of businessmen spirited out 100 Japanese to perform agricultural labor in Hawaii, Guam, and California. Subsequent waves of Japanese migrated from a small number of prefectures in the southwest of Japan. Arriving as contract workers in the wake of the Chinese Exclusion Act of 1882, the Japanese worked the sugar industry until the Organic Act of 1900 made the immigration of foreign nationals for contract labor illegal. Railroads, lumber mills, and farms in California and Washington formed the next stage of settlement for Japanese immigrants. However, the Gentlemen's Agreement of 1907 further curtailed their immigration.

Many Japanese immigrants carved out a niche in agriculture and horticulture. Early Japanese immigrants to California arrived with mulberry trees, silkworm cocoons, tea plants, bamboo roots, and other products, and became heavily involved with the burgeoning agricultural labor movement during the 1920s and 1930s.

World War II changed the dynamic of relationships between Japanese Americans and the rest of the nation. Executive Order 9066 paved the way for the removal of all persons of Japanese descent from western coastal areas to internment camps in the interior of the country. This policy effectively eliminated many of the Japantowns and other Japanese enclaves that sustained Japanese and Japanese American culture. These areas would never fully recover. Later, postwar urban renewal and highway act projects would finish what internment had begun by putting roads and highways through Japanese American neighborhoods (and other minority neighborhoods), further disintegrating the cultural essence of those places. Many Japanese chose either to relocate to the Midwest or move to the East Coast.

1.   This passage is written from the perspective of…

2.   In the context of the passage, what is the meaning of the word "spirited" (line 1)?

3.   In your own words, how did the construction of roads and highways mentioned in lines 15-16 affect Japanese Americans?

4.   What is the main idea of the third paragraph?

Cyprian was not to be found in the cutlery department when his aunt in due course arrived there, but in the crush and bustle of anxious shoppers and busy attendants it was an easy matter to miss anyone. It was in the leather goods department some quarter of an hour later that Adela Chemping caught sight of her nephew, separated from her by a rampart of suit-cases and portmanteaux and hemmed in by the jostling crush of human beings that now

5   invaded every corner of the great shopping emporium. She was just in time to witness a pardonable but rather embarrassing mistake on the part of a lady who had wriggled her way with unstayable determination towards the bareheaded Cyprian, and was now breathlessly demanding the sale price of a handbag which had taken her fancy.

"There now," exclaimed Adela to herself, "she takes him for one of the shop assistants because he hasn't got a hat on. I wonder it hasn't happened before."

10   Perhaps it had. Cyprian, at any rate, seemed neither startled nor embarrassed by the error into which the good lady had fallen. Examining the ticket on the bag, he announced in a clear, dispassionate voice:

"Black seal, thirty-four shillings, marked down to twenty-eight. As a matter of fact, we are clearing them out at a special reduction price of twenty-six shillings. They are going off rather fast."

"I'll take it," said the lady, eagerly digging some coins out of her purse.

15   "Will you take it as it is?" asked Cyprian; "it will be a matter of a few minutes to get it wrapped up, there is such a crush."

"Never mind, I'll take it as it is," said the purchaser, clutching her treasure and counting the money into Cyprian's palm.

Several kind strangers helped Adela into the open air.

20   "It's the crush and the heat," said one sympathiser to another; "it's enough to turn anyone giddy."

When she next came across Cyprian he was standing in the crowd that pushed and jostled around the counters of the book department. The dream look was deeper than ever in his eyes. He had just sold two books of devotion to an elderly Canon.

5.   What is the relationship between Cyprian and Adela?

6.   In what time period do you expect that this story may have taken place? Why?

7.   In lines 5-7 ("She was just in time...fancy"), what is the embarrassing mistake that the lady made? What was Adela's reaction to that mistake?

8.   In line 19, why does Adela need help?

9.   How would you describe the tone of this story?

Society is commonly too cheap. We meet at very short intervals, not having had time to acquire any new value for each other. We meet at meals three times a day, and give each other a new taste of that old musty cheese that we are. We have had to agree on a certain set of rules, called etiquette and politeness, to make this frequent meeting tolerable and that we need not come to open war. We meet at the post-office, and at the sociable, and about the

5   fireside every night; we live thick and are in each other's way, and stumble over one another, and I think that we thus lose some respect for one another. Certainly less frequency would suffice for all important and hearty communications. Consider the girls in a factory—never alone, hardly in their dreams. It would be better if there were but one inhabitant to a square mile, as where I live. The value of a man is not in his skin, that we should touch him.

10. Why does the author refer to "old musty cheese" in line 2?

11. When the author uses the phrase "open war," he is most likely describing…

12. What is the main point of the passage?

The business man the acquirer vast,
After assiduous years surveying results, preparing for departure,
Devises houses and lands to his children, bequeaths stocks, goods, funds for a school or hospital,
Leaves money to certain companions to buy tokens, souvenirs of gems and gold.

5   But I, my life surveying, closing,
With nothing to show to devise from its idle years,
Nor houses nor lands, nor tokens of gems or gold for my friends,
Yet certain remembrances of the war for you, and after you,
And little souvenirs of camps and soldiers, with my love,
10 I bind together and bequeath in this bundle of songs.

13. In your own words, how does the poet describe the "business man"?

14. What is the likely meaning of the word "Devises" as it is used in line 3?

15. In the second stanza, "remembrances of the war" and "little souvenirs" are examples of…

16. What is the main idea of the poem?

17. Based on your answer to the last question, what would be an appropriate title for this poem?

It was Joe Dillon who introduced the Wild West to us. He had a little library made up of old numbers of *The Union Jack*, *Pluck* and *The Halfpenny Marvel*. Every evening after school we met in his back garden and arranged Indian battles. He and his fat young brother, Leo, held the loft of the stable while we tried to carry it by storm; or we fought a pitched battle on the grass. But, however well we fought, we never won siege or battle and all our bouts
5   ended with Joe Dillon's war dance of victory. His parents went to eight-o'clock mass every morning in Gardiner Street and the peaceful odor of Mrs. Dillon was prevalent in the hall of the house. But he played too fiercely for us who were younger and more timid. He looked like some kind of an Indian when he capered round the garden, an old tea-cosy on his head, beating a tin with his fist and yelling: "Ya! yaka, yaka, yaka!"

No one could believe it when it was reported that he had entered the priesthood. Nevertheless it was true.
10   We banded ourselves together, some boldly, some in jest and some almost in fear: and of the number of these latter, the reluctant Indians who were afraid to seem studious or lacking in robustness, I was one. The adventures related in the literature of the Wild West were remote from my nature but, at least, they opened doors of escape.

18. The narrator of the story is probably

    (A) a young boy
    (B) a grown man
    (C) an American Indian
    (D) still friends with Joe Dillon
    (E) a cowboy

19. The author mentions Mrs. Dillon's "peaceful odor" (line 6) in order to

    (A) ridicule her lack of cleanliness
    (B) contrast with the odor of his own house
    (C) contrast with Joe Dillon's fierceness
    (D) impress the reader with his sense of smell
    (E) all of the above

20. Why could no one believe that Joe Dillon entered the priesthood?

    (A) He had never attended church.
    (B) He did not believe in God.
    (C) Everyone thought that he would move to the Wild West and fight Indians.
    (D) He seemed too violent to become a priest.
    (E) All of the above.

21. Why did the narrator join in the Indian battle games?

    (A) He was of American Indian ancestry.
    (B) He was afraid his friends would make fun of him if he did not.
    (C) He was basically a violent person.
    (D) He hated Joe Dillon.
    (E) He also hoped to join the priesthood.

On October 1, 1949, the People's Republic of China was formally established, with its national capital at Beijing. "The Chinese people have stood up!" declared Chairman Mao as he announced the creation of a "people's democratic dictatorship." The people were defined as a coalition of four social classes: the workers, the peasants, the middle class, and the capitalists. The four classes were to be led by the Chinese Communist Party (CCP). At that
5   time the CCP claimed a membership of 4.5 million, of which members of peasant origin accounted for nearly 90 percent. The party was under Mao's chairmanship, and the government was headed by Zhou Enlai (1898-1976) as premier of the State Administrative Council (the predecessor of the State Council).

For the first time in decades a Chinese government was met with peace, instead of massive military opposition, within its territory. The new leadership was highly disciplined and, having a decade of wartime administrative
10   experience to draw on, was able to embark on a program of national integration and reform. In the first year of Communist administration, moderate social and economic policies were implemented with skill and effectiveness. The leadership realized that the overwhelming and multitudinous task of economic reconstruction and achievement of political and social stability required the goodwill and cooperation of all classes of people. Results were impressive by any standard, and popular support was widespread.

22. The main purpose of the passage is

   (A) to persuade the reader to adopt a point of view
   (B) to inform the reader about a subject
   (C) to frighten the reader into taking action
   (D) to condemn the reader for his/her ignorance of a subject
   (E) to distract the reader from the real issues

23. By saying "The Chinese people have stood up!" Mao seems to mean that

   (A) they are cheering him for his leadership
   (B) many of them had been engaged in "sit-down" strikes against the government
   (C) he will have difficulty acting as their leader
   (D) the people have taken power into their own hands
   (E) the people oppose economic reconstruction

24. It can be assumed that "multitudinous" (line 12) means

   (A) having more than one color
   (B) unimportant
   (C) many-sided
   (D) one-dimensional
   (E) life-threatening

25. The author states that the Chinese Communists' first tasks were

   (A) creating national unity and economic reform
   (B) killing their enemies and imprisoning their families
   (C) defeating military opposition and building the army
   (D) recruiting Party members and spreading propaganda
   (E) electing a leader and state council

26. The author would likely agree with which of the following statements?

   (A) Mao was better suited to leadership than Zhou Enlai.
   (B) The Chinese Communists had no right to run the country.
   (C) The Chinese Communists were unfair to the peasants.
   (D) The Chinese Communists met with success at first.
   (E) The Chinese economy was worse under Mao than it had been before.

The picture of Robin Hood that is widely held today contrasts in many respects with that of the outlaw of medieval legend. While the modern image was created by dramatists and writers during the sixteenth and seventeenth centuries, the medieval Robin Hood, who was probably the creation of wandering minstrels, is a more elusive figure who lives principally in early ballads and a handful of historical sources.

5   From the very start, there appear to have been contradictory elements in the character of the legend of Robin Hood. To the 15th century writer Wyntoun, Robin Hood was an outlaw; to Walter Bower, who wrote at the same time, he was an assassin whose name could be used as a term of abuse and whose deeds were celebrated only by foolish people; yet to John Major, writing in 1520, Robin Hood was the kindliest of robbers.

      In an endeavor to date the origin of the Robin Hood tales, many historical Robin Hoods have been searched for.
10   The "outlaw hero" has rarely if ever been purely a fictional creation; and the activities of the leader of some group of outlaws may lie behind the legends of Robin Hood. It was in this way that legends grew up around modern outlaws like Jesse James and Sam Bass, and such may be the case with the original of Robin Hood. Nonetheless, attempts to identify a historical Robin Hood have on the whole been unsuccessful.

27. According to the passage, when was the "modern" image of Robin Hood created?

   (A) during this century
   (B) in medieval times
   (C) in the sixteenth and seventeenth centuries
   (D) around the year 1000 AD
   (E) in the year 1520

28. The author implies that the real Robin Hood

   (A) definitely never existed
   (B) was well known to the writer Wyntoun
   (C) was probably a wandering minstrel
   (D) has not been positively identified
   (E) was an assassin

29. The author mentions the writers Wyntoun, Bower, and Major in order to

   (A) prove that Robin Hood is completely fictional
   (B) show the contradictory views of Robin Hood
   (C) support his argument that Robin Hood was an evil character
   (D) counter arguments that 16th century writers knew Robin Hood's real identity
   (E) deny any personal knowledge of Robin Hood's crimes

30. Which of the following, if true, would contradict the author?

   (A) A manuscript discovered in the 1930s establishing Robin Hood's real identity.
   (B) Jesse James was never convicted of any crime.
   (C) Walter Bower had no personal knowledge of Robin Hood.
   (D) Robin Hood only robbed from the rich.
   (E) Robin Hood came from a family of noblemen.

31. The word "elusive," as used in line 4, most nearly means

   (A) hard to capture
   (B) flexible
   (C) extremely fast moving
   (D) very old
   (E) illegal

Who does not love the *Titanic?*
If they sold passage tomorrow for that same crossing,
Who would not buy?

To go down…We all go down, mostly
5   alone. But with crowds of people, friends, servants,
well fed, with music, with lights! Ah!

And the world, shocked, mourns, as it ought to do
and almost never does. There will be the books and movies
to remind our grandchildren who we were
10   and how we died, and give them a good cry.

Not so bad, after all. The cold
water is so anesthetic and very quick.
The cries on all sides must be a comfort.

We all go: only a few, first-class.

32. What is the tone of this poem?

   (A) Solemn
   (B) Mournful
   (C) Terrified
   (D) Sentimental
   (E) Ironic

33. This poem suggests that

   (A) life is short, and luxury makes life worth
       living
   (B) people should not remember the Titanic
       because it will only make them sad.
   (C) love is the only thing that lasts, it is stronger
       than death.
   (D) dying for a good cause is better than life.
   (E) cruise ships are better than airplanes.

34. "To go down… We all go down, mostly alone"
    is a reference to

   (A) the depths of the ocean
   (B) depression
   (C) solitude
   (D) death
   (E) the nature of love

35. The writer of this poem is most likely

   (A) an actual passenger of the Titanic
   (B) a fan of the blockbuster movie
   (C) a person living at the same time as the
       sinking of the ship
   (D) a person looking back on an historical event
   (E) a deep sea diver

Some 2,300 years ago the Greek philosophers Democritus and Leucippus proposed that if you cut an object, such as a loaf of bread, in half, and then in half again until you could do it no longer, you would reach the ultimate building block. They called it an atom.

The atom is infinitesimal. Your every breath holds a trillion atoms. And because atoms in the everyday world
5   we inhabit are virtually indestructible, the air you suck into your lungs may include an atom or two gasped out by Democritus with his dying breath.

To grasp the scale of the atom and the world within, look at a letter "i" on this page. Magnify its dot a million times with an electron microscope, and you should see an array of a million ink molecules. This is the domain of the chemist. Look closely at one ink molecule and you would see a fuzzy image of the largest atoms that compose it.
10   Whether by eye, camera, or microscope, no one has ever seen the internal structure of an atom: Minute as atoms are, they consist of still smaller subatomic particles. Protons, carrying a positive electric charge, and electrically neutral particles called neutrons cluster within the atom's central region, or nucleus – one hundred-thousandth the diameter of the atom. Nuclear physicists work at this level of matter.

36. According to the passage, the internal structure of an atom is

(A) a 20th century concept
(B) found primarily in bread and ink
(C) infinite and immense
(D) studied by nuclear physicists
(E) easily seen

37. The passage implies that chemists

(A) have a job that is less important than physicists
(B) study subatomic particles
(C) study molecules
(D) make great discoveries
(E) understand Greek philosophy

38. The word "infinitesimal" in line 4 most closely means

(A) minuscule
(B) eternal
(C) numerical
(D) containing oxygen
(E) multitudinous

39. The tone of the passage is most like that found in

(A) a highly technical scientific journal
(B) a Greek textbook
(C) a magazine article on popular science
(D) a press release
(E) laboratory report

40. According to the passage no one

(A) has ever written about this topic before
(B) believed Democritus until his dying breath
(C) wants to study molecules anymore
(D) grasps the importance of scientific inquiry
(E) can see the subatomic structure of an atom

(The following passage was written by the composer Ludwig van Beethoven.)

Oh you men who think or say that I am malevolent or stubborn, how greatly do you wrong me. You do not know the secret cause which makes me seem that way to you. From childhood on, my heart and soul have been full of the tender feeling of goodwill, and I was ever inclined to accomplish great things. But, think that for six years
5   now I have been hopelessly afflicted, made worse by senseless physicians, from year to year deceived with hopes of improvement, finally compelled to face the prospect of a lasting sickness (whose cure will take years or, perhaps, be impossible). Though born with a fiery, active temperament, even receptive to the diversions of society, I was soon compelled to withdraw myself, to live life alone. If at times I tried to forget all this, oh how harshly I was I flung back by the doubly sad experience of my bad hearing. Yet it was impossible for me to say to people, "Speak louder, shout, for I am deaf."
10   Ah, how could I possibly admit an imperfection in the one sense which ought to be more perfect in me than others, a sense which I once possessed in the highest perfection, a perfection such as few in my profession enjoy or ever have enjoyed. Oh I cannot do it; therefore forgive me when you see me draw back when I would have gladly mingled with you. Oh fellow men, when at some point you read this, consider then that you have done me an injustice; someone who has had misfortune can console himself to find a similar case to his, who despite all the
15   limitations of Nature nevertheless did everything within his powers to become accepted among worthy artists and men.

41. In the 3ʳᵈ sentence, the word "inclined" most nearly means

(A) tilted
(B) discouraged
(C) eager
(D) opposed
(E) prejudiced

42. The main purpose of the passage is to

(A) allow Beethoven to explain himself
(B) accuse others of unkindness
(C) show Beethoven's hatred of humanity
(D) explain Beethoven's musical decline
(E) prove that deaf people can play music

43. According to Beethoven, if not for his deafness

(A) he would have written more music
(B) he would have been a better person
(C) he would have sought out the company of others more
(D) he would never have written music
(E) he would have lived in the country

44. A fitting title for this selection would be

(A) The Power of Music
(B) Deafness: Its Causes and Cure
(C) The Sounds of Silence
(D) A Hater of Humanity
(E) A Plea for Understanding

45. The tone of the passage is

(A) sarcastic
(B) congratulating
(C) grateful
(D) threatening
(E) pleading

There were very few schools in the United States 150 years ago. If a child's parents were rich, they hired a tutor to teach the child reading, writing, spelling, and simple arithmetic. Often several children met at the teacher's house to be taught together. Because most of the teachers had also gone to inadequate schools, they knew little more than their pupils. Other children met in church and were taught by the minister. Their only school book was the Bible.

5   But if a child's parents were poor, he might never go to school at all. Instead, he had to work very hard. Some boys and girls worked on their families' farms, while others worked in mills and factories. They had little time to play. In fact, many children were forced to work such long hours that child labor laws were passed to set a limit on how long a boy or girl could work. In 1842, a law was passed in Massachusetts which said that children under 12 could work only 10 hours a day.

10   Some common schools did exist, and like our public schools of today, they were open to anyone. But conditions in American schools were very bad. They were cramped and uncomfortable. There were no maps, charts, or blackboards. In one Boston school of 400 students, there were about 65 whippings a day. Most of the school's windowpanes were broken and the floors were covered with mud.

46. The passage mentions all of the following schools EXCEPT

(A) schools taught by the minister in the church
(B) private tutors for children of rich parents
(C) boarding schools to prepare students for college
(D) common schools that were open to anyone
(E) several children meeting at a teacher's house

47. It can be inferred from the passage that before 1842

(A) children under 12 were not allowed to work
(B) all children spent 5 hours a day in school
(C) rich children worked more than poor children
(D) children were only allowed to work 10 hours a day
(E) some children under 12 were working more than 10 hours a day

48. As used in line 3, the word "inadequate" means

(A) subtracted
(B) lacking
(C) not helpful
(D) nearby
(E) gifted

49. This passage is primarily about

(A) religious education in Massachusetts
(B) the hard lives of poor children
(C) the creation of child labor laws in the United States
(D) how Boston teachers punished bad students
(E) American schools in the 1800s

50. The author mentions the 65 whippings a day (lines 12) in order to

(A) show how effective school discipline was
(B) call for stricter child abuse laws
(C) convince readers that schools are a bad idea
(D) demonstrate the harsh conditions in the school
(E) persuade people to move to Boston

51. Which of the following best describes the tone of this passage?

(A) playful
(B) nostalgic
(C) informative
(D) sarcastic
(E) bored

Every human language has been shaped by, and changes to meet, the needs of its speakers. In this limited sense, all human languages can be said to be both equal and perfect. Some Inuit languages, for example, have many different words for different types of snow: wet snow, powdery snow, blowing snow, and so forth. This extensive vocabulary obviously results from the importance of snow in the Inuit environment and the need to be able to talk

5   about it in detailed ways. In Chicago, where snow is just an occasional annoyance, we get along quite nicely with only a few basic terms—snow, slush, and sleet—and a number of adjectival modifiers. Richard Mitchell has described a certain primitive society where the main preoccupation is banging on tree-bark to harvest edible insects, and this particular people has developed a large, specialized vocabulary for talking about the different kinds of rocks and trees that are involved in this process. In each of these cases, the language in question is well adapted to the

10   needs of its speakers. Each language allows its speakers to easily talk about whatever it is important to discuss in that society.

52. The primary purpose of this passage is to

(A) suggest that some languages are superior to others
(B) show that each language adapts to its society
(C) compare how different cultures talk about snow
(D) show the way languages remain constant over time
(E) contrast primitive and modern languages

53. According to the passage, why do some Inuit languages have several words for "snow?"

(A) They have been influenced by other foreign languages.
(B) Inuit want more variety in their language.
(C) Inuit are more educated than other cultural groups.
(D) Snow is an important part of Inuit life and culture.
(E) Inuit languages change more quickly than other languages.

54. The word "preoccupation" in line 7 most nearly means

(A) frustration
(B) activity
(C) education
(D) anxiety
(E) distraction

55. Which of the following questions is answered by the information in the passage?

(A) How many different languages are there in the world?
(B) Who recorded all the different Inuit terms for snow?
(C) Where did the tree-banging primitive society live?
(D) What is the most commonly-used language?
(E) Why does Chicago have relatively few words for snow?

56. The author mentions which of the following influences on language?
   I. Climate and weather
   II. Food and survival
   III. Education

(A) II only
(B) III only
(C) I and II only
(D) II and III only
(E) I, II, and III

I wanted to be a cauliflower,
all brain and ears,
thinking on the origin of gardens
and the divinity of him
5   who carefully binds my leaves.

With my blind roots touched
by the songs of the worms,
and my rough throat throbbing
with strange, vegetable sounds,
10   perhaps I'd feel the parting stroke
of a butterfly's wing . . .

Not like my cousins, the cabbage,
whose heads, tightly folded,
see and hear nothing of this world,
15   dreaming only on the yellow
and green magnificence
that is hardening within them.

--John Haines

57. In this poem, being a cauliflower would include all of the following EXCEPT

(A) thinking great thoughts
(B) contemplating one's existence
(C) cutting oneself off from others
(D) being in tune with the world
(E) being involved with one's surroundings

58. The main literary technique used in this poem is

(A) metaphor
(B) rhyme
(C) irony
(D) sarcasm
(E) repetition

59. As used in line 4, "divinity" most nearly means

(A) sacrifice
(B) ignorance
(C) godliness
(D) concentration
(E) sweetness

60. The contrast between cauliflower and cabbages in this poem can best be described as the difference between

(A) happiness and sadness
(B) hearing and seeing
(C) poetry and prose
(D) faith and doubt
(E) awareness and isolation

61. With which of the following statements would the narrator be most likely to agree?

(A) We should focus on studying ourselves.
(B) Cauliflower is better to eat than cabbage.
(C) We should open ourselves up to experience the world.
(D) Too much thinking is a dangerous thing.
(E) People are not very different from vegetables.

"Look at me well! I am still alive and by the grace of God I shall yet prove victor!" His harsh voice rising above the din of battle, William pushed back his helmet and bared his face to his retreating troops who thought him slain. Inflamed by their leader's ardor, the Normans then surrounded their pursuers and rapidly cut them down so that not one escaped.

5   This episode marked the turning point of a blood-splashed October day nine centuries ago—a day which so changed the course of events that it is impossible to reckon our history without those few furious hours. For when darkness fell on Senlac Hill, near the seaside town of Hastings on the southeast coast of England, William, Duke of Normandy, had earned the lasting sobriquet of "Conqueror." And a flow of concepts began that would influence men's lives for centuries to come. William's victory at Hastings made England once more a part of Europe, as it had

10   not been since the better days of the Roman Empire. The Scandinavian influence on England began to give way to the political and cultural ideas of the Latin world. Besides feudalism and a new aristocracy, the Normans implanted in England much of their law, architecture, and social customs. Ultimately, the Conquest would affect the New World. Such terms as "justice," "liberty," and "sovereign" crossed the English Channel with William. Indeed, the Conquest left its mark forever on the language you are now reading.

62. In line 1, the purpose of William's speech was to

(A) calm the din of battle
(B) persuade retreating troops to take him with them
(C) inspire his armies to continue fighting
(D) leave a last statement before his death
(E) frighten his enemies into retreating

63. Which of the following best describes the main idea of this passage?

(A) William the Conqueror was a great fighter.
(B) The Norman Conquest changed the course of English history.
(C) The Normans drove the Scandinavian influence out of England.
(D) English history consists of many bloody battles like Hastings.
(E) The Roman Empire continued in England much longer than in other countries.

64. A "sobriquet" (line 8) is probably a kind of

(A) medical treatment
(B) fuel for cooking
(C) curse
(D) payment
(E) nickname

65. The author would most likely agree that

(A) The Norman army was victorious in spite of William's weak leadership
(B) William's greatest strength was his desire for peace at any cost
(C) Unlike most Europeans, William did not believe in God
(D) William was a passionate and effective military leader
(E) The Normans were displeased with William as a leader

66. According to the passage, the Conquest had which of the following effects?

  I. Restored England's ties to the rest of Europe
  II. Replaced Latin culture with Scandinavian political and cultural ideas
  III. Stopped the development of English society and language

(A) I only
(B) II only
(C) I and II only
(D) I and III only
(E) I, II, and III

Mr. Webster made an impression upon the people of Massachusetts, in his time, as of a demi-god. His magnificent presence, his stateliness of manner, his dignity, from which he never bent, even in his most convivial and playful moments, his grandeur of speech and bearing, the habit of dealing exclusively with the greatest subjects, enabled him to maintain his state. His great, sane intelligence pervades everything he said and did. But he has left
5   behind few evidences of constructive statesmanship.

There is hardly a great measure of legislation with which his name is connected, and he seems to us now to have erred in judgment in a great many cases, especially in undervaluing the great territory on the Pacific. He consented readily to the abandonment of our claim to the territory between the forty-ninth parallel and that of fifty-four forty, which would have insured our supremacy on the Pacific, and have saved us from the menace and rivalry there of the
10   power of England. He voted against the treaty by which we acquired California. That, however, is a proof of a larger foresight than that of any of his contemporaries. Alone he foresaw the terrible Civil War, to which everybody else of his time was blind.

What even he did not foresee was the triumphant success of the Union arms. It is hardly to be doubted that if the Civil War had come in 1850 or 1851 instead of 1861 its result would have been different. But Mr. Webster's great
15   service to the country, a service second to that of Washington alone, is that he inspired in the people to whom union and self-government seemed but a doubtful experiment, the sentiment of nationality, of love of the flag, and a passionate attachment to the whole country. When his political life began, we were a feeble folk, the bonds of the Union resting lightly upon the States, the contingency of disunion contemplated without much abhorrence by many leading men, both North and South. Mr. Webster awoke in the bosom of his countrymen the conception of national
20   unity and national greatness.

67. The author is primarily concerned with

(A) criticizing the faults of Mr. Webster
(B) explaining Mr. Webster's entrance into American politics
(C) describing some of Mr. Webster's strengths and weaknesses over his political career
(D) Mr. Webster's uncanny ability to foresee future events
(E) the factors that made Mr. Webster famous in Massachusetts

68. The purpose of the second paragraph is to

(A) show that Mr. Webster's political legacy is imperfect
(B) give evidence of the ways that Mr. Webster inspired nationalism in his countrymen
(C) describe the many laws that Mr. Webster passed as a legislator
(D) discuss the effect that his speeches had on the American people
(E) talk about the laws named after Mr. Webster

69. This passage was probably taken from

(A) a speech in a play
(B) a political advertisement
(C) a biographical text
(D) a government contract
(E) a news report

70. The author's claim that Mr. Webster dealt "exclusively with the greatest subjects" (line 3) most likely means that Mr. Webster was

(A) influenced by wealth and power
(B) not interested in trivial gossip
(C) bored with the common people
(D) misunderstood by his contemporaries
(E) swayed by his religious beliefs

71. According to the passage, what was Mr. Webster's greatest achievement?

(A) He predicted the Civil War.
(B) He was seen as a demi-god.
(C) He voted against useless treaties.
(D) He was a grand and stately figure.
(E) He inspired political unity and nationalism.

Baxter was, perhaps, the most scholarly member of the club. A graduate of Harvard, he had traveled extensively, had read widely, and while not so enthusiastic a collector as some of us, possessed as fine a private library as any man of his age in the city. He was about thirty-five when he joined the club, and apparently some bitter experience—some disappointment in love or ambition—had left its mark upon his character. With light, curly
5   hair, fair complexion, and gray eyes, one would have expected Baxter to be genial of temper, with a tendency toward wordiness of speech. But though he had occasional flashes of humor, his ordinary demeanor was characterized by a mild cynicism, which, with his gloomy pessimistic philosophy, so foreign to the temperament that should accompany his physical type, could only be accounted for upon the hypothesis of some secret sorrow such as I have suggested. What it might be no one knew. He had means and social position, and was an uncommonly
10   handsome man. The fact that he remained unmarried at thirty-five furnished some support for the theory of a disappointment in love, though this the several intimates of Baxter who belonged to the club were not able to verify.

72. According to the passage, which of the following is true?

(A) Baxter suffered from a failed romance.
(B) The members of the club refused to share Baxter's secrets.
(C) Baxter had a genial temper.
(D) At 35 years old, Baxter was concerned with marriage.
(E) Baxter's appearance did not seem to match his personality.

73. As he is described in the passage, Baxter appears to be

(A) the most avid member of the club
(B) talkative and humorous
(C) somber and educated
(D) secretive and friendless
(E) sorrowful and bashful

74. The word "fine" (line 2) most closely corresponds to

(A) passable
(B) humble
(C) impressive
(D) unrefined
(E) shabby

75. The narrator's relationship with Baxter is most likely that of a

(A) great friend and confidant
(B) former romantic interest
(C) fierce competitor
(D) fellow club member
(E) family member

I believe I must have been born believing in the full right of women to all the privileges and positions which nature and justice accord to her in common with other human beings. Perfectly equal rights—human rights. There was never any question in my mind in regard to this. I did not purchase my freedom with a price; I was born free; and when, as a younger woman I heard the subject discussed, it seemed simply ridiculous that any sensible, sane
5   person should question it. And when, later, the phase of woman's right to suffrage came up it was to me only a part of the whole, just as natural, just as right, and just as certain to take place.

And whenever I have been urged, as a petitioner, to ask for this privilege for woman, a kind of dazed, bewildered feeling has come over me.

Of whom should I ask this privilege? Who possessed the right to confer it? Who had greater right than woman
10   herself? Was it man, and if so, where did he get it? Who conferred it upon him? He depended upon woman for his being, his very existence, nurture and rearing. More fitting that she should have conferred it upon him.

Was it governments? What were they but the voice of the people? What gave them that power? Was it divinely conferred? Alas! No; or they would have been better, purer, more just and stable.

Was it force of arms—war? Who furnished the warriors? Who but the mothers? Who reared their sons and
15   taught them that liberty and their country were worth their blood? Who gave them up, wept their fall, nursed them in suffering and mourned them dead?

Was it labor? Women have always, as a rule, worked harder than men.

Was it capital? Woman has furnished her share up to the present hour. Who then, can give the right, and on what basis? Who can withhold it?

---

76. The attitude of the author towards "woman's right to suffrage" can best be described as

    (A) doubtful and resigned
    (B) optimistic and supportive
    (C) indecisive and curious
    (D) cheerful and festive
    (E) apathetic and passive

77. What best summarizes the main point of the passage?

    (A) Human rights for all people cannot be dictated by males alone.
    (B) The author is unsure of her opinion on the issue.
    (C) Women work harder than men, so they deserve the same rights.
    (D) Men have been given their rights by a divine power.
    (E) Women need to support each other in the pursuit of freedom.

78. Why does the author ask the questions in lines 9-19?

    (A) To illustrate reasons why it is bewildering that women do not have suffrage rights
    (B) To show that men should have the ability to decide women's rights issues
    (C) To argue that there are good reasons why women do not have certain rights
    (D) To invite the audience to answer the questions aloud
    (E) To introduce a comical tone to the speech

79. The author states all of the following EXCEPT

    (A) women work harder than men
    (B) men depend upon women for their very existence
    (C) it is ridiculous to question that women deserve equal suffrage rights
    (D) the power to decide suffrage rights is divinely conferred
    (E) women furnish and teach warriors

I will go up the mountain after the Moon:
She is caught in a dead fir-tree.
Like a great pale apple of silver and pearl,
Like a great pale apple is she.

5   I will leap and will clasp her in quick cold hands
And carry her home in my sack.
I will set her down safe on the oaken bench
That stands at the chimney-back.
And then I will sit by the fire all night,
10 And sit by the fire all day.
I will gnaw at the Moon to my heart's delight,
Till I gnaw her slowly away.

And while I grow mad with the Moon's cold taste,
The World may beat on my door,
15 Crying "Come out!" and crying "Make haste!
And give us the Moon once more!"
But I will not answer them ever at all;
I will laugh, as I count and hide
The great black beautiful seeds of the Moon
20 In a flower-pot deep and wide.

Then I will lie down and go fast asleep,
Drunken with flame and aswoon.
But the seeds will sprout, and the seeds will leap:
The subtle swift seeds of the Moon.
25 And some day, all of the world that beats
And cries at my door, shall see
A thousand moon-leaves sprout from my thatch
On a marvellous white Moon-tree!

Then each shall have moons to his heart's desire:
30 Apples of silver and pearl:
Apples of orange and copper fire,
Setting his five wits aswirl.
And then they will thank me, who mock me now:
"Wanting the Moon is he!"
35 Oh, I'm off to the mountain after the Moon,
Ere she falls from the dead fir-tree!

80. What literary technique does the poet
    employ in line 3: "Like a great pale apple of
    silver and pearl"?

    (A) melodrama
    (B) similarity
    (C) personification
    (D) simile
    (E) alliteration

81. The meaning or theme of the poem can best
    be expressed as:

    (A) the benefits of some actions are not
        immediately obvious
    (B) it is sometimes best to sleep on an issue
    (C) planets can be grown similarly to plants
    (D) people should not share their wealth
        with others
    (E) big deeds can have unpleasant
        consequences

82. The poet's reaction to "The World" in (lines
    13-20) can best be described as

    (A) consensus
    (B) encouragement
    (C) whimsical
    (D) forgiveness
    (E) evasive

83. When discussing the Moon, what is one way
    that the poem used personification?

    (A) the Moon cries for help
    (B) the Moon grows into a plant
    (C) the main character carries the Moon
    (D) the poem refers to the Moon as "she"
    (E) the Moon gets caught in a tree

At an early hour, the carriage, which was to take Emily and Madame Cheron to Tholouse, appeared at the door of the chateau, and Madame was already in the breakfast-room, when her niece entered it. The repast was silent and
5   melancholy on the part of Emily; and Madame Cheron, whose vanity was piqued on observing her dejection, reproved her in a manner that did not contribute to remove it. It was with much reluctance, that Emily's request to take with her the dog, which had been a favorite of her father, was granted. Her aunt, impatient to be gone, ordered the carriage to draw up; and, while she passed to the hall door, Emily gave another look into the library, and another farewell glance over the garden, and then followed. Old Theresa stood at the door to take leave of her young lady.
10 "God for ever keep you, ma'amselle!" said she, while Emily gave her hand in silence, and could answer only with a pressure of her hand, and a forced smile.

At the gate, which led out of the grounds, several of her father's pensioners were assembled to bid her farewell, to whom she would have spoken, if her aunt would have suffered the driver to stop; and, having distributed to them almost all the money she had about her, she sunk back in the carriage, yielding to the melancholy of her heart. Soon
15 after, she caught, between the steep banks of the road, another view of the chateau, peeping from among the high trees, and surrounded by green slopes and tufted groves, the Garonne winding its way beneath their shades, sometimes lost among the vineyards, and then rising in greater majesty in the distant pastures. The towering precipices of the Pyrenees, that rose to the south, gave Emily a thousand interesting recollections of her late journey; and these objects of her former enthusiastic admiration, now excited only sorrow and regret. Having gazed on the
20 chateau and its lovely scenery, till the banks again closed upon them, her mind became too much occupied by mournful reflections, to permit her to attend to the conversation, which Madame Cheron had begun on some trivial topic, so that they soon travelled in profound silence.

84. In line 4, "reproved" most nearly means
   (A) encouraged
   (B) relieved
   (C) scolded
   (D) ignored
   (E) confirmed

85. The reader can infer that the relationship between Madame Cheron and Emily is
   (A) loving
   (B) strained
   (C) enthusiastic
   (D) respectful
   (E) envious

86. From which viewpoint was this passage most likely written?
   (A) Emily
   (B) Madame Cheron
   (C) Old Theresa
   (D) An outside narrator
   (E) The carriage's driver

87. According to the passage, which of the following statements is NOT true?
   (A) Emily and her aunt left the chateau.
   (B) Madame Cheron attempted to talk to Emily in the carriage.
   (C) Emily did not feel like talking to her father's pensioners.
   (D) Madame Cheron did allow Emily to take her dog on the trip.
   (E) Emily was less excited about the scenery than she used to be.

88. It can be inferred that
   (A) Madame Cheron cares deeply about Emily's happiness
   (B) Emily is not expecting to come back to the chateau soon
   (C) The views outside of the carriage window made Emily feel cheerful
   (D) Emily was thrilled to finally leave the chateau
   (E) Emily would miss the library and gardens of the chateau more than she would miss the people

Writing

General Information

❏ The SSAT gives you 25 minutes to develop a clear and focused writing sample.

❏ You will have a choice between two writing prompts.

Middle Level tests have two creative prompts. These prompts give you the first sentence to be used in a story.

> *Nobody could have guessed that this would have happened to him.*

Upper Level tests have a creative prompt and a formal prompt. The formal prompt asks a question that usually relates to your own thoughts or opinions.

> *What are the best qualities of a person you admire?*

❏ **Your writing is not scored, but is sent directly to the schools to which you apply.** Even though individual readers may have differing opinions on what makes a good writing sample, most readers are looking for clear, correct writing and a logical response to the topic.

❏ Directions are as follows:

Middle Level

> *Schools would like to get to know you better through a story you tell using one of the ideas below. Please choose the idea you find most interesting and write a story using the idea as your first sentence. Please fill in the circle next to the one you choose.*

Upper Level

> *Schools would like to get to know you better through an essay or story using one of the two topics below. Please select the topic you find most interesting and fill in the circle next to the topic you choose.*

SSAT Structure

Writing Sample – 25 minutes

Quantitative – 30 minutes

MATHEMATICS																								
1	2	3	4	5	6	7	8	9	10	11	12	13	14	15	16	17	18	19	20	21	22	23	24	25
EASY → MEDIUM → DIFFICULT																								

Reading Comprehension – 40 minutes

READING PASSAGES																																							
1	2	3	4	5	6	7	8	9	10	11	12	13	14	15	16	17	18	19	20	21	22	23	24	25	26	27	28	29	30	31	32	33	34	35	36	37	38	39	40
NOT IN ORDER OF DIFFICULTY																																							

Verbal – 30 minutes

SYNONYMS																													
1	2	3	4	5	6	7	8	9	10	11	12	13	14	15	16	17	18	19	20	21	22	23	24	25	26	27	28	29	30
EASY → MEDIUM → DIFFICULT																													

ANALOGIES																													
31	32	33	34	35	36	37	38	39	40	41	42	43	44	45	46	47	48	49	50	51	52	53	54	55	56	57	58	59	60
EASY → MEDIUM → DIFFICULT																													

Quantitative – 30 minutes

MATHEMATICS																								
1	2	3	4	5	6	7	8	9	10	11	12	13	14	15	16	17	18	19	20	21	22	23	24	25
EASY → MEDIUM → DIFFICULT																								

What Are Your Readers Looking For?

❏ The SSAT writing sample is not scored, but copies of the writing sample will be sent to the admissions offices of schools to which you are applying.

Make sure that your penmanship is clean and clear. Remember that it will be read by someone who is unfamiliar with your handwriting.

❏ Typically, writing sample readers are checking that your writing is focused and well-organized. Make sure that you express your thoughts clearly. Strong writing is more important than length; however, don't be too brief or else you won't have time to explain your thoughts.

The writing sample is an opportunity for you to show something about yourself. Your writing sample may show your knowledge, experiences, interests, or personality. Admissions offices are interested in learning about you, so the writing sample is a great opportunity to show your interests, personality, and strengths.

❏ Different schools have different standards when judging writing samples. Contact the admissions offices of the schools you are applying to and ask about what they look for in SSAT writing samples.

Creative or Formal?

❑ For the Upper Level writing sample, your first decision is whether you choose the creative prompt or the formal prompt.

❑ The **creative** prompt is for a short story. This may be a good option if you know how to create an interesting narrative and if you enjoy descriptive writing.

> *It was the most embarrassing moment of his life.*
>
> *She had never seen something so beautiful.*
>
> *They were all waiting for me to speak.*
>
> *She had always been a hard worker, but she had never faced such a difficult challenge.*

❑ The **formal** prompt is for an essay. This may be a good option if you are skilled at defending arguments and enjoy logic and reason.

> *What class or subject in school do you enjoy most? Why?*
>
> *Who is someone you respect? Explain why you feel this way.*
>
> *Explain a hobby you have that makes you special.*
>
> *Which two historical figures would you like to meet and why?*

❑ Try writing both types of prompts. You may feel more comfortable with one type, which is important to know when preparing for the official test.

Preparing a Creative Story

❑ Most stories have three essential parts: setup, confrontation, and resolution.

The **setup** is used to introduce characters, describe settings, and establish situations. This usually comes first because it is needed to understand the rest of the story.

The **confrontation** is the main source of drama and tension in the story. Stories need some type of problem or conflict. This can be a personal desire, a disagreement, a difficult challenge, etc.

The **resolution** shows the outcome of the story. This is where the characters make important decisions, where relationships break apart or come together, where heroes succeed and problems are finally resolved.

❑ Before you begin writing your story, make sure that you know what will happen.

Take some time to plan and outline your story. This will ensure that your writing is focused and your time is managed effectively.

Prompt: *Nobody could have guessed that this would have happened to him.*

Nobody could have guessed that this would have happened to him. Just a week before, Frank had shoved him into the cold, dark depths of his own locker. For years, Frank had teased and tormented Kyle. Now, Kyle had the chance to play on the same team as Frank, the star quarterback of the school football team.

The coach of the football team had explained a few days earlier that one of their star players wasn't able to play anymore. The wide receiver had been injured in a recent practice, severely damaging his ankle, and wouldn't be returning for the rest of the season. Kyle was the wide receiver on the junior varsity team, and now the coach needed him to help fill the position on the varsity team.

> SETUP

Kyle's mind was filled with worries. Would he be able to play well enough? Most of the players were at least a year older than him, so they were more experienced. Would Frank bully him? He was tired of Frank calling him names and pushing him around. However, the situation could also be a great opportunity. Maybe he could show his skills, succeed, and have more of a chance to get an athletic scholarship. He had accepted the coach's offer because, more than anything, he wanted to prove to himself and to Frank that he was a strong player.

On the night of his first varsity game, Kyle nervously watched his teammates play. He sat on the hard bench on the sidelines and awaited his chance to shine. After the other team fumbled the ball early in the game, Kyle was able to get on the field with the offensive team. The players gathered in a huddle and Frank started barking out orders.

"Are you sure you can handle this, rookie?" Frank said, looking harshly at Kyle.

"Just get the ball to me," Kyle said with confidence. "I'm faster than anyone on the other team."

> CONFRONTATION

The players gathered on the line of scrimmage. Frank called the play, the linebacker snapped the ball, and Kyle was off running. His jersey waved in the cool air. He looked back and saw Frank look up toward him. For a second, he doubted that Frank would pass to him, but then the ball was launched, spiraling tightly toward him. Kyle sprinted on and snatched the ball out of the air. The other players were already far behind him, and he ran with the bright lights shining on him and the crowd cheering.

At the end zone, Kyle stood triumphant. Frank ran up to him and patted him on the back.

"Wow, I didn't know you were that fast," Frank said.

Kyle knew that he had earned Frank's respect. He had been afraid to join the varsity team, but he knew he could prove that he was as good as anyone.

> RESOLUTION

The Setup

❑ Use the beginning of your story to describe the characters and the situation.

Think about what kind of person your main character is. It is more important to describe your character's personality or relationships than his/her appearance.

Your character should be dealing with a problem, difficulty, or choice. The setup explains what this situation is <u>before</u> the character faces this problem and takes an action.

Consider what happened before the confrontation of the story. What events led to the main tension? How did it all begin?

❑ Your setup should show who the characters are and explain the situation they are in. A great setup will make your reader want to keep reading to find out how the characters handle the situation.

> *That moment changed everything. In an instant, my whole social life was undone, and it was years before I found my place in the world again.*
>
> *It all started back in the fourth grade. If I could do anything over again, I would change that year. I became friends with a group of people who were considered the "cool kids" in the school. Although these people were nice to me, they were cruel and condescending to many of the other students. They regularly bullied, teased, and gossiped about my classmates, and I am ashamed to say that I also took part in this. The unofficial leader of the group, Leslie, was a small girl whose greatest talent was criticizing others, usually the people who were unusual or unique in any way. As terrible as we were, there was a feeling of respect that we got from the rest of the students. Eventually, however, it all fell apart.*

TRY IT OUT

Write a setup for a short story using each of the following prompts:

1. *It seemed like it was going to be an ordinary day.*

    _____

    _____

    _____

    _____

    _____

    _____

    _____

    _____

    _____

    _____

    _____

2. *It was over almost as soon as it started.*

    _____

    _____

    _____

    _____

    _____

    _____

    _____

    _____

    _____

    _____

    _____

The Confrontation

❑ Usually, the biggest piece of a story focuses on the problem or conflict that the main character faces.

Something should happen to your character. If he/she wants to accomplish something, maybe something gets in the way; if he/she disagrees with someone, maybe they get in an argument; if he/she is afraid of something, maybe he/she finally his to face this fear. There should be an event that creates tension and drama in your story.

Your character should make a decision or take an action.

❑ Your confrontation should show what happens to the character and how he/she responds to it.

Although the outcasts were her usual prey, Leslie sometimes went for some of her friends, me included. One day during the lunch hour, Leslie asked me if I was rich. I had never considered this before, and my family has never seemed to struggle with money, so I said yes, that my family was wealthy. Leslie then smiled mischievously and told me, "Well, you don't look like it. You dress like a homeless person." Although now I can see that this comment was just a shallow attack, it hit me hard back then. I was humiliated, and for a long time I worked extra hard to get Leslie's approval, because I didn't want her to criticize me again.

Finally, after months of worrying about my clothes, I realized that I didn't need to please Leslie. I liked the clothes I wore, and that was all that mattered. My clothing style was unique, and that wasn't a bad thing. I finally decided that I liked being a bit different, and I wasn't going to let anyone make me feel bad about it. So, I stopped associating with Leslie and all of her friends. This was difficult at first, because I was losing most of my friends, but I knew it would be better for me, because I didn't like the person they were turning me into.

TRY IT OUT

Continue your short stories by writing confrontations:

1. *It seemed like it was going to be an ordinary day.*

_____

_____

_____

_____

_____

_____

_____

_____

_____

_____

_____

2. *It was over almost as soon as it started.*

_____

_____

_____

_____

_____

_____

_____

_____

_____

_____

_____

The Resolution

❑ The end of a story shows what happened as a result of the character's actions.

Something should have changed since the beginning of the story. In resolutions, characters often have a new realization or understanding. If the character has learned something, describe how he/she has changed or what he/she has learned. If the character has handled an issue, explain how the situation has changed.

❑ Your resolution should make the story feel complete, with no loose ends.

> *Looking back, I sometimes regret the time I spent being Leslie's friend. I wish I hadn't been a bully and that I hadn't lived with such low self-esteem because of her. I have a hard time accepting that I let myself be such a close friend to her. However, although I wish I could change my past, it has made me the person I am today. Because of what I have gone through, I have learned to be more accepting of others and of myself. I never judge or criticize my peers, and I also have more confidence in myself because I don't worry about the opinions of others. In the end, it has become one of my life's most important lessons.*

TRY IT OUT

Complete your short stories by writing resolutions:

1. *It seemed like it was going to be an ordinary day.*

_____

_____

_____

_____

_____

_____

_____

_____

_____

_____

2. *It was over almost as soon as it started.*

_____

_____

_____

_____

_____

_____

_____

_____

_____

_____

Preparing a Formal Essay

❑ Most essays have three essential parts: introduction, body, and conclusion.

The **introduction** establishes the main idea and focus of your essay. It includes your thesis, which is your essay's central argument or point.

The **body** is used to explain your argument and describe how your examples support that argument.

The **conclusion** summarizes your essay and connects your examples back to your main idea.

❑ Before you begin writing your essay, make sure that you know what your thesis and examples will be.

Take some time to plan and outline your essay. This will ensure that your writing is focused and your time is managed effectively.

Prompt: *Describe an experience that has inspired you.*

When I was eleven years old, I saw a group of boys harassing a girl in the hallway at my school. I pretended not to notice, as did most of my fellow students. However, one student, a fellow sixth-grade boy, stepped between the girl and her harassers and told the other boys to leave the girl alone. After making a couple of threats and insulting the boy, the group of boys walked away. The girl was upset, but okay, and when the boy verified that she was all right, he went back to his locker to get his things and head to class. Most people went back to their conversations and forgot all about it, but I was deeply affected by what had happened. This simple event made me change who I am so that I can be the type of person who will also stand up for others.

INTRODUCTION

This experience inspired me for a few reasons. One reason was that the boy who helped this girl wasn't friends with her. They didn't hang out in the same groups at all. He stepped in because it was the right thing to do, and for no other reason. It showed me that there are people who care about others even when they have no specific reason to do so. In our society, we often seek to protect and help those only in our "group," which is why major problems in other countries so often go ignored. This boy's attitude showed that he was willing to get involved to help people who had little in common with him. I was impressed by this selflessness, and since then I have tried to be the same way.

Another reason that this experience moved me was that it showed real character for him to step in between the girl and several boys (some of whom were known for getting into fights) when no one else had shown a willingness to get involved. I was too scared to get involved. I was worried about being beaten up, but also just of being made fun of in front of everyone. I allowed my fear to paralyze me and prevent me from stepping up and doing the right thing. I knew, though, that this other boy also would have been afraid of the same things, but he helped the girl anyway. I realized that there was nothing stopping me from also doing the right thing in a situation that scared me. Since then, I have tried to face my fear so that I won't be intimidated by people who need to be stopped.

BODY

Because of this single experience years ago, I have changed myself. In my memory, the boy who tried to help that girl is a great hero. He showed me a type of courage that I'll never forget. Now, I also try to help out people who need it, even if it scares me. It's the right thing to do.

CONCLUSION

The Introduction

❑ The purpose of the introduction is to state the main idea of your essay. In the introduction, you define and limit what you are going to discuss.

The introduction is like a preview of your whole essay. It should mention the example you'll be discussing and it should state your thesis.

❑ **Basic Introduction:** The simplest way to begin your essay is to state your thesis, which is usually an answer or response to the essay prompt. Continue your introduction by describing your example and how it connects to your thesis. You don't need many details or specifics yet; these will be covered in the essay body.

> *A hobby I have that makes me special is rock climbing. This sport has taught me a lot about myself, because it has made me aware of my physical and mental strengths. It has also made me stronger and braver, and it has been an inspiration for how I live my life.*

❑ **Inverted Funnel:** A more advanced method for writing an introduction is to begin with a general statement about the topic, then narrow the topic until you end with a statement of your thesis, specifically identifying the examples.

> *I grew up playing basketball, swimming, and attempting to play softball. All of these sports gave me an appreciation for healthy competition and team camaraderie, but I never felt a special connection with any of these. Rock climbing is different. It's individualistic, which means you have to trust and rely on your own strength and intelligence. Because of this, it teaches you a lot about your strengths and your limits. Climbing has taught me more about myself than any team sport I've played and it continues to do so.*

TRY IT OUT

Write an introduction for an essay using each of the following prompts:

1. *Describe an experience that has inspired you.*

_____

_____

_____

_____

_____

_____

_____

_____

_____

_____

2. *Discuss a problem in the world that you would like to solve and how you would solve it.*

_____

_____

_____

_____

_____

_____

_____

_____

_____

_____

_____

The Body

❑ In the body of your essay, you should explain how your examples support your main idea. Only include the details and descriptions that you need in order to prove your point.

Don't write everything you know about an example or try to impress your reader with the depth of your knowledge. If you're writing about a book, for example, don't recount the whole plot, but stick to the relevant details that support your main idea.

> *Rock climbing makes me special because it helped me overcome a fear. For much of my life, I was frightened by any tall heights. After my first few attempts at rock climbing, I went from a girl who never went on roller coasters or ferris wheels or looked over the edge of a hill to someone who can climb up the side of a mountain and look around in appreciation and awe at the beauty of nature below her. I was terrified when I first pulled myself up the side of a tall cliff and looked down at the long drop back to the ground, but I overcame that fear. Now what I feel is pride for what I have accomplished and appreciation for the new strength I have found in myself.*
>
> *Of course rock climbing is physically challenging, but it is mentally challenging as well. With no two climbing routes being the same, the challenge is to figure out how to do the climb using both skill and strength. Along the same line, everyone has a different climbing style. That's what makes each climber unique. While I like to backstep and stem, another person may prefer to dyno and smear up the wall. I climb with people of all ages and backgrounds. Climbing does not discriminate. Sure, there is a lingo that everyone speaks and you have to learn, but it only adds to the thrill of the climb. Once you hear the word "crux" and you find yourself right in the middle of it on a climb and conquer it, you will truly know the meaning of the word.*

TRY IT OUT

Continue your essays by writing the body paragraphs:

1. *Describe an experience that has inspired you.*

_____

_____

_____

_____

_____

_____

_____

_____

_____

_____

2. *Discuss a problem in the world that you would like to solve and how you would solve it.*

_____

_____

_____

_____

_____

_____

_____

_____

_____

_____

The Conclusion

❑ The conclusion wraps up your essay. It should not introduce any new ideas and is essentially a restatement of your main idea.

❑ When possible, it is a good idea to end with a general statement about your main idea. For example, if you wrote about past events, you can finish your conclusion by describing what is happening now and how this confirms your main idea.

> *Rock climbing has provided some of the greatest challenges I have ever faced, and this has made me stronger. It has helped me to become braver and it has taught me about myself. This sport has inspired me to fearlessly work to achieve greater things and reach higher and higher. I've learned that, although life has many struggles, the best view can only be seen from the top.*

TRY IT OUT

Complete your essays by writing conclusions:

1. *Describe an experience that has inspired you.*

_____

_____

_____

_____

_____

_____

_____

_____

_____

_____

2. *Discuss a problem in the world that you would like to solve and how you would solve it.*

_____

_____

_____

_____

_____

_____

_____

_____

_____

_____

_____

Notes on Style

- Be clear.

- Be simple and direct.

- Don't use slang.

- Avoid fancy words, especially if you're not sure what they mean.

- Be natural. Don't be rude, arrogant, or breezy.

- Use transitions to connect your thoughts.

- Avoid qualifiers (e.g., very, so).

- Write neatly. Avoid cross-outs.

- Watch spelling and punctuation.

- Avoid incomplete or run-on sentences.

- Don't ramble or go off topic.

Read through the following essay and make edits. Note how the essay could be improved.

Prompt: *What are the best qualities of a person you admire?*

What does it mean to admire? I guess we all know what it means, but have you ever really looked past the simple six-letter word and tried to really understand why we do it? What are the qualities that make you admire someone? Of course, a person you admire must be a good person. But beneath that, deep down to the core of this phenomenon, there must be certain qualities. A person that is admired would have to have these qualities. They would have to be giving, successful, and humble. These really are the best qualities of a person I admire. I admire my uncle, and these are the qualities he has.

Humans, by nature, are very selfish beings, but an admirable person will go past their inner coding to something more. They will go past their own well-being for that of another. A good person has got to understand that as easy as it could be to run ahead of a slower person in life who has fallen, you must instead take the time to stop, dust them off, and give encouragements, even though that makes the whole run harder. Would you respect a person who is always greedy? Would you want to be friends with someone who only takes and takes? Wouldn't you rather be around a person who is generous and tries to help other people? I look up to my uncle very much because of all the great things that he does for people that he doesn't even know. There are a lot of examples of this.

Second, I am going to talk about how my uncle gives a whole lot to charities and always helps others, but he also is very successful. He manages his own construction company, which is a lot of hard work. A person you really admire should have this quality. Someone you can hope to become. Someone with good ethics. Someone who worked hard to earn all of his success and still gives to others. Can you believe that some people don't care about that? They are rich and do everything for more money, but they don't do anything to make the world better. That is why giving is also a quality in people I admire. People that you can trust and respect. You sure can't count on a person that is doing everything for themselves. That is my second reason I admire my uncle and wanna be more like him.

The last important quality is the simplest, yet still often forgotten. A person worth admiring is humble. Someone who doesn't think they're better than everyone else. One of the most amazing things about my uncle is how he never judges people or looks down on them. My uncle used to always say, "Not everyone is born as privileged as you and me." That is something that never really crossed my mind until now. It really makes you think. Is it fair that some people are so lucky that their family has a lot of money and security but other people are poor and have to struggle to get anything at all? Too many people take this for granted. I can't imagine how difficult that could be. How scary life could get. Thinking of this now makes me feel lucky to appreciate all the advantages I have had in life.

In conclusion, these are my main reasons I admire my uncle.

Prompt: *What are the best qualities of a person you admire?*

A lot of this introduction is not necessary. It's better to be direct than to ramble.

~~What does it mean to admire? I guess we all know what it means, but have you ever really looked past the simple six-letter word and tried to really understand why we do it?~~ What are the qualities that make you admire someone? Of course, a person you admire must be a good person. But beneath that, ~~deep down to the core of this phenomenon, there must be certain qualities.~~ A person that is admired would have to ~~have these qualities. They would have to~~ be giving, successful, and humble. These ~~really~~ are the best qualities of ~~a person I admire. I admire~~ my uncle, ~~and~~ ← whom I greatly admire. ~~these are the qualities he has.~~

This paragraph would be much stronger if it focused on one or two examples of how the uncle gives to others. Specific examples help create strong essays.

Humans, by nature, are very selfish beings, but an admirable person will go past their inner coding to something more. They will go past their own well-being for that of another. A good person ~~has got to~~   ← must understand that as easy as it could be to run ahead of a slower person in life who has fallen, you must instead take the time to stop, dust them off, and give encouragements, even though that makes the whole run harder. Would you respect a person who is always greedy? Would you want to be friends with someone who only takes and takes? Wouldn't you rather be around a person who is generous and tries to help other people? I look up to my uncle very much because of all the great things that he does for people that he doesn't even know. <u>There are a lot of examples of this.</u>

Rhetorical questions can be effective, but don't use too many of them. Usually, a strong statement is more effective than a question.

This paragraph would be stronger if it explained **why** hard work is an admirable trait in a person. Even if it seems obvious to you, it's important to explain in an essay.

~~Second, I am going to talk about how~~ my uncle gives a ~~whole~~ lot to charities and always helps others, but he also is very successful. He manages his own construction company, which is a lot of hard work. A person you really admire should ~~have this quality.~~ ^be^ Someone you can hope to become. ~~Someone~~ ^and^ with good ethics. ~~Someone~~ who worked hard to earn all of his success and still gives to others. ~~Can you believe that some people don't care about that? They are rich and do everything for more money, but they don't do anything to make the world better. That is why giving is also a quality in people I admire. People that you can trust and respect. You sure can't count on a person that is doing everything for themselves. That is my second reason I admire my uncle and wanna be more like him.~~

Try to avoid describing the organization of your essay ("Second, I am going to talk about…" or "In conclusion…"). Your reader can easily tell if you are moving on to a new example or if it's your conclusion by looking at your paragraphs.

The quote from the uncle is a strong detail. This paragraph could be improved by an explanation of **why** humility is worth admiring.

~~The last important quality is the simplest, yet still often forgotten.~~ A person worth admiring is humble. ~~Someone who doesn't think they're better than everyone else.~~ One of the most amazing things about my uncle is how he never judges people or looks down on them. My uncle used to always say, "Not everyone is born as privileged as you and me." ~~That is something that never really crossed my mind until now. It really makes you think.~~ Is it fair that some people are so lucky that their family has a lot of money and security but other people are poor and have to struggle to get anything at all? Too many people take this for granted. I can't imagine how difficult that could be. ^or^ How scary life could get. Thinking of this now makes me feel lucky to appreciate all the advantages I have had in life.

The conclusion should do more. For example, it could explain what the student has learned from his or her uncle.

~~In conclusion,~~ these are my main reasons I admire my uncle.

Evaluating Your Writing

❑ In general, your readers will consider five aspects of your writing sample: content, format, style, mechanics, and appearance. These five elements contribute to the reader's overall impression.

❑ Content

Does your answer make sense?

Do your ideas connect logically?

Are your examples appropriate?

❑ Format

Does your writing have clear body paragraphs with one topic in each?

❑ Style

Is your writing clear?

Does your writing flow smoothly?

Do you vary your sentence structure?

Do you use standard written English and good vocabulary?

❑ Mechanics

Does your writing have spelling errors?

Does your writing contain grammatical or usage errors?

❑ Appearance

Is your writing neat?

Are your paragraphs clear?

Are there cross-outs?

Do you stay in the margins?

Examples of Student Writing

TRY IT OUT

Read through the following writings and note strengths and weaknesses.
Mark any issues such as run-on sentences, incomplete sentences, misspelled words, or slang.
Describe any mistakes that have been made, such as off-topic rambling, repetition, or weak writing.
Offer suggestions for improvement.

Formal prompt: *What class or subject in school do you enjoy most? Why?*

Out of all the subjects in school, I would say that I enjoy my English classes the best. I would not say that the English classes are better, because I am lucky to have great teachers in all my classes, but I personally enjoy English the most. I am the kind of person who likes creativity and possibilities, and my English classes provide these.

It's important for every student to explore different subjects and determine which ones suit them best. Some students enjoy the subjects like math and science because the rules are very rigid and there isn't very much room for interpretation on answers. For some students, it is reassuring to know that 5+5 will always be 10 and the atomic number of carbon will always be 6. For me, however, there is no excitement in these absolute rules. I prefer questions with no definite answers. In my English classes, you can have lively debates involving some great literature. One classmate's interpretation of a Robert Frost poem might be completely different than my own, and they could both be valid. I've also been exposed to a wide variety of some great writers such as Shakespeare, Orwell, Fitzgerald, and many more. I may never have thought to read *1984* if I hadn't been assigned it in school, but now I'm glad that I have as it has opened my eyes to many new ideas. Most of what I've learned in English class is not about learning facts but learning different viewpoints and ways to think. I think this is what makes life interesting.

Most students that I know do not like writing assignment, but I enjoy my assigned papers, and hope to continue this in college one day by studying journalism. I enjoy the challenge of trying to communicate an idea or event in writing. It still amazes me that we are even able to share such complicated thoughts and details with series of words. Writing has been my passion for years, and I plan to make it my profession. I can be confident that I will always enjoy it because writing is an art that you can never be perfect at. You will always be learning, becoming a stronger writer, so it is a skill that will always be interesting.

I've learned a lot of interesting things in my math and science classes, but overall English is the subject for me.

Notes: _____

_____

_____

_____

_____

Creative prompt: *They didn't know if they would be able to do it.*

They didn't know if they would be able to do it. After a full six years of fighting the mighty Gauls, Julius Caesar and his men finally had reached the fort of Alesia where Vercingetorix, the "Great Warrior King," was based. The powerful Gallic leader had led his tribes to victory against the Romans before, but Caesar had grown more determined and desperate to conquer the Gallic forces.

The Galls were strongly fortified in Alesia, and Caesar knew he didn't have enough of a force to successfully attach the stronghold. In a display of his military genius, Caesar decided to build a wall and ring of trenches around Alesia. This would prevent anyone from leaving the city, and eventually the Gauls would starve.

It was a brilliant plan, but before the siege was ready a scout got out of Alesia and contacted other Gallic tribes to help fight the Romans. In order to defend his troops, Caesar ordered them to build another wall around them. This way, the inner wall would prevent the Gauls in Alesia from escaping and the outer wall would protect the Romans from any other Gallic tribes that might come attach them. Unfortunately, this meant the Romans were as trapped as the Gauls in Alesia.

Another problem for the Romans was a cliffside where they couldn't build a wall, and this created a weak point in their defenses. The Gauls discovered this weakness and knew it was their best chance to defeat Caesar's army.

After weeks of fighting, the Gauls organized a massive attack on the weak point in the Roman defense. Thousands of Gallic warriors from Alesia attacked the inner walls. At the same time, an even greater Gallic army came and attacked the outer walls in the same area. With a little fighting force left, the Romans were weary and their morale was low. Outnumbered and exhausted, the Romans had little chance of winning the battle.

Caesar, with his skills of oratory and strategy, managed to give his troops confidence and strength. When all hope seemed to be lost, Caesar personally led a small group of soldiers in a surprise attack against a large Gallic force.

"Those Gaulish pigs are the only things getting in the way of our victory!" said Caesar. "After we kill his barbarians, Vercingetorix will be marched all the way back to Rome for a public execution, and all of you will be heroes!" The legionnaires were shouting and talking amongst themselves in agreement. "Now, form ranks and seal the doom for any that stand in our way!"

Suddenly, the Romans were ready for battle again. They felt courageous, strong, and restored.

Julius Caesar was at the front with his horse, Maximus. "CHAAAAARGE!" screamed Caesar. Then, from the legion came an even louder cry that shook the heavens.

The Gauls were terrified to see the Romans suddenly charging them, led by the mighty Caesar. Even though the Gauls outnumbered the Romans ten to one, they became so afraid of the legionnaires that they ran away. Caeasar and his men chased the Gauls down and slaughtered them all. Seeing this victory, the rest of the Romans were encouraged and they defeated the rest of the Gallic forces.

Through his courage and intelligence, Caesar became an eternal symbol of power. He will always be remembered as an incredible leader, and his legendary ingenuity and bravery will forever inspire others.

Notes: _____

_____

_____

_____

_____

Chapter Review

❑ Format/Directions

"Schools would like to get to know you better through an essay or story using one of the two topics below. Please select the topic you find most interesting and fill in the circle next to the topic you choose."

The writing sample is not scored, but is sent directly to admissions committees.

Typically, writing sample readers are checking that your writing is focused and well-organized. Make sure that you express your thoughts clearly.

The writing sample is an opportunity for you to show something about yourself.

❑ Creative or Formal?

The Middle Level SSAT will let you choose between two creative prompts.

The Upper Level SSAT will let you choose between a creative and a formal prompt.

❑ Preparing to Write

Plan before you begin writing. Create an outline to guide you through the writing and make sure you manage your time.

❑ Creative

The setup is used to introduce characters, describe settings, and establish situations. This usually comes first because it is needed in order to understand the rest of the story.

The confrontation is the main source of drama and tension in the story. Stories need some type of problem or conflict. This can be a personal desire, a disagreement, a difficult challenge, etc.

The resolution shows the outcome of the story. This is where the characters make important decisions, where relationships break apart or come together, where heroes succeed and problems are finally resolved.

❑ Formal

The introduction establishes the main idea and focus of your essay. It includes your thesis, which is your essay's central argument or point.

The body is used to explain your argument and describe how your examples support that argument.

The conclusion summarizes your essay and connects it back to your main idea.

Writing Practice - Creative

❑ Creative prompts

1. *Nobody could have guessed that this would have happened to him.*

2. *It was over almost as soon as it started.*

3. *It was the most embarrassing moment of his life.*

4. *She had never seen something so beautiful.*

5. *They were all waiting for me to speak.*

6. *It seemed like it was going to be an ordinary day.*

7. *She had always been a hard worker, but she had never faced such a difficult challenge.*

8. *They didn't know if they would be able to do it.*

Use this page to plan your writing, and then use the next two pages to write.

Prompt: _____

Characters and source of drama: _____

_____

Outline:
    Setup

_____

_____

_____

_____

_____

    Confrontation

_____

_____

_____

_____

_____

    Resolution

_____

_____

_____

_____

_____

Writing Practice - Formal

❑ Formal prompts

1. *What are the best qualities of a person you admire?*

2. *What class or subject in school do you enjoy most? Why?*

3. *Who is someone you respect? Explain why you feel this way.*

4. *Describe an experience that has inspired you.*

5. *Discuss a problem in the world that you would like to solve and how you would solve it.*

6. *Explain a hobby you have that makes you special.*

7. *Which two historical figures would you like to meet and why?*

Use this page to plan your writing, and then use the next two pages to write.

Prompt: _____

Thesis and examples: _____

_____

Outline:
     Introduction

_____

_____

_____

_____

_____

     Body

_____

_____

_____

_____

_____

     Conclusion

_____

_____

_____

_____

_____

Vocabulary

Developing Vocabulary

❏ **Read books that give you a challenge**. The best way to develop a strong vocabulary is to read books that have words you do not already know. This method is time-consuming, but very effective and rewarding.

Learn words through groups and associations. If you are studying vocabulary, you should focus on connecting new words to words you know. Associate new words with synonyms, antonyms, or other known words that are related in some way.

For each new word you are learning, consider the following:

- Have you ever heard of the word before? If so, in what context?

- What does the word make you think of?

- What other words have the same meaning?

- Is this word more or less extreme than similar words?

- What words have the opposite meaning?

- Does the word have a root, suffix, or prefix? If so, what other words have the same?

- How could you use the word in a sentence?

The following vocabulary materials are divided into different exercises.

Prefixes and Roots – These exercises are useful for when you begin learning new words. These exercises will help you understand how parts of words develop meaning.

Word Groups – Word groups are the best way to learn a lot of words in a short period of time. Rather than studying words individually, you can learn the meanings of several related words at once. When learning words with similar meanings, pay special attention to the degree of intensity. For example, jovial and ecstatic both mean happy, but the second word is more extreme.

Vocabulary Lists – Each of these lists provides definitions and/or synonyms for 10 vocabulary words and also shows these words used in a sentence. The lists then require you to match each vocabulary word to a different synonym and use each word within a different sentence. Using words in multiple contexts is the best way to develop a strong vocabulary, though it requires more time than studying with word groups.

Extended Vocabulary List – The extended list of SSAT vocabulary words is a good resource for self-guided study. Use this list to track which words you know and which you still need to learn. One of the best ways to utilize this list is to create your own vocabulary flashcards.

Learned Words – These pages provide space for noting which words you have learned during your SSAT preparation. To ensure you do not forget new vocabulary words and their definitions, as well as any tricks you may have to help you remember definitions, you can record them here.

Prefixes

PREFIX	MEANING	EXAMPLES
a-, an-	not, without	amoral, atheist
ambi-, amphi-	both, around	ambidextrous
ante-	before	antedate, anteroom
anti-	against	antifreeze, antisocial
bene-	well, good	benefit, benediction
col-, com-, con-	together, with	collect, combine
contra-, contro-, counter-	against	contrast, controversy
de-	down	depress, degrade
dis-	not, apart from, opposite	dishonest, dislocate
dys-	bad	dysfunction, dysentery
ex-, exo-	out	exit, exoskeleton
extra-	outside, beyond	extravagant
fore-, for-	in front, before	foresee, forward
il-, im-, in-	not	illegal, inactive
im-, in-	into	immigrate, incision
inter-	between, among	international
intro-, intra-	within	introvert, intramural
mal-	bad	malfunction, malign
mis-	wrong	misspell, misinterpret
mono-	one	monotone
multi-	many	multicolored
neo-	new, modern	neologism, neophyte
omni-	all	omnipotent, omniscient
per-	through, thorough	perfume, perplex
poly-	many	polygon, polygamy
proto-	first	prototype, protoplasm
re-	back, again	refund, reread
syl-, sym-, syn-	together, with	symphony, synonym
trans-	across, over	transmit, translate

TRY IT OUT

In the spaces provided, list words that use the following prefixes:

PREFIX   EXAMPLES

a-, an-   _____ _____ _____ _____

ambi-, amphi-   _____ _____ _____ _____

ante-   _____ _____ _____ _____

anti-   _____ _____ _____ _____

bene-   _____ _____ _____ _____

col-, com-, con-   _____ _____ _____ _____

contra-, contro-, counter- _____ _____ _____ _____

de-   _____ _____ _____ _____

dis-   _____ _____ _____ _____

dys-   _____ _____ _____ _____

ex-, exo-   _____ _____ _____ _____

extra-   _____ _____ _____ _____

fore-, for-   _____ _____ _____ _____

il-, im-, in-   _____ _____ _____ _____

im-, in-   _____ _____ _____ _____

inter-   _____ _____ _____ _____

intro-, intra-   _____ _____ _____ _____

mal-   _____ _____ _____ _____

mis-   _____ _____ _____ _____

mono-   _____ _____ _____ _____

multi-   _____ _____ _____ _____

neo-   _____ _____ _____ _____

omni-   _____ _____ _____ _____

per-   _____ _____ _____ _____

poly-   _____ _____ _____ _____

proto-   _____ _____ _____ _____

re-   _____ _____ _____ _____

syl-, sym-, syn-   _____ _____ _____ _____

trans-   _____ _____ _____ _____

uni-   _____ _____ _____ _____

Roots

ROOT	MEANING	EXAMPLES
animus	life, spirit	animal, animated
annus, enn	year	annual, centennial
anthropos	human	anthropology
arche, archi	chief, first	architect, archangel
audire	to hear	audible, audit
bios	life	biology, antibiotic
capere	to take	capture, accept
ced, cess	to go, to yield	concede, secede
chronos	time	chronicle, chronometer
credere	believe	credence, discredit
dicere, dictum	to say, to speak	predict, dictate
ducere, ductum	to lead	deduce, educate
finis	boundary, limit	define, confine
fluere	to flow	fluid, fluent
greg	herd	gregarious, congregate
gress	to go	digress, progress
loqui	to speak	loquacious, eloquent
lucere	to be light	lucid, translucent
mittere, missum	to send	transmit, missile
pedis	foot	pedal, centipede
plicare	to fold	implicate, implicit
portare	to carry	deport, portable
scribere, scriptum	to write	postscript, subscribe
sentire, sensum	to feel	consent, sense
specere, spectum	to look at	inspect
tenere, tentum	to hold	tenure, intent
trahere, tractum	to draw, to pull	attract, tractor
venire, vention	to come, to go, to arrive	convene, venture
vocare, vocatum	to call	invoke, convocation

TRY IT OUT

In the spaces provided, list words that use the following roots:

ROOT   EXAMPLES

animus

annus, enn

anthropos

arche, archi

audire

bios

capere

ced, cess

chronos

credere

dicere, dictum

ducere, ductum

finis

fluere

greg

gress

loqui

lucere

mittere, missum

pedis

plicare

portare

scribere, scriptum

sentire, sensum

specere, spectrum

tenere, tentum

trahere, tractum

venire, vention

vocare, vocatum

SUMMIT
EDUCATIONAL
GROUP

Word Groups

Work through each word group in the following steps:

1. Look at the group title and think of similar or related words. Don't look at the SSAT words yet; cover them if necessary.

2. Once you've thought of words related to the group title, look at the SSAT words. See if there are any that you already thought of, then see if there are other words that you already know in the group.

3. Circle any words that you have never seen before or that you don't know how to define. Look at their definitions, and see if they have the same definition as any other words you know.

4. Try to sort each group of words by intensity. Most word groups have words with similar meanings but different levels of extremity.

Intelligent / Skilled

adept	skillful, proficient
adroit	skillful
aptitude	skill, ability
astute	wise, keen in judgment
competent	having sufficient skill, adequate, capable
deft	skillful, dexterous, smart
dexterous	skillful with the hands or body
erudite	scholarly, well-educated
ingenuity	cleverness, inventiveness
proficient	skillful
prodigy	person with extraordinary talent, highly skilled child
prowess	great skill or strength
sage	wise person
sagacious	wise, insightful
sapient	wise, insightful
shrewd	clever, keen, insightful
witty	clever, humorous

Unintelligent / Unskilled

ignorance	lack of knowledge
illiterate	unable to read or write
incompetent	unskilled, incapable, unqualified
inept	unskilled, clumsy
naïve	inexperienced, uninformed
novice	beginner, inexperienced learner
obtuse	slow to understand; or: insensitive

Happy

complacent	smug, satisfied
ecstatic	delighted, in a state of great joy
elation	joy, happiness
euphoric	intensely happy, elated
jovial	joyful, cheerful
jubilant	joyful, triumphant

Sad / Miserable

despondent	dejected, hopeless
dismal	gloomy, hopeless
doleful	sad, mournful, sorrowful
dreary	depressing, causing sadness; **or:** dull, boring
forlorn	miserable, unhappy
mope	to be gloomy, to pout
morose	gloomy, having a sullen disposition
somber	gloomy, serious, depressing
woeful	unhappy, sorrowful

Hatred / Anger

abhor	to hate, to despise
animosity	hatred
disdain	contempt, intense dislike, scorn
indignant	offended, angry about unfair treatment
irate	very angry, furious
livid	very angry, furious
loathe	to hate, to feel disgust for something
malice	hatred, spite
outraged	angered, offended

A Good Idea

feasible	capable of being done, practical, viable
meticulous	showing extreme care about details
novel	original, new
pragmatic	practical
prudent	careful, cautious, wise

A Bad Idea

futile	hopeless, useless
impetuous	acting without consideration, impulsive
implausible	unlikely, farfetched
inane	lacking sense, silly, mindless
tenuous	flimsy, weak, thin

Good Person

admirable	inspiring approval
compassionate	showing sympathy
empathy	understanding of the feelings of others
integrity	reliability; or: morality, honesty

Bad Person

abrasive	irritating, annoying; or: harsh, rough
cantankerous	argumentative, irritable, contentious
despicable	deserving contempt, hateful
hypocritical	claiming to have virtues one does not have
infamy	bad reputation, disgrace, opprobrium
notorious	unfavorably known, infamous, disreputable
pettiness	narrow-mindedness; or: stinginess
reprehensible	shameful, bad, deserving rebuke or censure
scoundrel	dishonorable person, villain

Honest / True

authentic	real, genuine
candid	honest, sincere
frank	honest, direct, blunt
legitimate	lawful, rightful
literal	explicit, exact, following the meaning of a word
objective	factual, without bias, not subjective
sincere	genuine, earnest, true, honest
valid	founded on facts

Fake / False

erroneous	incorrect, wrong
fallacious	incorrect, invalid; or: misleading, deceptive
feign	to pretend, to imitate
forgery	counterfeit, imitation, false reproduction
fraud	something false, impostor; or: deception, trickery
hoax	something intended to deceive
illusory	based on a false perception of reality, deceptive

Clear / Convincing

cogent	clear, convincing
coherent	clear, intelligible
lucid	clear, easy to understand

Unclear / Unknown

abstract	theoretical, not concrete, not easily grasped
ambiguous	having more than one possible meaning, uncertain
ambivalent	indecisive, of two minds about something
amorphous	shapeless
clandestine	secret, private, illicit, surreptitious
dubious	doubtful, unsure, not trustworthy
elusive	hard to catch, hard to understand or solve
enigma	puzzle, mystery
esoteric	understood only by a select few, mysterious
intangible	not capable of being touched, abstract
obscure	unclear, vague; or: hard to find

Support

advocate	to support, to speak in favor of, to recommend
buttress	to support, to encourage; or: reinforcement
champion	winner; or: to support
encourage	to inspire, to support
endorsement	support, sanction
nourish	to nurture, to sustain
promote	to encourage, to give a higher position

Praise

acclaim	praise, enthusiastic approval
extol	to praise
laud	to praise
revere	to respect
venerate	to respect

Criticism / Harsh Speech

chastise	to discipline, to criticize
chide	to express disapproval, to criticize
condescend	to talk down to, to act superior, to be patronizing
contradiction	assertion of the opposite, opposition, denial
denigrate	to criticize, to speak badly of, to defame, to belittle
diatribe	bitter speech or criticism, rant
rebuke	to express disapproval, to criticize
reprimand	formal criticism, disapproval
scold	to express disapproval, to criticize angrily
slander	strong criticism; or: false claims against a person
tirade	prolonged speech of abuse or condemnation

Make Better / To Calm

alleviate	to lighten, to relieve
ameliorate	to make better
appease	to calm, to make peace with
assuage	to calm, to ease
conciliate	to calm, to make peace, to reconcile,
mitigate	to make milder, to make less severe
mollify	to calm, to soften
placate	to calm
quench	to satisfy, to put out, to cool
soothe	to calm, to relieve, to comfort

Make Worse

aggravate	to make worse; or: to irritate
debilitating	weakening, incapacitating
deteriorate	to make worse, to disintegrate
detrimental	harmful, damaging
exacerbate	to make more severe or worse
impair	to make worse, to weaken or damage

Decrease / Reduce

abase	to humble, to reduce in rank
abate	to decrease, to weaken
abbreviate	to shorten, to reduce
abridge	to shorten, to reduce
atrophy	to waste away, to decline, to degenerate
diminish	to reduce, to make smaller, to lessen
dwindle	to become smaller, to shrink, to waste away
quell	to extinguish, to put an end to
recession	withdrawal, decline
retract	to withdraw, to take back
wane	to decrease, to decline
wither	to shrivel, to shrink, to decrease

Obstacle / To Hold Back

curtail	to cut short, to hold back
deterrent	something which prevents or discourages action
hamper	to impede, to get in the way, to fetter
hindrance	obstacle, something that impedes progress
impasse	dead end, situation in which progress is prevented
obstruct	to block, to hinder
prohibitive	discouraging, preventative, unaffordable
stymie	to block, to hinder

Stubborn

adamant	unyielding, inflexible
obdurate	stubborn
obstinate	stubborn, unbending
tenacious	stubborn, persistent

Agree

acquiesce	to go along with something, to consent, to agree
compliance	obedience, submissiveness
concur	to agree, to approve

Disagree

dissent	disagreement, difference of opinion, conflict
discord	disagreement, dispute

Join Together

amalgamation	combination, mixture
coalesce	to come together, to merge, to join
collaborate	to work jointly with others

Unchanging / Unmoving

dormant	inactive, hidden, resting
incessant	unceasing, continuous
stagnant	inactive, still
static	stationary, not moving
steadfast	loyal, constant

Changing

fluctuate	to shift back and forth, to change
capricious	unstable, whimsical, flighty
erratic	inconsistent, unpredictable
fickle	unpredictable, capricious, inconsistent, erratic
mercurial	rapidly changing, temperamental

Opinionated / Dedicated

biased	prejudiced, not neutral
bigot	intolerant or prejudiced person, dogmatist
dogmatic	stubbornly opinionated
zealot	fanatical partisan, passionate extremist

Unfeeling / Uncaring

apathetic	indifferent, uninterested
callous	insensitive, unfeeling
negligent	neglectful, careless, inattentive
stoic	unaffected by pleasure and pain, emotionless

Too Prideful

bombastic	proud, overstated
haughty	proud, arrogant
ostentatious	attempting to impress
pompous	arrogant, exaggeratedly self-important
pretentious	self-important, affected

Friendly

affable	friendly
amiable	friendly
congenial	friendly
gregarious	enjoying company, sociable

Disrespectful

flippant	not showing respect, lacking in seriousness
insolent	disrespectful, contemptuous, impudent
irreverent	disrespectful, impertinent

Starting Fights

antagonistic	acting in opposition, hostile
belligerent	warlike, aggressive
provoke	to cause to act, to rouse; or: to anger
pugnacious	inclined to fight
quarrelsome	inclined to argue
rancorous	vengeful, resentful

Attack / Damage / Destroy

assail	to assault
barrage	to attack, to bombard
debase	to demean, to degrade, to spoil
efface	to erase, to wipe out
eradicate	to destroy, to eliminate

Speech

articulate	expressed clearly
colloquial	conversational, characteristic of informal speech
decree	to command, to declare
eloquent	fluent in verbal expression
emphatic	strongly expressive, forceful
enunciate	to express clearly
gossip	idle talk, rumor
orator	public speaker
rhetoric	the art of speaking or writing effectively

Talkative

garrulous	excessively talkative, babbling
loquacious	talkative, garrulous
verbose	wordy, talkative

Brief

brevity	briefness, of short duration or length
concise	briefly and clearly stated, succinct
succinct	expressed in few words, laconic
terse	brief, pithy

Shy

introverted	shy, self-concerned
reticent	quiet, uncommunicative
taciturn	reserved, not talkative
timid	unconfident, shy

Get Started

coercion	use of force to compel an act or choice
compel	to force someone to do something
incentive	motivation, stimulus
incite	to cause to act, to provoke, to urge
initiate	to set in motion, to start
instigate	to stir up, to urge on
prompt	call to action, reminder

Give Up

abandon	to give up, to leave
abdicate	to give up a power or position
concede	to admit to be true; or: to forfeit
forsake	to give up, to leave, to quit
renounce	to give up
relinquish	to give up, to renounce
resign	to give up
surrender	to give up, to yield to another

Looking Forward

anticipation	prediction, expectation
forebode	to predict
imminent	happening soon, impending
inevitable	unavoidable, expected
ominous	threatening, warning of danger
portent	sign of something about to happen, omen
premonition	forewarning, intuition about the future
presumption	guess, assumption
prophesy	to predict, to foretell
unforeseen	unexpected

Looking Back

contrite	feeling guilt or regret, repentant
lament	to mourn, to feel regret
nostalgia	yearning for the past, homesickness
reminiscence	memory, recollection
remorse	guilt, shame
retrospect	reflection on the past, consideration of history

Boring / Common

banal	common, lacking originality, hackneyed
insipid	bland, boring, without zest
monotonous	without variety, tiresomely uniform
mundane	ordinary, dull, commonplace
pedestrian	common, dull, banal, unremarkable
tedious	boring, unpleasantly painstaking

Normal

conformity	matching in form, compliance with norm
conventional	matching accepted standards, ordinary
customary	according to custom, usual
uniformity	overall similarity, sameness

Odd / Weird

aberrant	abnormal, unusual, deviant
bizarre	unusual, weird
eccentric	deviating from the standard or norm
idiosyncratic	characteristic of a person, peculiar to an individual
peculiar	odd, strange, unusual

Differences

disparate	different, distinct
juxtapose	to place side by side for comparison
nuance	subtle difference

Rich

affluent	wealthy
opulent	wealthy, luxurious
prolific	productive, fertile, fecund
prosperous	successful, flourishing, wealthy, affluent

Poor

destitute	without food or shelter, deprived, needy
impoverish	to make poor, to deprive
indigent	without food or shelter, deprived, needy

Giving

altruism	unselfish interest in helping others
benevolent	good, kind-hearted
generous	liberal in giving or sharing, charitable

Wasteful

prodigal	extravagant, wasteful
squander	to spend extravagantly, to waste

Empty / Lacking

barren	not productive, infertile, depleted
desolate	deserted, inhospitable, bare
omission	something left out
scant	tiny amount, insufficient
scarce	not enough, insufficient
vacant	empty, void

Confusing / Challenging

arduous	requiring great effort, straining, difficult
bewilder	to confuse
confound	to confuse
perplex	to confuse
plight	difficult and unpleasant situation, struggle
predicament	difficult situation, dilemma
quandary	difficult situation, dilemma
strenuous	requiring great effort, straining, difficult

Tricky

beguile	to lure, to charm, to captivate
deceive	to cause someone to believe a lie, to mislead
guile	cunning, deceitfulness
wily	cunning, sly, crafty

Not A Problem

benign	harmless, beneficial, kind, gentle
frivolous	not serious, insignificant
indifferent	not concerned, not caring
latent	inactive, dormant; or: hidden
trivial	unimportant, insignificant

Calm

docile	easy to manage, obedient, submissive
placid	calm, serene
tranquil	calm, peaceful

Lazy / Tired

languid	slow, tired, drooping
lax	careless, slack, not strict
lethargic	lazy, lacking energy
listless	without energy or enthusiasm, uninterested
sluggish	lazy, slow to act
torpid	slow, inactive, hibernating

Vocabulary List 1

esoteric	understood only by a select few; **or**: mysterious
valid	founded on fact or evidence
biased	prejudiced, not neutral
prosaic	uninspired, dull, commonplace
steadfast	fixed, constant, unchanging; **or**: firmly loyal
intangible	abstract, not capable of being touched
pragmatic	practical
incoherent	unintelligible, unclear, confused
static	stationary, not moving
auspicious	favorable, positive

Columnist George Will has been accused of covering mainly **esoteric** political aspects of major current events, obscure points about which few but insiders would know.

On multiple-choice tests, working backwards from the answer choices is a **valid** method for solving problems.

Although Donald wanted to view both sides of the issue equally, his experiences gave him a **biased** opinion.

In the hopes of increasing sales by releasing more unique stories, the publisher is working on less **prosaic** titles for its large collection of books.

The captured spy was **steadfast** in his refusal to give details of his mission.

A company's good relations with its customers are an **intangible** asset, much harder to assign a value in dollars than physical assets like buildings or machines.

A rational and realistic person, Patty preferred to be **pragmatic** rather than try new or unusual methods.

She did not know Spanish very well, so whenever she tried to speak the language she was **incoherent**.

The price of the new stereo system is likely to remain **static** until a new model is introduced.

The discovery of solar power came at an **auspicious** time, when the world needed it most.

TRY IT OUT

For each word or definition, find the matching vocabulary word and write a sentence using that word:

1. illogical, jumbled   _____ _____

2. influenced, subjective   _____ _____

3. legitimate, true, official _____ _____

4. obscure, enigmatic, secret _____ _____

5. ordinary, banal   _____ _____

6. promising, fortunate   _____ _____

7. realistic, sensible   _____ _____

8. resolute, committed   _____ _____

9. unchanging, motionless   _____ _____

10. not concrete, nonphysical   _____ _____

Complete each of the following sentences by inserting one of the vocabulary words:

11. The software company's core value is to provide _____ and realistic solutions, rather than the unreasonable services offered by their competitors.

12. The speaker was clearly losing the interest of the audience who found his speech quite _____ and muddled.

13. Peter was hard to have a conversation with because he only talked about _____ topics that nobody else knew about.

14. With the new research and discoveries, the scientists proved that their theories are _____ and accurate.

15. My teacher was not able to consider any view other than her own, so all of her ideas were _____.

16. Unlike his first novel, which was unique and exciting, his latest novel is unfortunately _____.

17. Although people tried to make him change his opinions, the idealist was _____ and held onto his beliefs.

18. The most valuable things are _____; they are not physical things that can be bought.

19. Recent politics have not allowed changes to be made, so most laws and policies have remained _____.

20. On this _____ date, we celebrate the anniversary of a grand moment in our nation's history.

Vocabulary List 2

verbose	wordy, redundant
tedious	boring, unpleasantly painstaking
hypocritical	claiming to have virtues one does not have
tentative	not final, hesitant, uncertain
stoic	unaffected by pleasure and pain, emotionless
sporadic	infrequent, occurring in scattered single instances
cryptic	secret, hidden; **or**: mysterious, puzzling
morose	gloomy, having a sullen disposition
taciturn	quiet, saying little
prolific	producing abundantly, fertile, fecund

The lecture was **verbose** in parts, and many students stopped paying attention during the professor's lengthy ramblings.

Milo kept working on his long math assignment, even though he found doing fifty subtraction problems to be **tedious.**

The principal was **hypocritical** for making rules to enforce a dress code but not following the code.

At first Nicholas was **tentative** about entering the water, but once he realized it was warm he dove in.

The winning team was known for its **stoic** players, who were so focused and blank-faced that they seemed robotic.

Mamalluca is a good site for viewing **sporadic** meteor showers, which appear in sudden, irregular bursts.

Hidden in the cabinet, she discovered a letter with **cryptic** messages she could not decipher.

The movie had a **morose** tone, as the characters struggled through sad, dark times in their lives.

Despite Juan's usual **taciturn** nature, he was bouncing off walls with energy and conversation points today.

Compared to last year's drought, the Nebraska farmers had a **prolific** yield of corn this year.

TRY IT OUT

For each word or definition, find the matching vocabulary word and write a sentence using that word:

1. depressed   _____   _____

2. dull, tiresome   _____   _____

3. fruitful, creative   _____   _____

4. indifferent, calm   _____   _____

5. insincere, two-faced   _____   _____

6. intermittent, irregular   _____   _____

7. obscure, enigmatic   _____   _____

8. reserved, aloof   _____   _____

9. talkative   _____   _____

10. unsure, cautious   _____   _____

Complete each of the following sentences by inserting one of the vocabulary words:

11. Let's make a _____ plan on meeting at the zoo at 3pm, unless it rains.

12. Many critics complained that the book was too _____ because of its tendency to over-explain and repeat ideas.

13. Mark's job was _____; he had to do the same, easy tasks over and over.

14. When Susan accused her friend of procrastinating too much, she was being _____ because she was a much worse procrastinator.

15. No matter how difficult the situation became, the monk was peaceful and _____.

16. The newspaper had forecast constant rain and thunderstorms throughout the day, but the rain was light and _____.

17. We could not understand the _____ message because it used a complex code to disguise its information.

18. After the sad news of the disaster, the mood of the entire nation was _____.

19. While her sister was incredibly talkative, Karen was _____ and shy.

20. Roberto was a _____ artist, creating many paintings and sculptures in a short time.

Vocabulary List 3

satirical	sarcastic, mocking
virulent	very harmful, malignant, noxious
amiable	friendly
gullible	overly trusting, willing to believe anything
vulnerable	capable of being harmed
reclusive	shut off by oneself, solitary
marred	damaged, bruised, defaced, disfigured
reprehensible	shameful, bad, deserving rebuke or censure
haphazard	lacking a plan or order, by chance, random
terse	effectively brief, concise, pithy

Often his **satirical** writings, pretending simply to poke fun at people, revealed his **virulent** nature, as he viciously attacked anyone who disagreed with him.

His genuinely **amiable** character showed itself as he shook hands, chatted with all kinds of people, and even kissed a few babies.

The con artist used his city-wise cunning and wit to take advantage of the **gullible** farmer, who always expected people to deal with him honestly.

After his mother dipped Achilles in the magic river, no spear could penetrate his skin. The only place where he was **vulnerable** was his left heel, which his mother had held while she submerged him.

An intensely private, **reclusive** person, he would hide in his office for days at a time while he worked.

Don Corleone decided not to buy the tomato after he turned it over and saw it was **marred** by a large bruise on the underside.

Victor was sent to detention for two weeks because of his **reprehensible** behavior.

Our efforts haven't been very effective because we didn't plan enough, which made our actions **haphazard** and careless.

Hemingway is known for his **terse** writing, which creates strong, direct sentences with few words.

TRY IT OUT

For each word or definition, find the matching vocabulary word and write a sentence using that word:

1. abrupt, curt _____ _____

2. agreeable, sociable _____ _____

3. dangerous, poisonous _____ _____

4. disorganized _____ _____

5. guilty, sinful _____ _____

6. introverted, withdrawn _____ _____

7. naïve, easy to fool _____ _____

8. ridiculing _____ _____

9. spoiled, ruined _____ _____

10. susceptible _____ _____

Complete each of the following sentences by inserting one of the vocabulary words:

11. Without investing in defense research, our nation would be _____ to attacks from rival nations.

12. Since Isaac is so _____, people trick him all the time because they know he cannot spot a lie.

13. A lot of political commentary does not use direct criticism but instead is witty and _____.

14. The student harassed and mistreated his fellow students; his conduct was absolutely _____.

15. Judy has always been kind and _____, which is why she has developed so many great relationships.

16. The surface of the moon has been _____ by explosive collisions with meteorites.

17. Mandy does not like to be around a lot of people, so she has become unsocial and _____.

18. After prescribing her a new medication, the doctor wanted to continue monitoring Peggy's health to make sure she did not have any _____ reactions to it.

19. When she gets angry, she doesn't like to talk much; she becomes _____ and it's hard to get her to communicate.

20. My father doesn't like to follow instructions, so most of his construction projects are _____.

Vocabulary List 4

incessant	unceasing, continuous
conventional	ordinary, customary
futile	hopeless, useless
monotonous	without variety, tiresomely uniform
indifferent	not caring
relevant	related to the topic, pertinent
pedestrian	common, ordinary, banal
stringent	strict, severe
vehement	urgent, vigorous, forceful
subtle	hardly noticeable

The teacher droned on in an **incessant** lecture, without pausing once in the entire period.

He believed in following the customs of his family, so his life was **conventional**.

The revolutionaries had great hopes for their cause, but their actions were **futile** because they had no chance of succeeding.

At first, the tourists loved the prairies, but after a few days the sight of the same, flat grassland became **monotonous**.

Antisocial behavior can be defined as being **indifferent** and unconcerned for other people's feelings.

The Secretary of State derided the reporter for her question about local politics and asked that only questions **relevant** to the national situation be asked.

Hank thought his article contained new ideas, but the magazine publisher, who had seen hundreds just like it, rejected it because it was too **pedestrian** for her readers.

To address the safety problems with their products, the company has been enacting more and more **stringent** requirements in the interest of protecting the consumer.

The labor leader was **vehement** in urging restraint, yelling at the mob of workers for nearly 20 minutes so they would control themselves.

The soft, pale colors used in Sabrina's make up were **subtle** and flattering.

TRY IT OUT

For each word or definition, find the matching vocabulary word and write a sentence using that word:

1. apathetic, unconcerned _____ _____

2. applicable, significant _____ _____

3. faint, not obvious _____ _____

4. intense, passionate _____ _____

5. mundane, dull _____ _____

6. nonstop, never ending _____ _____

7. pointless _____ _____

8. repetitive, unvaried _____ _____

9. stern, harsh _____ _____

10. traditional, normal _____ _____

Complete each of the following sentences by inserting one of the vocabulary words:

11. Because there were _____ objections to the new policies, the governing committee decided to alter their rulings.

12. Despite his attempts to create incredible paintings, his work was mostly unimpressive and _____.

13. His essay was well-written, but its argument was weak because its examples were not _____ or connected to the main subject.

14. Usually, the most _____ methods work better than new methods that haven't been tested and proven.

15. The _____ music droned on with the same rhythm and notes.

16. The stranger tried to make him feel sympathy, but he was _____ to the stranger's troubles and did not offer any aid.

17. The villain left a series of _____ clues, and the detective had to use all of his skill to discover and interpret this hard-to-find evidence.

18. There was no chance that he could succeed; all of his efforts were _____.

19. The noise and commotion from the nearby apartment was _____; it continued for hours and hours.

20. With her parents' _____ rules, she was not allowed many freedoms.

Vocabulary List 5

zealot	fanatical partisan, passionate extremist
charlatan	quack, person pretending to have knowledge or ability
virtuoso	a master musician or artist
guile	cunning, deceitfulness
coercion	use of force to compel an act or choice
rhetoric	the art of speaking or writing effectively
humility	state of being humble, not proud or showy
respite	rest, pause, break
vacillation	wavering between choices
hindrance	obstacle, something that impedes progress

Frank is such a golf **zealot** that he will frequently get up at 5 AM just to play before work.

Mark Twain believed politicians were generally **charlatans**, not knowing more than a tiny fraction of what they claimed to know

The legendary Miles Davis is considered to be one of the great **virtuosos** of the Jazz world.

He didn't get to the top of the company ranks because he's a good worker, but he has a lot of **guile** and was able to trick and sabotage everyone in his way.

The largest and toughest kid on the playground used his strength as a **coercion** to make the other kids do whatever he wanted.

Abraham Lincoln is considered a master of **rhetoric**; his skill with words moved many people who heard him speak.

Humility is a great virtue that is only present in people who realize and appreciate their own limitations.

Cape Cod provides a pleasant **respite** from the August humidity for Bostonians.

Her **vacillation** on the topic showed that she hadn't made a strong decision yet and was switching from one side to the other.

Even when his captors resorted to **coercion**, hitting him repeatedly, he still would not say anything.

TRY IT OUT

For each word or definition, find the matching vocabulary word and write a sentence using that word:

1. eloquence, speech style   _____   _____

2. fake, impostor   _____   _____

3. indecision, fluctuation   _____   _____

4. lull, interval   _____   _____

5. modesty   _____   _____

6. obstruction, barrier   _____   _____

7. pressure, intimidation   _____   _____

8. prodigy, skilled person   _____   _____

9. slyness, deviousness   _____   _____

10. supporter, devotee   _____   _____

Complete each of the following sentences by inserting one of the vocabulary words:

11. Although he struggled with some forms of art, his incredible patience and talent with stonework made him a _____ in sculpture.

12. Dennis did not have any _____; he was not able to lie or trick anybody.

13. Sebastian had no _____; he thought that he was better than everyone else and that he couldn't make any mistakes.

14. Some political _____ will always follow their party and will never consider changing their ideals.

15. The business owner was criticized for not being able to make a decision between two types of insurance; his workers were frustrated by his _____.

16. The interrogator used his _____ skills to make the suspect reveal information about the crime.

17. The king used powerful _____ in his speeches in order to inspire and motivate his people.

18. The man claimed to be an expert, but his lack of skill showed that he was merely a _____.

19. The new economic restrictions have been a _____ to some large companies.

20. Two-thirds of the way up the mountain, the plateau provided a brief and much needed _____ where the hikers could catch their breaths.

Vocabulary List 6

enigma	puzzle, mystery
solitude	the state of being alone
adversary	opponent, enemy
acclaim	praise, enthusiastic approval
philanthropy	desire or effort to help humanity
nostalgia	yearning for the past, homesickness
animosity	hatred
epitome	perfect example, paradigm
connoisseur	expert, knowledgeable judge
hiatus	break, interruption

Despite the unmatched success of the detective in solving mysteries, this difficult case remained a complete **enigma** to him.

Henry David Thoreau is known for the year he spent in Walden Woods, living in **solitude** with no distractions from the outside world.

After a fierce battle against the villainous captain, Peter finally defeated his **adversary**.

Despite the widespread **acclaim** for the renowned author's recent best seller, he often started his guest lectures with some mild self-effacing humor about his "human side" and shortcomings.

Mrs. Sykes, who had donated a great deal of money to various causes, was commended by the local newspaper for her **philanthropy**.

Baby boomers look back on their childhoods with **nostalgia**, remembering a simple and easy life in contrast to today's complexities and difficulties.

In the serenity of the cathedral, it was impossible to envision a world of **animosity** and small-minded selfishness.

According to some, a dinner of steak, potato, and vegetables in the **epitome** of United States cuisine.

The food **connoisseur** was so knowledgeable that he was able to identify uncommon ingredients by taste and texture alone.

The television show will be on **hiatus** until Fall, when the next season will begin.

TRY IT OUT

For each word or definition, find the matching vocabulary word and write a sentence using that word:

1. applause, support _____ _____

2. authority, specialist _____ _____

3. charity _____ _____

4. essence, embodiment _____ _____

5. hostility, loathing _____ _____

6. reminiscence, memory _____ _____

7. pause _____ _____

8. riddle, secret _____ _____

9. rival, foe _____ _____

10. seclusion, privacy _____ _____

Complete each of the following sentences by inserting one of the vocabulary words:

11. Even though she became very famous, the young movie star did not let the _____ of her fans make her conceited or vain.

12. Herman Melville's Moby Dick is often seen as the _____ of American Literature as it has influenced countless other writers and novels.

13. Many artists seek lives of _____, so they don't have to worry about other people and can instead focus on their art.

14. My friend is a _____ of fine cheeses; she has an extensive knowledge and always knows the perfect one to match with any meal.

15. The _____ between Red Sox fans and Yankee fans is legendary, with them often getting into altercations.

16. The Gospel of Wealth was Andrew Carnegie's belief that wealthy people have a responsibility to promote _____ in order to support the rest of society.

17. The student-run magazine has a _____ during the summer when the students can no longer work on it.

18. The superhero had to always fight against his _____, who constantly tried to take over the world.

19. When I watch the old cartoons that I used to watch as a child, I am filled with a feeling of _____.

20. With no one theory universally agreed upon, the extinction of dinosaurs remains one of history's greatest _____.

Vocabulary List 7

disparity	inequality, difference
gravity	seriousness, weightiness
candor	honesty, sincerity
skeptic	a doubter
disinclination	a feeling of unwillingness or aversion
compliance	obedience, submissiveness
brevity	briefness, of short duration or length
remorse	guilt, regret, shame
disdain	contempt, intense dislike, scorn
tirade	a prolonged speech of abuse or condemnation

There is a large **disparity** between Jim's football skills and his opinion of himself; he thinks he's the best player on the team, but he has never shown much talent.

The president spoke with seriousness and **gravity** as he discussed the situation of the nation.

The photographer took pictures of people who were unaware they were being photographed, and so her photos captured moments of **candor** and reality.

At first, the audience was quite **skeptical,** but in time they would be persuaded by Dr. Magnamo's wild theory.

A peaceful person by nature, the new recruit had a **disinclination** to fighting in any battles.

Baking requires careful measuring, so **compliance** with recipes is important.

Since newspapers have a limited amount of space available, **brevity** is important in journalism.

Because Snake felt no **remorse** for his crime, he was not released for parole as originally scheduled.

The Cambridge city council's **disdain** for billboards led to their recommendation that every billboard in the city should be obliterated by next year.

It is a shame when parents lose their tempers and go off on long **tirades** against their children, yelling at them for anything and everything.

TRY IT OUT

For each word or definition, find the matching vocabulary word and write a sentence using that word:

1. agreement, conformity   _____ _____

2. disbeliever   _____ _____

3. hatred, lack of respect   _____ _____

4. variation, discrepancy   _____ _____

5. importance, significance   _____ _____

6. rant   _____ _____

7. reluctance, opposition   _____ _____

8. repentance, sorrow   _____ _____

9. shortness   _____ _____

10. truthfulness, frankness   _____ _____

Complete each of the following sentences by inserting one of the vocabulary words:

11. _____ with safety regulations is necessary for firefighters in order to keep themselves safe.

12. Henry had been a _____ of UFO sightings for years, but he finally believed in them when he saw unexplainable lights in the night sky.

13. If the gang members felt any _____, they certainly didn't show it, grinning up at the judge as he read them their sentences.

14. Interviewers hope to talk to people who will speak with openness and _____.

15. Many people feel _____ to going to the dentist because they worry that the experience will be uncomfortable.

16. Some people complain that there is a great _____ in different people's incomes, with some having much more wealth than others.

17. The Mayor's _____ on the poor state of schools in our city went on and on for hours.

18. The speaker was known for his _____; his speeches rarely lasted for more than a couple minutes.

19. Tommy showed _____ for the rules; he always got in trouble and refused to listen to authority.

20. When the citizens started complaining, the mayor finally realized the _____ of the situation.

Vocabulary List 8

blasphemy	irreverence toward a belief, disrespect
aesthetic	idea of what is beautiful, particular style
altruism	unselfish interest in helping others
diligence	persistent effort, working steadily
fervor	passion, great enthusiasm, ardor
deterrent	something which prevents or discourages action
nuance	subtle difference
chicanery	trickery, deceitfulness
bigot	intolerant or prejudiced person, dogmatist
strife	conflict, struggle

His offensive language against their culture was considered **blasphemy**.

They bought typewriters and an old-fashioned refrigerator to fit with the retro **aesthetic** of their home.

The knight showed **altruism** by refusing to accept payment for saving the villagers.

Although Scott completed his homework with great **diligence**, copying over each page for neatness and correctness, he was often lax when it came to other "non-school" work.

As the speaker delivered his powerful and inspiring speech, there was a **fervor** building in the crowd.

Worrying about instability and profits can be a **deterrent** that keeps investors from supporting new companies.

If you listen to the same music on different media, such as vinyl records, CDs, or cassette tapes, you can notice **nuances** in the sound quality.

The politician was accused of **chicanery** for misleading the voters and manipulating laws.

The old man held onto outdated beliefs and values, few people liked to associate with him because he was a **bigot**.

Even through the great **strife** of the economic depression, Apple computers have prospered and become bigger than ever.

TRY IT OUT

For each word or definition, find the matching vocabulary word and write a sentence using that word:

1. chauvinist, extremist   _____ _____

2. discord, trouble   _____ _____

3. fine detail, distinction   _____ _____

4. perseverance   _____ _____

5. philanthropy, kindness   _____ _____

6. profanity, sacrilege   _____ _____

7. restraint, restriction   _____ _____

8. treachery, fraud   _____ _____

9. artistic sense, taste   _____ _____

10. zeal, dedication   _____ _____

Complete each of the following sentences by inserting one of the vocabulary words:

11. I was surprised to learn of the awful _____ that people in other parts of the world have to endure.

12. Jeanna was praised for her _____; when others gave up, she continued to work hard.

13. Marigolds are sometimes planted around gardens as a _____ to pesky bugs who dislike the smell of these flowers.

14. Patricia's _____ was shown in her many efforts to support poor people and raise funds for charities.

15. She accused her father of being a _____ because he refused to change his controversial opinions.

16. She worried that, since she didn't know the customs of the people, her actions would be seen as _____.

17. The art scholar was able to distinguish an authentic painting from a fake replica by noticing very minor _____.

18. The clever spy was known for his _____.

19. The interior designer chose certain colors and styles of furniture in order to create a particular _____.

20. The new employee loved his job and worked with _____, excitedly doing his duties.

Vocabulary List 9

trivial	unimportant, insignificant
superficial	shallow, on the surface only
capricious	unstable, whimsical, flighty
viable	capable of living or growing, possible
superfluous	exceeding what is sufficient or necessary, surplus
abstract	theoretical, not concrete, not easily grasped
complacent	smug, satisfied
illusory	based on a false perception of reality, deceptive
objective	factual, without bias, not subjective
dubious	doubtful, unsure

Something that may be considered to be **trivial** for one person may actually be considered a catastrophe for another.

Fortunately, the wound was **superficial** and would not require any surgery.

Our newspaper delivery boy is a **capricious** character; depending on his mood, he either angrily hurls the paper at our kitchen window or politely brings it to our front door.

The new plan was more **viable**, and we all agreed that we could accomplish it.

The additional pages were considered **superfluous** and thus were removed from the treatise.

Abstract art is known for being unrealistic or unidentifiable and is often more concerned with ideas or impressions.

Others viewed Shana as **complacent** because it appeared she didn't really care about what was happening around her.

When one realizes how easy it is for locks to be picked and opened, the safety they provide might seem **illusory**.

An **objective** opinion is one that is based on facts rather than on ideas.

TRY IT OUT

For each word or definition, find the matching vocabulary word and write a sentence using that word:

1. conceptual, intangible   _____ _____

2. external, exterior   _____ _____

3. more than needed   _____ _____

4. feasible, doable   _____ _____

5. impulsive, variable   _____ _____

6. minor, inconsequential   _____ _____

7. not influenced by opinion   _____ _____

8. not real   _____ _____

9. uncertain   _____ _____

10. unworried, content   _____ _____

Complete each of the following sentences by inserting one of the vocabulary words:

11. At some point, every child must grow up to realize that the pleasant world seen in fairy tales is _____.

12. I like cows because of their _____ faces; they always look so calm and fulfilled, like they have no worries in the whole world.

13. If she has extra money available, she invests the _____ funds in the stock market.

14. Jeff had a great idea for a new invention, but without any funding it wouldn't be _____.

15. Lucinda likes math more than philosophy because she prefers to study something definite than to work with _____ ideas.

16. Scientists strive to ensure that their research is _____ and not affected by their own beliefs.

17. The crash only did _____ damage to the car, because the paint was scuffed but the body was unaffected.

18. The damage to the plane was _____; the plane could still fly perfectly well.

19. The supposed "expert" didn't actually have any knowledge of the subject, so was _____ about his theories.

20. When Courtney changed her college major several times, her family said that she was too _____ and needed to make a definite decision.

Vocabulary List 10

reticent	quiet, uncommunicative, taciturn
eccentric	deviating from the standard or norm
lucid	clear, easy to understand
grandiose	impressive, grand; **or**: pompous, pretentious
magnanimous	noble and generous
redundant	unnecessary, superfluous
adroit	skillful, adept, deft
comprehensive	inclusive, large in scope or content
impartial	unbiased, unprejudiced, disinterested
dogmatic	stubbornly opinionated

Although Ron was skeptical about the outcome, questioning every turn of events, he was **reticent**, not voicing his concern to the crew members.

Because he enjoyed doing crazy things in the classroom, Mr. Thompson was considered an **eccentric** old man by his students.

My favorite math teacher was able to give clear, **lucid** explanations of complex math concepts, which helped me to understand new ideas.

He was a **grandiose** figure – bigger than life.

The elderly statesman had given much for his country and was recognized and loved for his **magnanimous** nature.

Much of the evidence presented to support the theory of UFO's is **redundant**, always involving the same shadowy photographs of lighted discs.

The town performer was so **adroit** at twirling batons that a crowd had gathered to watch.

As a firm advocate of women's rights, she compiled a **comprehensive** list of all the companies in eastern Massachusetts in which women were underrepresented.

Although originally **impartial**, the judge took on a decided bias after the bribe offer.

Rebecca became **dogmatic** in her belief of the Easter Bunny; even as an adult, she stubbornly argued that it was real.

TRY IT OUT

For each word or definition, find the matching vocabulary word and write a sentence using that word:

1. broad, complete   _____ _____

2. coherent, logical   _____ _____

3. practiced, competent   _____ _____

4. extravagant, showy   _____ _____

5. giving, kind   _____ _____

6. neutral, fair   _____ _____

7. one-sided, narrow-minded _____ _____

8. reserved, not talkative   _____ _____

9. unneeded, repetitive   _____ _____

10. unusual, peculiar   _____ _____

Complete each of the following sentences by inserting one of the vocabulary words:

11. A good referee is _____, with no preference for either team.

12. After decades of practice and experience, the carpenter was amazingly _____ with woodworking.

13. Many fans were disappointed with the director's confusing and overly-complex movie, because his earlier movies had been so _____.

14. Many old churches are _____, with their incredible and excessive decorations and embellishments.

15. Norman was so shy that even around his family he was _____.

16. The game was fun at first, but it seemed boring and _____ after I realized it involved doing the same thing over and over.

17. The _____ king was charitable and gracious when dealing with his peasants.

18. When people are not exposed to other cultures or beliefs, they might hold too strongly onto their own ideas and become problematically _____.

19. While a standard dictionary has most words, the Oxford English Dictionary is far more _____; it endeavors to include every word in the language.

20. With his wild outfits and odd behavior, Walter gained a reputation as one of the most _____ members of his class.

Vocabulary List 11

furtive	secretive, stealthy, surreptitious
blithe	free-spirited, carefree, happy
frivolous	not serious, insignificant
benign	harmless, beneficial, kind, gentle
obscure	unclear, vague; **or**: hard to find
impoverished	poor, suffering from poverty
eloquent	articulate, fluent in verbal expression
ominous	threatening, warning of danger
fickle	unpredictable, capricious, inconsistent, erratic
banal	common, lacking originality, hackneyed

At the dinner table, the siblings exchanged **furtive** whispers, sharing secrets that their parents couldn't hear.

The **blithe** children played on the beach with no worries at all.

During the meeting, there were a few **frivolous** remarks, but nothing important was said.

Some illnesses may start as **benign**, but become harmful later.

Candlepin bowling is an **obscure** sport because it is not well known outside of New England and some parts of Canada.

Formerly proud and prosperous, the old mining town is now **impoverished**.

To sound beautifully **eloquent** should not be the primary goal of speech or writing.

On the edge of the horizon, **ominous** clouds warned of an upcoming storm.

He can never decide which clothes to wear because he is too **fickle** and keeps doubting his decisions.

Even though Marcus is an interesting person, he isn't good at holding a conversation because his stories are **banal** and boring.

TRY IT OUT

For each word or definition, find the matching vocabulary word and write a sentence using that word:

1. bankrupt, insolvent   _____ _____

2. well-said, persuasive   _____ _____

3. indefinable; intangible   _____ _____

4. indecisive, whimsical   _____ _____

5. trivial, silly   _____ _____

6. mild, not hurtful   _____ _____

7. sneaky, sly   _____ _____

8. trite, dull, ordinary   _____ _____

9. unconcerned, merry   _____ _____

10. worrying, foreboding   _____ _____

Complete each of the following sentences by inserting one of the vocabulary words:

11. Because he was unaware of the dangers involved, the _____ hero happily began his adventure.

12. He thought his music was exciting and unique, but it was disappointingly _____.

13. I tried to interpret his argument, but his logic was so _____ that I couldn't comprehend him.

14. Many horror movies use _____ music to set a creepy mood.

15. Martha is too concerned about _____ issues that are not important enough to worry about.

16. My _____ cousin always changes her mind.

17. Some snakes are awfully dangerous because of their poisonous venom, but other snakes are safe and _____.

18. The charity group hopes to strengthen weak economies in order to help the _____ people in the world.

19. Wanting to hide their relationship from others, the couple had _____ meetings in the middle of the night.

20. While Dawn is able to verbally express herself clearly and confidently, her writing skills are not nearly as _____.

Vocabulary List 12

ironic	unexpected; **or**: paradoxical, self-contradictory
concise	briefly and clearly stated, succinct
benevolent	good, kind-hearted, generous
languid	slow, tired, drooping, listless
prudent	careful, cautious, having practical wisdom
flagrant	intentionally offensive, noticeably bad, deliberate
austere	severe, stern, strict
elusive	hard to catch, hard to understand or solve
fastidious	not easy to please, overly critical, meticulous
astute	shrewd, wise, keen in judgment

It is **ironic** that for years Clark Kent tried so hard to hide his identity from Lois Lane, when all along she knew he was Superman.

The author's **concise** article was lauded by many literary critics for being so tight and well-written.

Mrs. Gill, a noted philanthropist, showed her **benevolent** character again when she donated 1.5 million dollars to the Homeless Veteran's Foundation.

The **languid** river moved so slowly that it seemed the water was still.

Jenny was a **prudent** shopper, always finding the best bargains and sales.

His **flagrant** abuse of rules caused such an uproar that the representative's entire constituency was in a state of shock.

Although living in an ornate monastery, the monks led **austere** lives in which only their most basic needs were met.

Eliminating the need of fossil fuels has been an **elusive** goal for many years, but we are getting closer to solving this problem.

She was a **fastidious** dresser, always making sure that her clothes matched perfectly and that she had perfect accessories to accentuate her outfits.

The **astute** lawyer, who seemed never to miss a trick, quickly pointed out the fallacious reasoning behind her opponent's inadequate argument.

TRY IT OUT

For each word or definition, find the matching vocabulary word and write a sentence using that word:

1. caring, compassionate   _____   _____

2. blatant, shameless   _____   _____

3. lazy, unhurried   _____   _____

4. picky, finicky   _____   _____

5. practical, sensible   _____   _____

6. satiric, sarcastic   _____   _____

7. serious, grave   _____   _____

8. smart, perceptive   _____   _____

9. terse, snappy   _____   _____

10. hard to pin down, baffling _____   _____

Complete each of the following sentences by inserting one of the vocabulary words:

11. By the appearance of his harsh face, it seems that my grandfather is _____, but in actuality he is a funny, goofy person.

12. By the story's conclusion, Scrooge has gone from being cruel and selfish to kind and _____.

13. I was exhausted after the game, and for the rest of the day I was _____.

14. Many scientists have spent years attempting to hunt down a live specimen of the _____ giant squid.

15. The business school is looking for _____ students who show good judgment in their decisions and investments.

16. The _____ crime was so cruel and shocking that it captured the attentions of the media and the public.

17. The instruction manual was very _____, with only a few brief descriptions and short explanations.

18. The _____ ending of the play was that the pair who hated each other most eventually fell in love.

19. The teacher was _____; no matter how hard his students tried or how well they performed, he always criticized them for every minor mistake they made.

20. When hiring new employees, you must be _____ and carefully analyze applicants in order to ensure you make a well-informed decision.

Vocabulary List 13

surpass	to be superior, to excel, to transcend, to outdo
disparage	to speak badly of, to belittle
retaliate	to get back at, to get revenge
refute	to disprove, to prove false
bolster	to support, to reinforce
acquiesce	to go along with something, to consent, to agree
allege	to assert without proof, to claim
evoke	to call forth, to bring to mind
chastise	to discipline, to reprimand
coalesce	to come together, to merge, to join

Uncle Nick is a successful investor, and his skills **surpass** those of all but the cleverest of the money managers.

Rather than **disparaging** others, you should be kind and supportive.

Finally, Ken had had enough and **retaliated** by punching one of the bullies in the nose.

When beliefs are held for a long time, some people will stubbornly ignore anything that **refutes** their ideas.

New types of metals will help **bolster** the strength and safety of automobiles.

When he realized that nobody else on the committee shared his opinion, he **acquiesced** and changed his vote to follow the others.

She **alleged** that her neighbor was a criminal, but she didn't have any proof to support this claim.

When I watch old movies from my childhood, they **evoke** memories and feelings from that time.

The teacher **chastised** his class for not studying enough in preparation for their big test.

In large cities, different cultures and ethnicities **coalesce** and intermingle.

TRY IT OUT

For each word or definition, find the matching vocabulary word and write a sentence using that word:

1. to comply, to accept   _____   _____

2. to contend, to declare   _____   _____

3. to counter, to contest   _____   _____

4. to criticize, to mock   _____   _____

5. to outdo, to exceed   _____   _____

6. to react, to strike back   _____   _____

7. to punish, to scold   _____   _____

8. to strengthen, to boost   _____   _____

9. to unite, to combine   _____   _____

10. to suggest, to induce   _____   _____

Complete each of the following sentences by inserting one of the vocabulary words:

11. After generations of being oppressed and victimized, the revolutionaries finally decided to _____ and fight against the people who had exploited them.

12. Analysts hope that the new tax reforms will _____ the economy by improving business investments.

13. Every year, new athletes _____ the performance of older athletes and set new records.

14. Hannah and her husband disagreed about where to go to dinner, but her husband was so stubborn that she decided to _____ and go where he wanted.

15. In the finest meals, all of the ingredients _____ in a perfect harmony.

16. Larry's parents often have to _____ him for all of the trouble and mischief he gets into.

17. Some athletes are more motivated by coaches that _____ and criticize them than coaches who are supportive and positive.

18. Some people _____ that unbelievable monsters live in the woods near our town, but they have no evidence.

19. Sometimes, new discoveries in science will _____ and replace old theories that were shown to be incorrect.

20. The best books _____ strong emotions, making the reader feel strong sympathy for the characters.

Vocabulary List 14

venerate	to regard with respect, adore
collaborate	to work jointly with others
corroborate	to support with evidence, to confirm
mitigate	to make milder, to make less severe
exacerbate	to make more severe or worse
repudiate	to reject, to disown, to not accept
scrutinize	to examine closely
dispel	to drive away by scattering, to dissipate
censure	to criticize harshly, to condemn
hamper	to impede, to get in the way, to fetter

An award was given to the **venerated** paleontologist when he retired after over 50 years of important contributions to the field.

Howard Roarke refused to **collaborate** with others; on the contrary, he preferred to work alone.

The evidence from the new dig site could **corroborate** the archaeologist's theory and make it much more credible.

Brian tried to **mitigate** the disagreement between his two friends, but instead his irritating manner **exacerbated** the argument, elevating it to a shouting match.

The defense lawyer **repudiated** the charges that the prosecution was making.

They were careful to **scrutinize** their path, checking to make sure it was safe, as they had been told of avalanches caused by careless hikers.

The strong winds **dispelled** the clouds and cleared the skies.

The young boy was **censured** by his parents for stealing toys from another child.

The bad weather **hampered** the family's plans, and they had to reschedule for another time.

TRY IT OUT

For each word or definition, find the matching vocabulary word and write a sentence using that word:

1. to aggravate   _____ _____

2. to alleviate, to ease   _____ _____

3. to cooperate   _____ _____

4. to deny   _____ _____

5. to inspect   _____ _____

6. to disperse, to dismiss   _____ _____

7. to obstruct, to hinder   _____ _____

8. to reprimand, to disapprove _____ _____

9. to revere, to idolize, to esteem _____ _____

10. to substantiate, to prove   _____ _____

Complete each of the following sentences by inserting one of the vocabulary words:

11. A selfish and bitter man, Jared _____ the idea that he should ever help other people.

12. Archaeologists _____ every artifact in order to learn as much as possible about ancient civilizations.

13. It can be difficult to _____ false rumors once people start believing in them.

14. Musicians often look for other musicians so they can _____ and make new music together.

15. My brother always tries to help whenever there is a problem, but he is so clumsy that he just _____ the situation instead of making it better.

16. Some cultures _____ great heroes by having certain days on which they remember and honor these great people.

17. The detectives searched for more facts that could help _____ the fact that the criminal was guilty.

18. The whole nation will _____ the actions of the traitor who betrayed his fellow people.

19. The worst illnesses cannot be cured, so doctors try to _____ the effects instead.

20. Willis is so determined that he will not let anything _____ his progress.

Vocabulary List 15

compromise	to agree by conceding; **or**: to expose to risk
solicit	to ask for, to request
alleviate	to lighten, to relieve
digress	to stray from the subject in speaking or writing
emulate	to copy something admired, to rival by imitating
engender	to create, to produce, to propagate
deride	to ridicule, to make fun of
nullify	to negate, to invalidate; **or**: to make unimportant
rejuvenate	to make youthful again
extol	to praise, to exalt

Jose Canseco may sit out the beginning of the baseball season if he and the management are unable to **compromise** on how much he should be paid.

At a loss for what to do, he decided to **solicit** advice from his parents.

His recent pay raise will help **alleviate** the burden of paying financial loans.

Although Donna had intended to discuss the Middle East situation, she **digressed** into a long story about her childhood.

Carol's admiration for Mother Teresa led her to try to **emulate** the saintly woman by devoting her life to aiding the poor and hungry.

Often a leader's great fervor will **engender** fanaticism among his or her followers.

The school bully was **deriding** the other students on the playground by calling them names.

With three seconds remaining, the Patriots scored, **nullifying** the Jets' lead and sending the game into overtime.

Ponce de Leon claims to have been **rejuvenated** when he bathed in the Fountain of Youth.

The hero was **extolled** for his noble actions.

TRY IT OUT

For each word or definition, find the matching vocabulary word and write a sentence using that word:

1. to admire _____ _____

2. to beg, to plead _____ _____

3. to cancel, to abolish _____ _____

4. to cooperate _____ _____

5. to disparage, to mock _____ _____

6. to lessen, to ease _____ _____

7. to mimic _____ _____

8. to revitalize, to refresh _____ _____

9. to stray, to wander _____ _____

10. to cause, to prompt _____ _____

Complete each of the following sentences by inserting one of the vocabulary words:

11. Beauty products claim they can _____ your skin and make you look years younger.

12. Joe's editorial piece in the school newspaper _____ much discussion on the nutritional value of food served in the cafeteria.

13. Once a year, the charity has a fund raiser to _____ people for more financial support.

14. Pain relief medication might not solve problems, but it can _____ some suffering.

15. The speech was only supposed to take a few minutes, but she continued to _____ and get distracted from the main topic, so she ended up speaking for nearly an hour.

16. The government's decision will _____ several laws, making them obsolete and no longer legitimate.

17. The salesman _____ the great qualities of the vacuum cleaner, trying to convince us it was the best product available.

18. The scholar's hypothesis was _____ by many experts who believed his ideas were foolish and absurd.

19. Training every day, Sandy worked hard to _____ the skills of her favorite gymnasts.

20. When it was apparent that neither side would give up, they had to _____ and find an agreement that would satisfy both of them.

Vocabulary List 16

concede	to admit to be true; **or**: to forfeit
advocate	to support, to speak in favor of, to recommend
laud	to praise, to extol
assuage	to soothe, to ease, to appease, to calm
condescend	to talk down to, to act superior, to be patronizing
efface	to erase, to wipe out
condone	to forgive, to overlook without censure or protest
provoke	to cause to act, to rouse; **or**: to anger
ameliorate	to make better, to improve
instigate	to stir up, to urge on, to initiate

After the harsh reviews, she **conceded** that the performance could have been better.

Doctors will **advocate** the use of medicines that they believe are particularly effective.

The successful new book was **lauded** by fans and reviewers.

She **assuaged** her hunger by eating a cheeseburger.

Alvin's father hardly ever addressed him as an equal, instead giving him advice in a **condescending** manner.

The burglar tried to **efface** all clues of his presence, but he accidentally left his fingerprints on the doorknob.

Although he had committed a crime, his actions were **condoned** because he had only tried to protect himself.

In spite—or perhaps because—of her weightlifting and kickboxing, Alice is not one to **provoke** a fight.

Morgan took aspirin to **ameliorate** her headache.

Steve **instigated** the fight by shouting insults and making threats.

TRY IT OUT

For each word or definition, find the matching vocabulary word and write a sentence using that word:

1. to admire, to revere

2. to disrespect

3. to give in, to yield

4. to ignore, to excuse

5. to irritate, to aggravate

6. to lessen, to alleviate

7. to promote

8. to start, to bring about

9. to upgrade, to enhance

10. to wear away, to eradicate

Complete each of the following sentences by inserting one of the vocabulary words:

11. A firm believer in the importance of education, he _____ for better salaries for teachers.

12. According to many studies, poverty may _____ an increase in crime and a decrease in the quality of public education.

13. After a lengthy and tiring argument, he finally _____ that she had been right all along.

14. Government officials are trying to agree on methods to _____ the recent economic problems.

15. Millennia of erosion have _____ the carvings and paintings that were once visible on the canyon walls.

16. The doctors gave him medication that _____ his soreness, making it easier to deal with the pain.

17. The general believed that many of his troops were uneducated, so he _____ to them by speaking in simple terms.

18. The orchestra's performance was _____ by the audience, which gave great applause.

19. The school's dean would no longer _____ student hazing, and she notified the students that it would now result in harsh punishment.

20. With tensions so high between the nations, some worry that even a slight dispute could _____ a large war.

Vocabulary List 17

prodigal	extravagant, wasteful
prodigious	enormous, extraordinary, marvelous
ambiguous	having more than one possible meaning, uncertain
ambivalent	indecisive, of two minds about something
ephemeral	short-lived, transitory, fleeting
despondent	dejected, hopeless
pretentious	pompous, self-important, affected
insipid	bland, boring, without zest
cursory	rushed, hurried, superficial, perfunctory
lax	careless, slack, not strict

The Count of Monravia was once quite wealthy; however he lost his fortune through **prodigal** living.

The **prodigious** storm covered the whole state in a thick blanket of snow.

The finale of the film was **ambiguous**, which lead fans to debate what had actually happened for years.

Scott was **ambivalent** about his relationship with Katie; they had fun together, but they also fought often.

The bloodroot is classified as an **ephemeral** plant due to the brevity of its life cycle.

Craig was **despondent** after he broke up with his girlfriend.

Daniel wouldn't stop talking during the meeting, and he constantly alluded to how successful and knowledgeable he was, which made him sound **pretentious**.

The professor droned on and on as if his every word augmented the world's supply of wisdom. Soon his **insipid** lecture put everyone to sleep.

Even a **cursory** look at the class statistics will show that the students are excelling in every area.

If you are **lax** on maintenance and repairs, your home could quickly start falling apart.

TRY IT OUT

For each word or definition, find the matching vocabulary word and write a sentence using that word:

1. casual, brief, hasty _____ _____

2. colossal, incredible _____ _____

3. dull, trite _____ _____

4. laidback, negligent _____ _____

5. sad, downhearted _____ _____

6. snobbish, ostentatious _____ _____

7. squandering, reckless _____ _____

8. temporary, momentary _____ _____

9. unclear, vague _____ _____

10. unsure, undecided _____ _____

Complete each of the following sentences by inserting one of the vocabulary words:

11. After losing her job, Carol was depressed and _____.

12. Although Fred is usually very opinionated, he feels _____ about music.

13. Melissa has always been _____, preferring to spend all her money right away than to save it.

14. Most people only give instruction manuals a _____ look and assume they can understand things on their own.

15. The banquet is always a _____ event, with a tremendous amount of food and hundreds of guests.

16. The factory employees were extremely careful because their strict manager was never _____ on rules and regulations.

17. The presenter wasn't _____, but was instead very genuine and modest.

18. The test results were _____; the doctors could not determine a diagnosis.

19. Unlike their first album, which was exciting and inspiring, the new album is _____.

20. Youth is an _____ blessing that should be enjoyed for the short time that it lasts.

Vocabulary List 18

eclectic	consisting of varied things, mixed, heterogeneous
haughty	proud, arrogant
laconic	using few words, concise, terse
mercurial	rapidly changing, capricious, temperamental
affluent	wealthy
placid	calm, docile, serene
wary	cautious, suspicious
spurious	false, fake
prudish	excessively proper, puritanical
obdurate	stubborn, adamant, obstinate

With everything from heavy metal to easy listening, Roger has an **eclectic** record collection.

Because they are wealthy and privileged, royalty are sometimes prideful and **haughty**.

The message on the card I got from my parents was short and **laconic**.

The state of the economy is **mercurial**, always shifting.

Property is very expensive in **affluent** neighborhoods.

Far from the noise and activity of the cities, Lake Solitude is a **placid** vacation spot on Mount Sunapee.

The sentry was supposed to stay **wary** of intruders all night, but he slowly began to drift off to sleep.

Spurious reports of alien sightings have been made all over the world, but what if one of them was true?

Prudish Victorians are known for strongly opposing the use of nude models in art.

Even though everyone tried to convince her try something else, she was **obdurate**.

TRY IT OUT

For each word or definition, find the matching vocabulary word and write a sentence using that word:

1. assorted, diverse   _____ _____

2. bogus, counterfeit   _____ _____

3. conceited, self-important _____ _____

4. distrustful, on guard   _____ _____

5. peaceful, mild   _____ _____

6. formal, straitlaced   _____ _____

7. inflexible, unyielding   _____ _____

8. rich, prosperous   _____ _____

9. short, to the point   _____ _____

10. unstable, unpredictable   _____ _____

Complete each of the following sentences by inserting one of the vocabulary words:

11. Catherine's jewelry collection is _____, with many different styles and fashions.

12. Customers were outraged by the company's _____ apology, which only offered a few words and a weak excuse.

13. If she remains _____, we will have to work harder to change her mind.

14. Instead of being consistent and predictable, her parents' moods were _____ and erratic.

15. The campground in the middle of the forest was quiet, restful, and _____.

16. The mayor lost support from the townspeople because he appeared too prideful and _____.

17. The salesman tried to trick customers into buying his bogus product by making _____ claims that it would cure all of their ailments.

18. When Frank declined the invitation to the wild party, people said he was _____.

19. When he won the lottery, the young farmer went from nearly bankrupt to incredibly _____.

20. While hiking, you should be _____ of bears, mountain lions, and uneven paths.

Vocabulary List 19

apathetic	indifferent, uninterested
cathartic	producing a release of emotions
indigenous	native
stalwart	strong, brave
livid	angered, infuriated
blatant	obvious, unashamed
opulent	wealthy, luxurious
pedantic	showy of knowledge, ostentatiously scholarly
loquacious	talkative, garrulous
tenacious	stubborn, persistent

The teenager was so **apathetic** that she didn't care when she failed all of her classes.

At the end of the movie, there was a **cathartic** scene where the two main characters realized that they loved each other.

There are still some **indigenous** tribes that have not been studied because they have always lived in very dangerous and remote areas that most people can't access.

The **stalwart** knight drank his mead before fearlessly entering into battle.

When I realized that someone stole my computer, I was **livid** and wanted to find and punish the thief.

His goofy expressions and idiotic remarks show that he is a **blatant** fool.

Ancient palaces are known for being astoundingly **opulent**; some of them had such expensive décor that they nearly bankrupted entire nations!

Professor Marquez's lectures were awfully **pedantic**; he used so many big words and tried so hard to show his intelligence that his classes were more about his boasting than our learning.

Case had a tendency to repeat and over-explain everything, which made him **loquacious**.

Lola has been **tenacious** in her pursuit of the gold medal, and for that she will be surely rewarded.

TRY IT OUT

For each word or definition, find the matching vocabulary word and write a sentence using that word:

1. aboriginal, local   _____ _____

2. know-it-all, pretentious   _____ _____

3. deliberate, transparent   _____ _____

4. determined, resolute   _____ _____

5. enraged   _____ _____

6. lavish, affluent   _____ _____

7. not caring, unconcerned   _____ _____

8. purgative, liberating   _____ _____

9. robust, rugged   _____ _____

10. wordy, long-winded   _____ _____

Complete each of the following sentences by inserting one of the vocabulary words:

11. Although potatoes were originally _____ to a small area of Peru, they are now grown across the globe.

12. As he argued with his brother, he became so _____ his face turned purple and hot.

13. As soon as Heather stepped into the _____ hotel, with its crystal chandelier and marble floors, she knew she wouldn't be able to afford a room.

14. Henry didn't care about either of the soccer teams, so he felt _____ while he watched the match.

15. His lies were so _____ that nobody was ever fooled.

16. Mia's _____ friend looks for any opportunity to correct people's grammar or share his knowledge of useless facts.

17. The lumberjack was such a _____ man that people talked about his strength and courage as if he was a legend.

18. When Cassandra finally confessed to her lies, she felt a _____ release that freed her from her worries, anxieties, and guilt.

19. Her _____ cousin was always looking for an opportunity to tell stories about himself.

20. Jack and Kyle have been _____ in their constant pursuit of artistic excellence.

Vocabulary List 20

circumspect	cautious, prudent
melancholy	depressing, sad
lethargic	lacking energy, lazy
erratic	inconsistent, unpredictable
erudite	scholarly, well-educated
inept	incompetent, clumsy
latent	inactive, dormant; **or**: hidden
intrepid	fearless, brave
cosmopolitan	worldly, sophisticated
deft	skillful, smart

Spies must always be **circumspect** in order to ensure that they aren't caught.

We had expected the movie to be funny and uplifting, but it was actually very **melancholy** and left us all downhearted.

Supposedly, eating turkey will make you sleepy and **lethargic** because it contains a lot of tryptophan.

Eric kept slamming into the walls on the go-cart course as his driving was much more **erratic** than the other racers.

Jim was one of the more **erudite** students at the school; he received straight A's in all of his classes.

Our taxi driver was **inept** and took twice as long as usual to find the way to our destination because he didn't know many of the roads well.

After years of being friends, her **latent** feelings of love for him were finally awakened.

I am **intrepid** when ordering from restaurants, so I have eaten some very odd foods.

After traveling around the world and experiencing many cultures, Carol was very **cosmopolitan**.

My uncle is a **deft** jazz musician because he is able to adapt and improvise with incredible skill.

TRY IT OUT

For each word or definition, find the matching vocabulary word and write a sentence using that word:

1. awkward, bumbling   _____ _____

2. clever, adroit   _____ _____

3. courageous   _____ _____

4. glum, miserable   _____ _____

5. idle; concealed   _____ _____

6. intellectual, knowledgeable _____ _____

7. irregular, changing   _____ _____

8. languid, sluggish   _____ _____

9. multinational   _____ _____

10. wary, careful   _____ _____

Complete each of the following sentences by inserting one of the vocabulary words:

11. A bad diet can make you feel sluggish and _____.

12. New York is a _____ city with many different cultures mixing and mingling.

13. Some people believe humans are capable of incredible powers that are still _____ because we have not discovered how to unlock them.

14. The _____ professor was incredibly well-educated and knowledgeable.

15. The _____ explorers went boldly into dangerous, uncharted lands.

16. The new business manager was so _____ that the company quickly went bankrupt.

17. The panther is a _____ hunter, silently stalking from the shadows and attacking in sudden, agile strikes.

18. Their guide was always _____ and cautious, carefully leading them through the dense jungle.

19. Weather can be _____ and unpredictable, which is why weather forecasts are uncertain.

20. When the team lost the tournament, the mood of the whole town was _____.

SUMMIT
EDUCATIONAL
GROUP

Vocabulary List 21

assessment	an estimate of value, appraisal, evaluation
presumption	guess, assumption
dissent	difference of opinion, conflict, discordance
diatribe	a bitter speech or criticism, rant
empathy	understanding of the feelings of others
iconoclast	person who opposes established institutions, freethinker
martyr	person who suffers for a cause
novice	beginner, inexperienced learner
platitude	unoriginal remark, cliché, banality
placebo	substance containing no medication

The job of an appraiser is to analyze property and make an **assessment** of its value.

I was under the **presumption** my husband liked my cooking; however, I recently found out that he was feeding scraps to the dog under the table.

The large protest march was an act of public **dissent** in order to show how upset people were with the state of the nation.

At half-time, the coach unleashed a **diatribe** because the team was falling behind.

Diagnosed with the disease herself, Theresa had a great deal of **empathy** for those suffering from Cystic Fibrosis.

Many of history's greatest heroes were revolutionaries and **iconoclasts** in their times.

Martyrs are honored and respected because they held onto their beliefs so strongly that they were willing to sacrifice themselves in order to maintain their faith.

Even the greatest athletes began as **novices**.

I believe that these are not just **platitudes** anymore; the Governor really means what he says this time.

Josefina will have no idea whether she received a **placebo** or not until the medical trials are complete.

TRY IT OUT

For each word or definition, find the matching vocabulary word and write a sentence using that word:

1. apprentice, neophyte   _____ _____

2. belief, conjecture   _____ _____

3. compassion   _____ _____

4. dispute, opposition   _____ _____

5. inactive; fake   _____ _____

6. measurement   _____ _____

7. overused expression, inanity _____ _____

8. rebel   _____ _____

9. sacrifice, victim   _____ _____

10. tirade, harangue   _____ _____

Complete each of the following sentences by inserting one of the vocabulary words:

11. During dinner, Howard's father gave a harsh _____ about the consequences of laziness and procrastination.

12. His lack of _____ makes it hard for him to understand people or develop good relationships.

13. Holly's decision to move to Colorado was made with the _____ that she could endure the cold winters better than the hot summers of New Mexico; however, it turned out that she hated the cold even more.

14. Many superheroes are _____ because they make incredible sacrifices for the sake of justice.

15. My grandfather is full of _____ that get more dull and obvious every time he tells them.

16. The doctor doubted that the patient was truly ill, so she prescribed a _____ instead of actual medication.

17. The famous actor's controversial political views made him an _____ because he criticized and opposed many institutions and beliefs.

18. The _____ chess player was hesitant to make moves and could not anticipate what his competitors would do next.

19. The physician used several tests to make a health _____ of the patient.

20. There were rumors of _____ among the sailors, and the captain worried that they would oppose him and would mutiny.

Vocabulary List 22

autonomy	self-government, independence
despot	ruler with absolute power, dictator
fiasco	failure, disaster, debacle
integrity	completeness, reliability; **or**: morality, honesty
archetype	prime example, epitome
prompt	call to action, reminder
surrogate	substitute, stand-in
amalgamation	combination, mixture
impudence	rudeness, lack of respect, insolence
squalor	filth, dirtiness

The colony petitioned for **autonomy** so that it could govern itself.

In my house, my mother was like a **despot**, with complete control over everything.

Their vacation was a **fiasco** because of problems with their car and canceled reservations.

I always use the products from this company because it has **integrity** and is reliable and trustworthy.

Shakespeare's dramas are **archetypes** that established characters and plots that have served as examples for many later stories.

The landlord called for a **prompt** reply to her request to reduce noise after 9:30pm or more drastic measures would be taken.

The **surrogate** Vice Chairman is doing a great job and is well respected by everyone, maybe we will end up keeping him!

Many people don't know that rock n' roll began as an **amalgamation** of blues and country music.

The teacher was frustrated by the student's **impudence**, because she could not get the young boy to follow the rules.

The **squalor** of the Favelas of Rio is contrasted by the shiny skyscrapers of Ipanema.

TRY IT OUT

For each word or definition, find the matching vocabulary word and write a sentence using that word:

1. authoritarian, tyrant   _____ _____

2. catastrophe, mess   _____ _____

3. disrespect   _____ _____

4. foulness   _____ _____

5. incitement, cue   _____ _____

6. sovereignty   _____ _____

7. replacement, alternate   _____ _____

8. standard, model   _____ _____

9. truthfulness   _____ _____

10. merger, blend   _____ _____

Complete each of the following sentences by inserting one of the vocabulary words:

11. A good politician should have _____ so she can be trusted.

12. After the king was assassinated, he was replaced by another _____.

13. In many large cities, slums and ghettos have been areas of poverty and _____ for generations.

14. It is important for high school students to learn responsibilities and develop some _____ before they go to college and have to depend on themselves.

15. Schopenhauer believed that reading could be bad for you because it is a _____ for thinking for yourself.

16. Several _____ and instructions guided me through the installation of the program.

17. The meal was an _____ of several styles of cooking; it showed influences from Mexican, Indian, and Spanish cuisines.

18. The party was a _____, with a fire starting in the kitchen and two of the guests getting in a fight.

19. The story of Beowulf is so well-known that even the villain has become a character _____.

20. The student had the _____ to demand that the teacher change her grade, but of course the teacher was not influenced by this disrespect.

Vocabulary List 23

attribute	inherent characteristic
rigor	difficulty, strictness, rigidity
exodus	a mass departure, emigration
ingenuity	cleverness, inventiveness
panacea	curative, remedy, cure-all
pettiness	narrow-mindedness; **or**: stinginess, ungenerousness
recession	withdrawal, decline
counterfeit	forgery, fake
precursor	person or thing that comes before, herald
glutton	person with great desire or capacity; **or**: overeater

Siblings are recognizable because they share **attributes** they inherited from their parents.

Some people appreciate the **rigor** of Army training because it promotes hard work and responsibility.

The mass of refugees left the area in a large **exodus**.

Many of the technologies that we rely on today are the result of past **ingenuity**.

Illnesses and diseases are so different that there is no **panacea** to cure all of them.

I am tired of the **pettiness** of the student council President; why can't she bring up any of the important issues?

After Christmas mass, the **recession** party proceeded down the center aisle and out through the double doors at the back of the church.

A talented artist tried to make money by copying famous paintings and selling these **counterfeits**.

The failure of several large banks was a **precursor** to the Great Depression.

Charlie doesn't like candy, but he is a **glutton** for honey-roasted almonds.

TRY IT OUT

For each word or definition, find the matching vocabulary word and write a sentence using that word:

1. concern for trivial things _____ _____

2. creativity, originality _____ _____

3. elixir, solution _____ _____

4. evacuation _____ _____

5. predecessor, forerunner _____ _____

6. imitation, sham _____ _____

7. foodie, gourmand _____ _____

8. severity, harshness _____ _____

9. slump, downturn _____ _____

10. trait, quality _____ _____

Complete each of the following sentences by inserting one of the vocabulary words:

11. A local criminal was caught creating _____ by bleaching five-dollar bills and printing the design for twenty-dollar bills on them.

12. Drops in profits and jobs have made people worry that the nation will experience an economic _____.

13. Graduate school is known for its _____, which makes some students question whether the degree is worth all of the work and stress.

14. Ivan only cared about things that directly affected him, and most people thought that his _____ was pathetic.

15. One _____ of a good relationship is a mutual feeling of trust.

16. Pigs are known for being _____ because they will eat almost anything and have huge appetites.

17. The many advancements and new inventions of the modern age are the product of great _____.

18. The _____ to political changes is usually public unrest that leads to the desire for new laws and policies.

19. Until medical scientists develop a _____ for all diseases, some illnesses will have to be treated with traditional medicines and techniques.

20. When war broke out, thousands of citizens evacuated the country in a sudden _____.

Vocabulary List 24

impediment	obstacle, hindrance
indictment	accusation
perfidy	treachery, deceit
profanity	irreverence, obscenity
stimulus	something that excites or incites
diversion	deviation; **or**: distraction, entertainment
contempt	disdain, bitter scorn, open disrespect
endorsement	support, sanction
malice	hatred, spite
infamy	bad reputation, disgrace, opprobrium

A major **impediment** to the progress of modernizing cities is that old infrastructure must be removed or adapted.

The police had a formal **indictment** which charged the suspect with the crime.

Carlotta was so enraged with her boyfriend's act of **perfidy** against her that she is considering bringing him up on charges with the local police department.

Mrs. Callahan reminded us not to use any forms of **profanity** during the debates this afternoon.

The axon conducts an electronic **stimulus** within our muscles.

The thief used fireworks to create a noisy, flashy **diversion** that distracted the police while he escaped.

My friend loves fine food, so he has **contempt** for cheap, fast-food cuisine.

After a series of controversial remarks, the mayoral candidate lost her **endorsement** from the local newspaper.

When someone is victimized, the pain they experience will turn to **malice** and possibly a desire for revenge.

Robert Ford earned his **infamy** for cowardly killing the outlaw Jesse James.

TRY IT OUT

For each word or definition, find the matching vocabulary word and write a sentence using that word:

1. amusement, hobby _____ _____

2. approval _____ _____

3. betrayal, dishonesty _____ _____

4. catalyst, encouragement _____ _____

5. condemnation, denunciation _____ _____

6. disapproval, dislike _____ _____

7. hostility, malevolence _____ _____

8. notoriety, disrepute _____ _____

9. obstruction, barrier _____ _____

10. vulgarity, curse _____ _____

Complete each of the following sentences by inserting one of the vocabulary words:

11. A star athlete's _____ of this new product should convince audiences of its effectiveness.

12. Although he claims his criticism was without _____, it is clear that he intended to damage her reputation.

13. Dogs can be trained much more easily when they are offered the simple _____ of a tasty treat.

14. In order to cover his fellow inmate's escape, the prisoner created a _____ in the courtyard to distract the guards' attention.

15. The boss discovered his employee's _____ when he stumbled upon the worker sharing company secrets with a competitor.

16. The government made an official _____ of the terrorists who had endangered civilians.

17. The international criminal's _____ for horrible acts is well-known to citizens and police officers alike.

18. The school has a strict policy regarding _____, so students who use swear words in the classroom can expect punishment.

19. The storm tore down trees, which lied across the roads and were an _____ to traffic.

20. They looked down upon him, treating him with _____ due to his low birth.

Vocabulary List 25

meticulous	showing extreme care about details
mundane	ordinary, dull, commonplace
vacuous	lacking content, empty
subjective	affected by interpretation, not objective
tenuous	flimsy, weak, thin
bombastic	self-important, ostentatious, pompous
copious	abundant, plentiful
affable	friendly, pleasant, genial
cynical	distrustful and critical of others, pessimistic
lavish	abundant, extravagant

Watchmakers have to be **meticulous**, carefully checking every detail for absolute precision.

Even the most beautiful landscapes can seem **mundane** if you see them every day.

The **vacuous** film I saw at the film festival really underwhelmed me.

The saleswoman was excessively **subjective** when promoting her new line of vehicles.

Woodrow Wilson holds a **tenuous** place in U.S. History; more people should recognize the great work he did as President.

The politician made a **bombastic** speech about what a great candidate he could be, and it was clear he was promising more than he could deliver.

Some college courses cover so much information so quickly that students must take **copious** notes and then review all of them in order to absorb everything.

The receptionist was **affable** and made everyone feel comfortable as soon as they entered the office.

William's **cynical** nature makes him very negative and untrusting.

The **lavish** feast had a remarkable array of fine dishes.

TRY IT OUT

For each word or definition, find the matching vocabulary word and write a sentence using that word:

1. biased   _____ _____

2. blank   _____ _____

3. boring, everyday   _____ _____

4. grand, splendid   _____ _____

5. not humble, not modest   _____ _____

6. numerous, bountiful   _____ _____

7. skeptical, doubting   _____ _____

8. slim, delicate   _____ _____

9. sociable   _____ _____

10. thorough, careful   _____ _____

Complete each of the following sentences by inserting one of the vocabulary words:

11. Although the student's opening paragraph was strong, her weak evidence and flimsy conclusion revealed a _____ grasp of the subject matter.

12. Her hard experiences have given her a _____ view of the world, so she tends to distrust others and expect the worst.

13. His _____ nature allows him to make friends quickly almost anywhere he goes.

14. If one wants to score a perfect grade on this test, one must be _____ in one's calculations, checking and double-checking answers carefully for errors.

15. In a debate based on logic and hard evidence, one must be careful not to rely on _____ opinions or personal stories.

16. Nora had volunteered in order to gain exciting experience, but she quickly grew bored with the _____ nature of her repetitive office tasks.

17. She was not content with a simple wedding, organizing instead a _____ 4-hour ballroom ceremony and inviting hundreds of guests.

18. The book's main character is quite _____; he offers no intelligent insights and performs no interesting tasks.

19. The orator spoke in a _____ style, using flowery language and exaggerated gestures.

20. The Thanksgiving table was loaded with _____ amounts of food, almost groaning under the weight of it all.

Vocabulary List 26

adamant	immovable, obstinate, obdurate
bourgeois	middle-class, conventional
irate	very angry, furious
clandestine	secret, private, illicit, surreptitious
docile	easy to manage, obedient, submissive
eminent	well-known, renowned
ornate	elaborately decorated, embellished
explicit	clearly expressed, definite, unambiguous
innocuous	harmless, inoffensive
lugubrious	mournful, gloomy, melancholy

Her daughter was **adamant** in her belief of Santa Claus and wouldn't consider the idea that he isn't real.

The developing nation finally had normal **bourgeois** comforts, like air conditioning, public education, and health insurance.

He was **irate** when he heard the bad news, screaming and cursing in red-faced anger.

One of Chekhov's best stories is about a **clandestine** affair between a selfish man and a woman who hides the relationship from her husband.

It takes a lot of effort to make a wild horse **docile** so it can be ridden safely.

Standing at 20,320 feet tall, Mount McKinley stands as the **eminent** peak of Alaska's Denali National Park.

Her bracelet was incredibly **ornate**, with many small gems and delicate filigree.

The recipe book gave thorough, **explicit** directions so amateur cooks could easily understand even the most complicated recipes.

This species of spider looks terrifying, but actually it's **innocuous** so you shouldn't worry if you see one.

The day had a **lugubrious** mood because the clouds and rain made everything feel dark and depressing.

TRY IT OUT

For each word or definition, find the matching vocabulary word and write a sentence using that word:

1. adorned, lavish   _____ _____

2. certain, understandable   _____ _____

3. common, average   _____ _____

4. compliant, tame   _____ _____

5. concealed, covert   _____ _____

6. incensed, enraged   _____ _____

7. inflexible, unyielding   _____ _____

8. reputed, distinguished   _____ _____

9. sad, depressed   _____ _____

10. safe, mild   _____ _____

Complete each of the following sentences by inserting one of the vocabulary words:

11. Ever since her boyfriend broke up with her, she's been listening to sad songs and writing _____ poems about the hopelessness of lost love.

12. Having worked her way up from the very bottom, she now enjoys a respected position as an _____ politician.

13. He was _____ in his refusal to compromise, and it became clear that negotiations would fall apart if he did not get his way.

14. I thought that my comment was _____, but she took offense and I had to apologize.

15. The 18th-century mansion was filled with _____ furniture and objects of art, each more beautiful and valuable than the last.

16. The _____ government operation was kept secret from all but those directly involved.

17. The general gave _____ orders to his troops, leaving no detail unexplained.

18. These mild-mannered sheep are very _____, and can be directed easily by a single shepherd.

19. They were not rich but not poor, living a fairly standard but comfortable _____ lifestyle.

20. When he realized one of his students had cheated, the teacher was _____ and had to calm himself down before he spoke to her.

Vocabulary List 27

perfunctory	automatic, without thought; **or**: unenthusiastic
somber	gloomy, dark, depressing
succinct	concise, terse, laconic
emphatic	strongly expressive, forceful
trenchant	sharp, incisive, forceful
adjunct	associated, additional, attached
contingent	dependent on something, conditional
belligerent	warlike, aggressive, pugnacious
callous	insensitive, unfeeling
dormant	inactive, hidden, resting

Trevor has a general disdain for the theater, however he decided to accompany his girlfriend to the performance as a **perfunctory** courtesy.

On a **somber** occasion such as this, we reflect on our past and what we could have done better.

The pamphlet served the general public perfectly, **succinct** and to the point, so it was easy to comprehend.

Ben was **emphatic** in denying the charges despite overwhelming evidence against him.

The **trenchant** critique from the media was far more than any person should have to deal with, especially when it was not deserved.

Skilled artisans believe that technologies should only be **adjunct** to traditional tools and methods so that the old ways can be preserved.

Our picnic plans are **contingent** on the weather, because we can't go if it's rainy or too windy.

The rebel faction was **belligerent** and constantly tried to battle the government forces.

Oliver is so **callous** that he has never been saddened, excited, or captivated by a good book.

The virus was **dormant** inside of him, and the doctors could not predict when it would activate.

TRY IT OUT

For each word or definition, find the matching vocabulary word and write a sentence using that word:

1. accessory, extra   _____   _____

2. argumentative, quarrelsome   _____   _____

3. brief   _____   _____

4. heartless   _____   _____

5. insistent, assertive   _____   _____

6. latent, sleeping   _____   _____

7. possible, reliant   _____   _____

8. severe   _____   _____

9. solemn, grave   _____   _____

10. unthinking, mechanical   _____   _____

Complete each of the following sentences by inserting one of the vocabulary words:

11. Churchill's _____ use of language cut right to the core, offending some people but always conveying a clear message.

12. He signed that week's fourth birthday card in a _____ manner, without any real thought or attention to detail.

13. Her speech was _____, conveying a complicated message effectively in a short period of time.

14. I thought he was a sensitive person, but he revealed his _____ nature when he verbally abused a homeless beggar.

15. Our final decision is _____ upon next week's results; we can't proceed until we have more information.

16. Polly was _____ in her performance of the play's climactic line, speaking each word forcefully and brimming with emotion.

17. The _____ professor knew she wasn't a critical member of the faculty, and she desperately wanted a more secure and respectable position.

18. The generals are eager for war, and their _____ behavior has scared neighboring countries.

19. The team's defeat in the state championships had a _____ effect on the entire school, and the hallways were no longer filled with shouting and laughter.

20. The volcano has lain _____ for many years, but now geologists are worried it may awake and erupt.

Vocabulary List 28

imminent	happening soon, impending
arduous	difficult, strenuous
obstinate	stubborn, unbending
ostentatious	attempting to impress, pretentious
quixotic	impractically idealistic, unrealistically romantic
stagnant	inactive, still
tacit	understood without being said, implied, unspoken
wily	cunning, sly, crafty
frugal	not wasteful, thrifty, prudent
gregarious	enjoying company, sociable

The pressure to buy gifts is high when the holiday season is **imminent**.

Jobs in construction are **arduous** and labor-intensive.

My younger brother is **obstinate**, which is why he always gets what he wants.

The wedding decorations were so expensive and overly fancy that they seemed tacky and **ostentatious**.

The biopic describes the actor's **quixotic** adventure from the cornfields of Oklahoma to the Hollywood big screens in a way that is so emotional and dramatic it is hard to believe.

If the economic conditions remain **stagnant**, we may need another federal bailout.

The decision was met with **tacit** approval, by this time next year; our family will be living in Hawaii.

Wily as a fox, Arturo crept through the small opening and entered the building, unseen and unheard by anyone around.

If you live **frugally** by using coupons, spotting sales, and never buying more than you have to, you'll save a lot of your money.

The **gregarious** socialite was always going to parties and making new friends and acquaintances.

TRY IT OUT

For each word or definition, find the matching vocabulary word and write a sentence using that word:

1. assumed, inferred   _____ _____

2. economical, penny-pinching _____ _____

3. extroverted, outgoing   _____ _____

4. foolish, dreaming   _____ _____

5. forthcoming, looming   _____ _____

6. inflexible, fixed   _____ _____

7. laborious, hard   _____ _____

8. motionless   _____ _____

9. scheming, clever   _____ _____

10. showy, not modest   _____ _____

Complete each of the following sentences by inserting one of the vocabulary words:

11. Building the Great Wall of China was an _____ task, and many peasants died of exhaustion during its construction.

12. He saved money through _____ living habits, and, even though he is now a millionaire, he still lives very simply.

13. He was _____ in his position, and our appeals to reason and emotion all failed to change his mind.

14. I wanted a simple answer, but he gave a long and _____ response, which was clearly intended to impress the audience.

15. It had not rained for months, and the stream had dried out into a few _____ pools full of scum and mosquito larvae.

16. She was shy in high school but is _____ in college, and she goes out to gatherings and parties almost every night.

17. The building is damaged and I fear a collapse is _____—we have to get out of here right now!

18. The coach did not openly call for a new game plan, but a quick nod to the team captain signaled his _____ approval of new tactics.

19. The _____ possum had somehow anticipated the hunter's trap, and escaped once again.

20. We need a realistic and reasonable strategy, not a _____ plan which focuses on imaginary enemies and impractical techniques.

Vocabulary List 29

denounce	to condemn openly
feign	to pretend, to imitate
infer	to reason, to draw a conclusion, to surmise
juxtapose	to place side by side for comparison
revere	to respect, to venerate
satiate	to satisfy, to fill
wane	to decrease, to decline
discern	to recognize, to perceive
conform	to comply with norms, to become similar
stymie	to block, to hinder

After it was discovered that the king's advisor was actually a traitor, he was **denounced** and banished from the kingdom.

She didn't want her friend to know that she had already heard the rumors, so she **feigned** ignorance.

If you read books carefully, you may be able to **infer** the opinions and beliefs of the author.

The DJ **juxtaposed** old and new music, showing the bonds between different generations and styles.

All of the grandchildren in the family **revered** their grandmother with a special honor.

Following the great feast of autumn, the **satiated** king retreated to his quarters for a nap.

As the daylight **waned** and nighttime arrived, I knew that it would soon be bedtime, and I could relax after my long day.

She had a **discerning** eye for quality and could spot cheap items quickly.

Some people find comfort in **conforming** to stereotypes because it lets them easily fit in to a group.

Hopefully the typhoon will not **stymie** the progress of the simian researchers in the jungles of Papua New Guinea.

TRY IT OUT

For each word or definition, find the matching vocabulary word and write a sentence using that word:

1. to admire   _____ _____

2. to assume, to suppose   _____ _____

3. to contrast   _____ _____

4. to criticize, to censure   _____ _____

5. to detect, to distinguish   _____ _____

6. to diminish, to get smaller _____ _____

7. to fake   _____ _____

8. to impede, to stall   _____ _____

9. to obey rules, to match   _____ _____

10. to quench, to please   _____ _____

Complete each of the following sentences by inserting one of the vocabulary words:

11. As winter _____ and springtime begins, the icicles begin to melt and green buds begin to appear.

12. By _____ this painting with others from the same time period, we will gain a broader understanding of the artist's message.

13. George was _____ by the test question, and when time ran out he just had to guess.

14. He _____ sickness in order to avoid a test that morning, but his plan backfired when he had to spend the whole day in a hospital waiting room.

15. He tried three different brands, but was unable to _____ any difference between the three types of vanilla ice cream.

16. Henry ate three burgers, two milkshakes, and a pile of fries, but was somehow still not _____.

17. She refused to _____ to her classmates' clothing preferences, and wore unusual outfits every day.

18. She was not appreciated during her lifetime, but she is now _____ as the grandmother of that political movement.

19. The politician _____ his opponent constantly, accusing him of every possible misdeed and moral shortcoming.

20. We can often _____ from a person's tone of voice and body language what their words do not tell us directly.

Vocabulary List 30

subvert	to undermine, to sabotage
circumvent	to go around, to avoid
embellish	to adorn, to enhance
ascertain	to find out, to learn, to make certain
harangue	to speak angrily, to give a diatribe
innovate	to introduce something new
fluctuate	to shift back and forth, to change
debunk	to expose as being false
abhor	to hate, to despise
placate	to calm, to pacify

It is our hope that our interest in hiring new staff will not **subvert** our efforts in training our existing staff.

Many new technologies are used to **circumvent** the stress of labor and make our lives easier.

The writer faced immense pressure from his critics to apologize after it was revealed that he **embellished** many details in his autobiography to sell more copies.

With all of the clues finally within his grasp, the detective was able to **ascertain** the identity of the murderer.

The police officer **harangued** the boys for causing trouble, and this harsh speech was enough of a punishment.

The old techniques are no longer effective, so if we are unable to **innovate** we will soon be out of business.

It is normal for people's interests to **fluctuate** as they grow older and find new passions.

With the new research, we have finally **debunked** the idea that the Loch Ness Monster exists.

Ivan doesn't just dislike asparagus, he **abhors** it.

Whether we support banning pesticides or not, we must **placate** the farming lobbies in order to garner more votes.

TRY IT OUT

For each word or definition, find the matching vocabulary word and write a sentence using that word:

1. to corrupt _____ _____

2. to criticize, to berate, to rant _____ _____

3. to determine _____ _____

4. to disprove, to demystify _____ _____

5. to decorate, to exaggerate _____ _____

6. to evade, to elude _____ _____

7. to invent, to renew _____ _____

8. to loathe, to detest _____ _____

9. to soothe _____ _____

10. to vary, to alternate _____ _____

Complete each of the following sentences by inserting one of the vocabulary words:

11. As new illnesses appear, scientists must _____ new drugs that can keep people healthy and safe.

12. His mother was very upset, but he was able to _____ her with soothing words and promises.

13. I absolutely _____ that song, and I'm going to leave the room if I hear it on the jukebox.

14. Intelligence units are working around the clock, but have thus far been unable to _____ the target's whereabouts.

15. It is far easier to _____ the mountain than it is to climb up and over to the other side.

16. She was slightly shocked when her long-held belief was _____ through scientific observation.

17. The defendant _____ his false story with details, hoping they would make his defense more believable.

18. The government's best efforts to stop drug use among teens have been _____ by musicians who celebrate the use of recreational drugs.

19. The stock market _____ daily, making investors millionaires one day and penniless the next.

20. The wife _____ her husband every time he came home late, but her fierce scolding never seemed to have an effect on his habits.

Vocabulary List 31

belie	to show to be untrue, to contradict
beguile	to lure, to charm, to attract
aggravate	to make worse; **or:** to irritate
expedite	to speed up, to hasten
reconcile	to resolve, to make a person accept something
curb	to hold back, to restrain
debase	to demean, to degrade, to spoil
confound	to confuse
discriminate	to note differences, to distinguish
lament	to mourn, to feel regret

The beauty of the old forest **belies** the dangers of the animals and plants within it.

The audience was **beguiled** by the enchanting music.

When the athlete played another game instead of resting and healing, he **aggravated** his injury.

In order to finish the project sooner, more assistants were hired to **expedite** progress.

The couple ending up **reconciling** their differences in the end, and their marriage was saved.

After all of the negative reviews I heard, my enthusiasm for seeing the movie was **curbed**.

Some believe that people are **debased** if they are in the company of others who are immoral.

Astronomers were **confounded** by the new findings, which seem to disprove their understanding of the universe.

The admissions committee did not look at any of the applicants' personal information in order to ensure that they did not **discriminate** based on gender, race, or other factors.

Jeremy still **laments** the loss of his scholarship; he regrets not working harder to keep his grades high.

TRY IT OUT

For each word or definition, find the matching vocabulary word and write a sentence using that word:

1. to annoy; to exacerbate _____ _____

2. to bewilder, to puzzle _____ _____

3. to categorize, to judge _____ _____

4. to disprove _____ _____

5. to entice, to captivate _____ _____

6. to grieve _____ _____

7. to corrupt, to lower _____ _____

8. to limit, to curtail _____ _____

9. to rush _____ _____

10. to settle, to resolve _____ _____

Complete each of the following sentences by inserting one of the vocabulary words:

11. She refuses to _____ herself by doing manual labor, but, if she doesn't find work, she'll go broke.

12. She spent many hours _____ the poor score she received on her last test, but she took no realistic steps to raise her grade.

13. The con artist _____ the old couple with fantastic promises of high investment returns and used their trust to steal all their savings.

14. The couple across the street has _____ since their screaming match the other day, and they can now be seen holding hands and smiling.

15. The detective was _____ by a complete lack of clues at the crime scene, and he never solved the case.

16. The expert was able to _____ between different varieties of wine, even identifying individual vineyards by taste alone.

17. The politician made public statements without checking the facts, and careful research later _____ his false claims.

18. The project deadline is drawing close, and we won't make it if we don't _____ a few important tasks.

19. The strict laws on texting while driving are designed to _____ rising rates of car accidents.

20. We thought he would help us resolve the conflict, but his bad attitude has only _____ the problem.

Vocabulary List 32

assail	to assault
conjecture	to conclude or assume from incomplete evidence
obstruct	to block, to hinder
curtail	to cut short, to hold back
abate	to decrease, to weaken
abase	to humble, to reduce in rank
eradicate	to destroy, to eliminate
bewilder	to confuse, to confound
foster	to promote growth
imply	to suggest, to hint

The army of soldiers **assailed** the castle gates, bashing it with an enormous battering ram.

The researcher was not willing to **conjecture** because he wanted absolute proof before he made a statement.

Passage along the river was **obstructed** by a tree that had fallen into the water.

Some worry that the new laws and restrictions will **curtail** the freedoms of citizens.

A car's muffler is used to **abate** the noise of the exhaust from the engine.

She felt sympathy for the man when she saw him being insulted and **abased**.

The organization's mission is to **eradicate** hunger in the city of Boston by providing food for families in need.

A good riddle can **bewilder** even the smartest people because they are a test of cleverness and creativity more than knowledge.

The store's great sales will **foster** more business and hopefully some big profits.

My teacher never tells us things directly; instead, she **implies** things and makes us figure out what she really wants us to learn.

TRY IT OUT

For each word or definition, find the matching vocabulary word and write a sentence using that word:

1. to attack   _____   _____

2. to baffle, to puzzle   _____   _____

3. to cultivate, to encourage   _____   _____

4. to decline, to lessen   _____   _____

5. to demean, to humiliate   _____   _____

6. to exterminate   _____   _____

7. to give evidence, to insinuate _____   _____

8. to guess, to infer   _____   _____

9. to impede, to hamper   _____   _____

10. to limit, to restrict   _____   _____

Complete each of the following sentences by inserting one of the vocabulary words:

11. Even his hometown team's string of losses couldn't _____ John's burning passion for rugby.

12. If Congress's new budget does not _____ out-of-control spending, our country will sink deeper into debt.

13. Our hope is that kind treatment will _____ a sense of hope among homeless youth.

14. She did not say so directly, but her words _____ a deep disappointment.

15. She used a laser pointer to _____ her cat, who couldn't understand its rapid movements.

16. Ted was thoroughly _____ by his teacher's harsh words, and he would not act arrogantly again.

17. The convoy slowly came to a halt, _____ by a herd of sheep crossing the road.

18. The harsh weather _____ the peasants' crops, and many starved that winter.

19. The mayor had been caught up in a scandal, and when he left the office he was _____ by reporters' angry questions.

20. Without solid proof, any conclusions we reach are merely a matter of _____.

Vocabulary List 33

voracious	extremely hungry, ravenous
debilitating	weakening, incapacitating
sanctimonious	self-righteous, making a display of devotion
ineffable	incapable of being expressed, indescribable
replete	full, stuffed
prosperous	successful, flourishing, wealthy, affluent
pious	devout, religious, reverent
cantankerous	argumentative, irritable, contentious
detrimental	harmful, damaging
judicious	sensible, thoughtful, practical

Homer has a **voracious** appetite for donuts and can eat half a dozen in one sitting.

The accident was **debilitating**, leaving him seriously injured.

The Senator from Nebraska adopted a **sanctimonious** stance, criticizing the morals of his fellow Congressmen.

When she finally returned to her childhood home, she was filled with an **ineffable** feeling, a mix of so many emotions she couldn't describe it.

The school cafeteria was **replete** with every kind of food and drink imaginable.

After many years of operating in the red, the chocolate factory finally became **prosperous** after they came out with the popular mint nougat bar.

Nikki has such a **pious** persona that many have wondered why she never went into the clergy.

As he grew older he got more **cantankerous** and would complain or start arguments whenever he had the chance.

Too much exercise can be **detrimental** to the body because it can overstrain muscles and joints.

Judicious use of spices is important for making meals that are savory but not overwhelming.

TRY IT OUT

For each word or definition, find the matching vocabulary word and write a sentence using that word:

1. bad-tempered, cranky   _____ _____

2. crippling   _____ _____

3. dedicated, zealous   _____ _____

4. gluttonous, insatiable   _____ _____

5. negative, destructive   _____ _____

6. packed, jammed   _____ _____

7. preachy, smug   _____ _____

8. shrewd, astute, cautious   _____ _____

9. thriving   _____ _____

10. unspeakable, beyond words _____ _____

Complete each of the following sentences by inserting one of the vocabulary words:

11. Growing children can have _____ appetites—sometimes it seems as if they never stop eating.

12. He is a _____ man, who makes all day-to-day decisions according to his religious beliefs.

13. He suffers from _____ back pain, which can be so bad that some days he cannot rise from bed.

14. He used his money _____ for many years, and his good judgment resulted in a comfortable retirement.

15. Her _____ old neighbor would look for any excuse to pick a fight, and simply wouldn't listen to reason.

16. It is now generally recognized that smoking is _____ to one's health, and many smokers are trying to quit.

17. Overcome by an _____ sense of joy, she had no words to express her happiness.

18. The preacher gave a _____ speech about the evils of alcohol, but we all know he can be found at the local bar most weekday evenings.

19. The rough draft of this paper is _____ with errors, and it will take hours to correct.

20. This is a _____ town, with wealthy citizens and well-funded schools.

Vocabulary List 34

insolvent	out of money, impoverished
ravenous	extremely hungry, famished
aberrant	abnormal, unusual, deviant
impetuous	acting without consideration, impulsive
congenial	friendly, pleasant
indignant	offended, angry about unfair treatment
tangential	slightly connected or related, digressive
ardent	passionate, enthusiastic
sparse	thinly distributed, meager, scanty
quarrelsome	inclined to disagree, belligerent

Years of debt and recent troubles have left the family **insolvent**.

Frederica was so **ravenous** that she ate the whole pepperoni pizza in one sitting.

At the family reunion, my uncle's behavior was **aberrant** and everyone thought he was acting oddly.

While it is usually a good idea to be rational and careful, it can be exciting to sometimes be **impetuous**.

The clerk at the hotel was very kind and **congenial**, offering to help us with anything we needed.

Norman was **indignant** when the stranger insulted him for no reason.

Even though it's a long book, not much happens in the story because most of it is **tangential** information that is not important to the main narrative.

She was an **ardent** supporter of the sports team, going to every game and cheering wildly.

Because of North Dakota's **sparse** population, locations such as Fargo have been touted for starting a new business and not being fearful of significant competition.

The **quarrelsome** couple next door has such loud arguments that I can't sleep when they are fighting.

TRY IT OUT

For each word or definition, find the matching vocabulary word and write a sentence using that word:

1. disgruntled, resentful   _____ _____

2. argumentative, cantankerous   _____ _____

3. fervent, zealous   _____ _____

4. financially ruined, bankrupt   _____ _____

5. affable, amiable, nice   _____ _____

6. peculiar, odd   _____ _____

7. peripheral, not central   _____ _____

8. reckless, rash, hasty   _____ _____

9. scarce, bare   _____ _____

10. starving, voracious   _____ _____

Complete each of the following sentences by inserting one of the vocabulary words:

11. After a series of bad business deals and years of rising costs, the company became _____ and failed to pay its bills.

12. All of the ducklings followed their mother in a neat row, except one _____ little bird that kept wandering off.

13. His _____ expression of love was so moving that she immediately agreed to marry him.

14. I would advise against working with _____ teammates, as their unpredictable nature can be a danger to project goals.

15. Most hosts go out of their way to be _____ towards guests, doing their best to put visitors at ease.

16. Our teacher is easily distracted, and he often strays slightly from the topic at hand to discuss _____ matters.

17. Plants are _____ in this part of the desert due to lack of rain.

18. She hadn't eaten for days, and was _____ when she finally attacked a full meal.

19. She was an honest student, and she was _____ when someone claimed that she had cheated.

20. The couple which lives next to me is _____, and I can hear their nightly arguments through the thin walls.

Vocabulary List 35

insolent	disrespectful, contemptuous, impudent
negligent	neglectful, careless, inattentive
prohibitive	discouraging, preventative, unaffordable
rancorous	vengeful, resentful
anomalous	deviating from the normal, irregular
arcane	known by few, esoteric
precocious	ahead in development, gifted, talented
stupefying	astonishing, amazing, stunning
incompetent	unskilled, inept
nefarious	evil, wicked

The teenager was **insolent** in the face of criticism, and he boldly responded to scolding with insults and smart remarks.

If you are **negligent** of your plants, they may wilt, because they need care and nourishment.

If Jorge's apartment complex was not so **prohibitive**, he would have had many parties already.

There is no concrete evidence to suggest that baboons living in **rancorous** societies will live shorter lives than those living more tranquil lives in zoos.

Since he usually runs 3 miles every morning and lifts weights every night, any day he doesn't exercise is **anomalous**.

Studying ancient texts can reveal **arcane** beliefs or stories that were lost in history.

Sandra was a **precocious** child; she was reading John Grisham novels by age nine.

Despite all of his great success, the artist was **stupefied** by the crowd that was gathered before him.

When you start learning a new skill, you may feel **incompetent**, but, with more practice, you'll become proficient.

In many fairytales, there is a **nefarious** witch who manipulates or threatens the protagonist.

TRY IT OUT

For each word or definition, find the matching vocabulary word and write a sentence using that word:

1. advanced, unusually smart   _____   _____

2. inconsistent, not ordinary   _____   _____

3. astounding, incredible   _____   _____

4. rude, insulting   _____   _____

5. despicable, vile, heinous   _____   _____

6. lacking ability   _____   _____

7. lazy, unconcerned   _____   _____

8. obscure, mysterious   _____   _____

9. restrictive   _____   _____

10. unforgiving   _____   _____

Complete each of the following sentences by inserting one of the vocabulary words:

11. Despite his parent's attempts to teach him to be well-mannered, the child was _____.

12. He has been _____ in his responsibilities, and will be punished for failing to fulfill his duties.

13. John was good at his last job but _____ at this one, messing up even the simplest tasks.

14. The high costs of luxury goods are _____ to most people, who simply can't afford to purchase them.

15. She had not expected her opponent to express aggression or hatred, so his _____ attitude shocked and frightened her.

16. Such ancient and _____ knowledge is familiar to only a few experts worldwide.

17. Supporters of nuclear power are quick to claim that meltdowns are quite _____, and that residents close to power plants have little to fear.

18. The music was incredibly loud, _____ everyone in front of the loudspeakers into numb silence.

19. The _____ five-year-old child held her own in conversation with adults, impressing all within earshot.

20. The townsfolk had heard news of the arriving villain's _____ deeds, and they all hid inside their homes.

Vocabulary List 36

averse	having a feeling of opposition, reluctant
notorious	unfavorably known, infamous, disreputable
ethereal	extremely delicate, airy, ghostly
obsolete	out of use, not current, antiquated
legitimate	lawful, rightful
impulsive	acting on sudden desires or whims, reckless
devious	not sincere, deceitful, scheming
feasible	capable of being done, practical, viable
antagonistic	acting in opposition, hostile
flamboyant	showy, ostentatious, ornate

Paul dislikes crowds, but he is not **averse** to going to parties occasionally.

After his many crimes, the outlaw was **notorious** throughout the West.

The sculpture had an **ethereal** beauty; its elaborate, fine details made it look hauntingly real.

Whenever a new gadget or device comes out, people believe that the previous version is suddenly **obsolete** and inferior.

Because the king did not come from a royal lineage, people did not believe he had a **legitimate** place on the throne.

Willis often gets in trouble because he is **impulsive** and doesn't plan before he acts.

My mother cautioned me to avoid people who seem **devious** and not trustworthy.

The teacher's class schedule was not **feasible** because there wasn't enough time to accomplish all she needed to do.

When Russell gets irritated he becomes **antagonistic** and starts arguments with everyone.

The musical had **flamboyant** costumes with vibrant colors and incredible designs.

TRY IT OUT

For each word or definition, find the matching vocabulary word and write a sentence using that word:

1. old-fashioned, outdated   _____ _____

2. dishonest, crafty   _____ _____

3. disinclined, unenthusiastic   _____ _____

4. flashy, gaudy, colorful   _____ _____

5. justifiable   _____ _____

6. light, heavenly   _____ _____

7. realistic, possible   _____ _____

8. scandalous, dishonorable   _____ _____

9. spontaneous   _____ _____

10. unfriendly, aggressive   _____ _____

Complete each of the following sentences by inserting one of the vocabulary words:

11. Beatrice was the _____ owner of the stolen vehicle, and she provided a title and a bill of sale as proof.

12. Drew can be quite _____, making sudden decisions at the drop of a hat.

13. Her _____ singing voice seemed to the audience as if it had drifted down from heaven on a ray of sunlight.

14. His _____ clothes and behavior are designed to draw as much attention as possible.

15. Oliver avoided answering his accusers' answers directly, responding with _____ half-truths and excuses.

16. Paul had become _____ for cheating at cards, so all the other poker players watched him carefully for suspicious movements.

17. She was completely _____ to socializing with his friends, and refused to acknowledge their greetings.

18. Technology evolves so quickly that some computers become _____ within a few years and are given away in favor of more up-to-date ones.

19. The proposed plan is simply not _____, and we need to come up with a more realistic method of accomplishing our goals.

20. The two debaters were highly _____, attacking each other at every opportunity.

Vocabulary List 37

indelible	cannot be erased, indestructible
pejorative	derogatory, negative
idiosyncratic	characteristic of a person, peculiar to an individual
unorthodox	untraditional, unconventional
abrasive	harsh, rough; **or**: irritating, annoying
intricate	having many parts, complex
irreverent	without respect, impertinent
lackadaisical	without interest, lazy, careless
assiduous	hard-working, diligent
authentic	real, genuine

The president's memorable term will leave an **indelible** mark on history; it won't be forgotten.

The political candidates stooped as low as to use **pejorative** statements against one another, in order to prove that their opponent was an inferior candidate.

My friend's unusual fashion sense is **idiosyncratic** because nobody else looks like her.

Daniel's behavior would probably be considered to be **unorthodox** anywhere else, but in New York City, anything goes!

He can be rude and arrogant, so some people think he's **abrasive**.

Clocks are incredibly **intricate**, with many small, precise components that all work together in perfect harmony.

When the substitute teacher arrived, the students were **irreverent** and misbehaved all day.

The new worker was **lackadaisical**, and his fellow workers were upset that he didn't care about the job.

The **assiduous** farmer worked from sunrise to sunset in order to maintain and protect his crops.

Heather thought the antique was **authentic**, but she later realized it was a fake.

TRY IT OUT

For each word or definition, find the matching vocabulary word and write a sentence using that word:

1. apathetic, easy-going _____ _____

2. coarse, rude _____ _____

3. complicated _____ _____

4. credible, legit _____ _____

5. debasing, derisive _____ _____

6. insolent, rude _____ _____

7. distinctive, particular _____ _____

8. nonconformist, abnormal _____ _____

9. permanent _____ _____

10. tireless, industrious _____ _____

Complete each of the following sentences by inserting one of the vocabulary words:

11. Bradley gave his son an _____ 19th-century pocket watch, originally owned by his great-grandfather.

12. Having lost his respect for authority, he spoke to parents and teachers alike in an _____ tone.

13. Having stained her shirt with _____ ink, she sighed and threw the ruined garment away.

14. His odd habit is quite _____, and as you get to know him better you will learn of his other quirks as well.

15. Lawrence's _____ personality rubs many people the wrong way, and some become so annoyed that they refuse to work with him.

16. Only _____ study, night after night, will lead to mastery of such a difficult subject.

17. The _____ lace had been carefully woven into complex and beautiful shapes.

18. The teacher's methods are _____, and they draw criticism from those who prefer traditional ways.

19. Veronica has been _____ in her studies, and her laziness has caused her grades to fall.

20. Wanda described him in _____ language, making it very clear that she looked down upon him.

Vocabulary List 38

evanescent	tending to disappear quickly, short-lived
obtuse	insensitive; **or**: slow to understand
polemic	controversial
inevitable	unavoidable, expected
ubiquitous	existing everywhere, omnipresent
contrite	feeling guilt or regret, remorseful, repentant
repugnant	disgusting, offensive
adept	skillful, proficient
shrewd	astute, keen, clever, insightful
destitute	without basic necessities, needy, impoverished

Many of the greatest joys in life are **evanescent**, only lasting for a brief moment before they fade away.

Jack didn't know that Jill was interested in him, because with relationships he was unfortunately **obtuse**.

The **polemic** ideas of the rebel forces are creating great confusion in this country.

While people try their best to stay youthful, old age is **inevitable**.

These days, every time I change the channel on my TV, presidential campaign advertisements are **ubiquitous**.

When he realized how cruel he had been, he was **contrite** and apologized.

The odor coming from those shoes was so **repugnant** they had to be thrown in the bin.

After years of practice, he is an **adept** soccer player and may get a sports scholarship.

A **shrewd** businessman knows when it is the best time to buy or sell a product.

After the hurricane, many families lost everything and were **destitute**.

TRY IT OUT

For each word or definition, find the matching vocabulary word and write a sentence using that word:

1. adroit, practiced   _____ _____

2. perceptive, wise   _____ _____

3. creating arguments   _____ _____

4. fleeting, momentary   _____ _____

5. foreseeable, certain   _____ _____

6. pervasive, in all places   _____ _____

7. poor, insolvent   _____ _____

8. revolting, repulsive   _____ _____

9. simple-minded   _____ _____

10. sorry, apologetic   _____ _____

Complete each of the following sentences by inserting one of the vocabulary words:

11. Advertisements are so _____ that no matter where one goes, one is constantly being instructed to purchase a product or service.

12. Diana finds lizards _____, and she avoids the reptile house when she goes to the zoo.

13. Evan was an _____ student, and the teacher found it necessary to explain concepts many times before he understood.

14. He was _____ in his apology and genuinely wished to make up for the harm he had caused.

15. Isaac is an _____ cook, capable of making a wide variety of dishes for many guests.

16. More and more people entered the _____ debate, until it seemed that everyone in the room was arguing.

17. She realized that failure was _____ and decided to get it over with instead of putting off the unavoidable.

18. She was a _____ negotiator, and she eventually convinced the salesman to sell at her desired price.

19. She was struck by an _____ moment of déjà vu, which went as quickly as it came.

20. The poor man was utterly _____, and he slept cold and hungry on the street.

Vocabulary List 39

caustic	sharply derogatory, with cutting wit; **or:** burning
immutable	not able to be challenged, undeniable
inane	lacking sense, empty, shallow
profound	deep, insightful, of emotional or intellectual depth
garrulous	excessively talkative, babbling, loquacious
innate	inborn, inherited
amorphous	shapeless
didactic	instructive, educational
fallacious	illogical, erroneous; **or:** misleading, deceptive
novel	original, new

My sister has a **caustic** personality; she is so sarcastic and insulting that most people don't like to be around her.

Physicists seek to define the **immutable** truths of the laws that control everything.

Some people said the book was silly and **inane**, but I thought it was good for some casual reading.

The team suffered a **profound** loss when their star pitched decided to hang up his glove and retire.

Dan loves to tell stories because he has a naturally **garrulous** personality.

We all have **innate** qualities that define us and are passed down to us from our parents.

The **amorphous** sculpture was unrecognizable, even up close.

Within her simple stories there was always a lesson to be learned, each entertaining adventure having a **didactic** purpose behind it.

The salesman made **fallacious** claims, promising his product would somehow solve all of my problems.

My favorite television shows have **novel** ideas that I've never seen before.

TRY IT OUT

For each word or definition, find the matching vocabulary word and write a sentence using that word:

1. absurd, ridiculous   _____ _____

2. chatty   _____ _____

3. false, untrue   _____ _____

4. formless, nebulous   _____ _____

5. indisputable, absolute   _____ _____

6. informative, academic   _____ _____

7. instinctive, natural, intrinsic _____ _____

8. scathing, harsh   _____ _____

9. thoughtful   _____ _____

10. unique, fresh   _____ _____

Complete each of the following sentences by inserting one of the vocabulary words:

11. Although cities rose and fell, the _____ mountain remained unchanged by human progress.

12. Creativity is an _____ trait, found in infinite forms and impossible to define.

13. Graham is a _____ talker, and we all grow weary of his non-stop chatter.

14. Her _____ argument contained many holes and errors, and her opponent picked it apart point by point.

15. His _____ descriptions of popular figures were both clever and cruel, and we all hoped we would not be the next target of his biting remarks.

16. I've had it with her _____ comments, and will tolerate no more of her silliness.

17. It is an _____ ability which all humans possess, and which we all may develop with practice.

18. It was a _____ idea, which her peers had never encountered before.

19. Mr. Thompson instructed the class in a flat and _____ tone, giving his students no chance to find our own paths.

20. Ryan was a deep thinker, and his _____ observation made us all stop and consider his words.

Vocabulary List 40

mediate	to settle an agreement, to reconcile
decree	to command, to declare
barrage	to attack, to bombard
ruminate	to think, to ponder, to contemplate
vex	to annoy, to irritate; **or**: to confuse
reprove	to admonish, to castigate, to scold
belittle	to consider less important or valuable, to disparage
retract	to withdraw, to take back
squander	to spend extravagantly, to waste
renounce	to give up, to quit, to relinquish

The counselor talked to the brother and sister so he could **mediate** their argument and help resolve their problems.

The mayor has **decreed** that there will be a new town holiday, and the townspeople were excited by the declaration.

When the actor made an offensive remark, he was **barraged** with harsh criticisms from many people who had been fans.

The mathematician **ruminated** on the problem for hours before he thought of a solution.

The **vexing** questions of the child were trying Ms. Petticoat's patience.

As soon as I made the mistake, I knew that my parents would **reprove** me for what I'd done.

Bullies will try to **belittle** people and make them feel bad about themselves.

The politician **retracted** his statement because he wanted people to forget what he'd said.

Patrick once had a lot of money, but he **squandered** it on expensive food and clothes.

When the first sailor traveled around the world, people had to **renounce** their belief that the world is flat.

TRY IT OUT

For each word or definition, find the matching vocabulary word and write a sentence using that word:

1. to abandon, to surrender   _____   _____

2. to criticize, to reprimand   _____   _____

3. to assault   _____   _____

4. to back off, to recall   _____   _____

5. to bother, to irk   _____   _____

6. to contemplate, to consider   _____   _____

7. to demean, to deride   _____   _____

8. to intervene, to referee   _____   _____

9. to order, to announce   _____   _____

10. to throw away, to use up   _____   _____

Complete each of the following sentences by inserting one of the vocabulary words:

11. An adult stepped in to _____ between the two arguing children, who eventually settled their disagreement and reached a compromise.

12. After finals ended, she had more than a month to relax and to _____ on her future after college, considering the many opportunities and options available to her.

13. Bob _____ his inheritance, and, after years of wasteful spending, he had not a penny left.

14. He is insecure about his own accomplishments, so he _____ others to make himself look better by comparison.

15. He _____ his leadership position, giving up the heavy responsibility to spend more time with his family.

16. Several major problems _____ him, but he has a solution to only one of them.

17. The audience hated the performer, and, when he came on stage, they greeted him with a _____ of rotten eggs and fruit.

18. The professor _____ her favorite pupil for making a simple error, but she scolded him so gently that he was barely embarrassed.

19. The royal _____ made local townships responsible for the collection of taxes.

20. Today's newspaper _____ yesterday's error, apologizing for the mistake and publishing the correct information.

Extended Vocabulary List

This list of 1600 words includes most of the words that are likely to appear on the SSAT. This list includes the 400 words in the previous vocabulary lists.

Check off all the words you already know. Study the definitions of words you do not know.

☐ abase	☐ acquaint	☐ agitate	☐ analogous
☐ abash	☐ acquiesce	☐ ailment	☐ analyze
☐ abate	☐ acquire	☐ aimless	☐ anatomist
☐ abbreviate	☐ acquit	☐ ajar	☐ androgynous
☐ abdicate	☐ acrid	☐ akin	☐ anesthesia
☐ aberrant	☐ acrobat	☐ alacrity	☐ anguish
☐ abhor	☐ acumen	☐ alias	☐ animated
☐ abide	☐ acute	☐ alibi	☐ animosity
☐ abode	☐ adage	☐ allege	☐ annihilate
☐ abolish	☐ adamant	☐ alleviate	☐ annoy
☐ abomination	☐ adapt	☐ alliance	☐ anonymous
☐ abound	☐ adept	☐ allotment	☐ antagonistic
☐ abrasive	☐ adhere	☐ allusion	☐ anticipation
☐ abridge	☐ adjunct	☐ ally	☐ antidote
☐ abrupt	☐ administer	☐ aloof	☐ anxious
☐ abscond	☐ admirable	☐ alter	☐ apathetic
☐ absolve	☐ admonish	☐ alternating	☐ aplomb
☐ abstract	☐ adroit	☐ altruism	☐ apologist
☐ absurd	☐ adversary	☐ amalgamation	☐ apostate
☐ abundance	☐ advocate	☐ amass	☐ apparatus
☐ abyss	☐ aesthetic	☐ ambiguous	☐ apparition
☐ accessible	☐ affable	☐ ambivalent	☐ appease
☐ acclaim	☐ affiliation	☐ ambush	☐ apprehensive
☐ accolade	☐ afflict	☐ ameliorate	☐ approbation
☐ accompany	☐ affluent	☐ amenable	☐ approve
☐ accost	☐ agenda	☐ amend	☐ aptitude
☐ accountable	☐ aggrandizement	☐ amiable	☐ arbitrate
☐ accrue	☐ aggravate	☐ amicable	☐ arcane
☐ accumulate	☐ aggregate	☐ amnesty	☐ archaic
☐ accusation	☐ aghast	☐ amorphous	☐ archetype
☐ acoustic	☐ agility	☐ amplify	☐ ardent

- arduous
- arid
- armistice
- aroma
- arrogance
- articulate
- ascertain
- asphyxiation
- aspire
- assail
- assault
- assertive
- assessment
- assiduous
- assist
- assuage
- astute
- atonement
- atrophy
- attain
- attribute
- audacious
- augment
- auspicious
- austere
- authentic
- autonomy
- avarice
- averse
- avoidance
- awkward
- babble
- badger
- baleful
- banal
- banish
- bargain
- barrage
- barren
- barter
- battery

- bedlam
- beguile
- behold
- belie
- belittle
- bellicose
- belligerent
- benefactor
- beneficial
- benevolent
- benign
- bestow
- bewilder
- biased
- bide
- bigot
- bizarre
- bland
- blandish
- blasphemy
- blatant
- bleak
- blithe
- blockage
- boast
- boisterous
- bolster
- bombastic
- boorish
- boundary
- bounty
- bovine
- brandish
- brash
- brawl
- brazen
- breach
- brevity
- brittle
- broach
- buffoon

- bulwark
- burden
- burgeon
- burnish
- buttress
- cache
- cajole
- calamity
- calculation
- callous
- camaraderie
- camouflage
- candid
- candor
- cantankerous
- caprice
- capricious
- capsize
- captivate
- catastrophe
- cathartic
- caustic
- cauterize
- cautious
- celestial
- certainty
- certify
- censure
- chagrin
- charlatan
- chastise
- chattel
- cherish
- chicanery
- chide
- chiropractic
- chivalry
- chronic
- chronological
- circumspect
- circumvent

- clandestine
- classify
- clemency
- clique
- clumsy
- coalesce
- coarse
- coax
- coddle
- coercion
- cogent
- cognizant
- collaborate
- collate
- collateral
- colloquial
- colossal
- combustible
- commence
- comparable
- compassion
- compel
- compensate
- competent
- complacent
- complementary
- compliance
- complicit
- complimentary
- comprehensive
- comprise
- compromise
- compulsion
- compulsive
- concede
- conciliate
- concise
- concur
- condemn
- condense
- condescend

❑ condone	❑ contraction	❑ dawdle	❑ deplore
❑ conduit	❑ contradiction	❑ debacle	❑ deprive
❑ confer	❑ contrary	❑ debase	❑ deride
❑ confidant	❑ contrite	❑ debilitating	❑ descendant
❑ confide	❑ convene	❑ debunk	❑ desolation
❑ confidential	❑ conventional	❑ decadent	❑ desperate
❑ confine	❑ convert	❑ deceive	❑ despicable
❑ confirmation	❑ conviction	❑ deception	❑ despondent
❑ confiscate	❑ convince	❑ decimate	❑ despot
❑ conflagration	❑ convoluted	❑ decipher	❑ destiny
❑ conform	❑ cooperate	❑ decomposition	❑ destitute
❑ confound	❑ copious	❑ decree	❑ detach
❑ confront	❑ corpulent	❑ decry	❑ detain
❑ congenial	❑ correlated	❑ dedicate	❑ deteriorate
❑ congest	❑ correspondence	❑ deface	❑ deterrent
❑ congregate	❑ corroborate	❑ defect	❑ detrimental
❑ conjecture	❑ corruption	❑ deference	❑ devious
❑ conjunction	❑ corsair	❑ defiance	❑ devour
❑ conjure	❑ cosmopolitan	❑ deficient	❑ devout
❑ conniving	❑ counsel	❑ deflect	❑ dexterous
❑ connoisseur	❑ counterfeit	❑ defraud	❑ diagnosis
❑ conscientious	❑ courtship	❑ deft	❑ diatribe
❑ conscious	❑ coy	❑ defunct	❑ didactic
❑ consequence	❑ crass	❑ dehydrate	❑ diffuse
❑ conserve	❑ craven	❑ dejected	❑ dignity
❑ considerate	❑ credible	❑ dejection	❑ digress
❑ consist	❑ crestfallen	❑ delegate	❑ dilapidated
❑ conspicuous	❑ crisis	❑ deleterious	❑ dilate
❑ conspiracy	❑ criticize	❑ deliberation	❑ diligence
❑ constellation	❑ crude	❑ delicate	❑ dilute
❑ constrict	❑ crumble	❑ delighted	❑ diminish
❑ constructive	❑ cryptic	❑ delude	❑ din
❑ consume	❑ culinary	❑ deluge	❑ diplomatic
❑ contagious	❑ culpable	❑ delusion	❑ disburse
❑ contaminate	❑ cultivate	❑ demolish	❑ discern
❑ contemplation	❑ curb	❑ demonstrate	❑ discipline
❑ contempt	❑ cursory	❑ denigrate	❑ disclaim
❑ contention	❑ curtail	❑ denounce	❑ disclosure
❑ contingent	❑ customary	❑ dense	❑ discontent
❑ contort	❑ cynical	❑ depict	❑ discord
❑ contour	❑ daunting	❑ deplete	❑ discreet

- discriminate
- disdain
- disguise
- disinclination
- disjointed
- dismal
- dismantle
- disparage
- disparity
- dispassionate
- dispel
- dispersal
- disperse
- disruptive
- disseminate
- dissent
- dissertation
- distortion
- distract
- diverge
- diversion
- diverted
- divest
- divisive
- divulge
- docile
- dogmatic
- doleful
- domestic
- dominate
- dormant
- downtrodden
- dreary
- dubious
- duplicate
- duration
- dwindle
- dynamic
- earnest
- eccentric
- eclectic

- ecstatic
- ecumenical
- edible
- edifice
- efface
- efficiency
- effusive
- egregious
- egress
- elaborate
- elastic
- elation
- elegant
- elegy
- elevate
- elicit
- elongate
- eloquent
- elucidate
- elude
- elusive
- emaciated
- emancipate
- embark
- embellish
- embezzle
- embrace
- embroider
- eminent
- empathetic
- emphasize
- emphatic
- emulate
- enchant
- encompass
- encounter
- encourage
- encroach
- encumber
- endeavor
- endorse

- endorsement
- endowment
- endurance
- engage
- engender
- engrave
- enhance
- enigma
- enlist
- enrage
- enthusiasm
- entice
- entity
- entourage
- entreat
- enunciate
- envious
- ephemeral
- epilogue
- epitome
- equitable
- eradicate
- erode
- erratic
- erroneous
- erudite
- eruption
- esoteric
- essential
- eternal
- ethereal
- euphoric
- evacuate
- evade
- evanescent
- evasion
- evict
- evident
- evoke
- evolve
- exacerbate

- exacting
- exaggerate
- exalt
- exasperate
- excess
- exclusive
- excursion
- exemplary
- exhibit
- exhilarate
- exhort
- exodus
- exonerate
- expectation
- expedient
- expedite
- expel
- expenditure
- explicit
- exploit
- expunge
- exquisite
- extent
- extinct
- extinguish
- extol
- extort
- extraction
- extraordinary
- extravagant
- exuberance
- exuberant
- fabricate
- facet
- facile
- fallacious
- fanatic
- fascinate
- fastidious
- fatal
- fatigue

- ❏ feasible
- ❏ feign
- ❏ feint
- ❏ ferocious
- ❏ fertile
- ❏ fervor
- ❏ festive
- ❏ fiasco
- ❏ fickle
- ❏ fidelity
- ❏ fierce
- ❏ finesse
- ❏ flabbergast
- ❏ flagrant
- ❏ flamboyant
- ❏ flammable
- ❏ flattery
- ❏ fleeting
- ❏ flexible
- ❏ fling
- ❏ flippant
- ❏ flourish
- ❏ fluctuate
- ❏ fluent
- ❏ forage
- ❏ forebode
- ❏ forgery
- ❏ forgo
- ❏ forlorn
- ❏ formidable
- ❏ forsake
- ❏ fortify
- ❏ fortunate
- ❏ foster
- ❏ foundation
- ❏ founder
- ❏ fractious
- ❏ fragile
- ❏ frail
- ❏ frank
- ❏ frantic

- ❏ fraud
- ❏ frenetic
- ❏ frequent
- ❏ fret
- ❏ friction
- ❏ frivolous
- ❏ frugal
- ❏ fugitive
- ❏ fumble
- ❏ furious
- ❏ furtive
- ❏ futile
- ❏ gallant
- ❏ gargantuan
- ❏ garment
- ❏ garrulous
- ❏ gauche
- ❏ gaunt
- ❏ gauntlet
- ❏ generous
- ❏ genesis
- ❏ genteel
- ❏ genuine
- ❏ gimmick
- ❏ girth
- ❏ glutton
- ❏ goad
- ❏ gossip
- ❏ gracious
- ❏ grandiose
- ❏ gratify
- ❏ gratitude
- ❏ gravity
- ❏ gregarious
- ❏ grieve
- ❏ grim
- ❏ grotesque
- ❏ guile
- ❏ gullible
- ❏ habitat
- ❏ habitual

- ❏ haggard
- ❏ halcyon
- ❏ hallucinate
- ❏ halt
- ❏ hamper
- ❏ haphazard
- ❏ hapless
- ❏ harangue
- ❏ harass
- ❏ harbinger
- ❏ harmony
- ❏ harsh
- ❏ haughty
- ❏ hazardous
- ❏ heed
- ❏ herculean
- ❏ hesitation
- ❏ hiatus
- ❏ hideous
- ❏ hilarious
- ❏ hindrance
- ❏ hoard
- ❏ hoax
- ❏ hospitable
- ❏ hostile
- ❏ hostility
- ❏ hovel
- ❏ hue
- ❏ humid
- ❏ humility
- ❏ humongous
- ❏ hyperbole
- ❏ hypocritical
- ❏ icon
- ❏ iconoclast
- ❏ idiosyncratic
- ❏ idle
- ❏ ignorance
- ❏ illicit
- ❏ illiterate
- ❏ illuminate

- ❏ illusory
- ❏ imbibe
- ❏ imbue
- ❏ imitate
- ❏ immaculate
- ❏ immense
- ❏ imminent
- ❏ immunity
- ❏ immutable
- ❏ impair
- ❏ impartial
- ❏ impasse
- ❏ impeccable
- ❏ impediment
- ❏ impending
- ❏ impetuous
- ❏ implausible
- ❏ implement
- ❏ imply
- ❏ impose
- ❏ imposition
- ❏ impoverished
- ❏ impractical
- ❏ impromptu
- ❏ impudence
- ❏ impulsive
- ❏ inadvertent
- ❏ inane
- ❏ incapacitated
- ❏ incendiary
- ❏ incentive
- ❏ incessant
- ❏ incident
- ❏ incinerate
- ❏ incision
- ❏ incisive
- ❏ incite
- ❏ inclement
- ❏ incline
- ❏ incoherent
- ❏ incompetent

- ❑ inconsolable
- ❑ incorrigible
- ❑ incredulous
- ❑ increment
- ❑ incumbent
- ❑ indecent
- ❑ indelible
- ❑ indemnify
- ❑ indicate
- ❑ indictment
- ❑ indifferent
- ❑ indigenous
- ❑ indigent
- ❑ indignant
- ❑ indispensable
- ❑ indisposed
- ❑ indulge
- ❑ industry
- ❑ ineffable
- ❑ inept
- ❑ inert
- ❑ inevitable
- ❑ infallible
- ❑ infamy
- ❑ infer
- ❑ inferior
- ❑ infinite
- ❑ influential
- ❑ infuse
- ❑ ingenuity
- ❑ inhabit
- ❑ initiate
- ❑ inkling
- ❑ innate
- ❑ innocuous
- ❑ innovate
- ❑ inquire
- ❑ insatiable
- ❑ inscribe
- ❑ insinuation
- ❑ insipid

- ❑ insolent
- ❑ insolvent
- ❑ inspiring
- ❑ instigate
- ❑ instinctive
- ❑ insult
- ❑ insurrection
- ❑ intangible
- ❑ integrate
- ❑ integrity
- ❑ interfere
- ❑ interim
- ❑ interloper
- ❑ interminable
- ❑ intermission
- ❑ interrogate
- ❑ intersect
- ❑ intervene
- ❑ intimidate
- ❑ intrepid
- ❑ intricate
- ❑ intriguing
- ❑ introverted
- ❑ intrude
- ❑ intrusion
- ❑ intuition
- ❑ inundate
- ❑ invert
- ❑ inveterate
- ❑ invigorating
- ❑ invincible
- ❑ irate
- ❑ irk
- ❑ ironic
- ❑ irrelevant
- ❑ irresponsible
- ❑ irreverent
- ❑ irritable
- ❑ itinerant
- ❑ jabber
- ❑ jaded

- ❑ jargon
- ❑ jaunt
- ❑ jeer
- ❑ jeopardize
- ❑ jeopardy
- ❑ jocular
- ❑ jovial
- ❑ jubilant
- ❑ judicious
- ❑ jumble
- ❑ junction
- ❑ jurisdiction
- ❑ justify
- ❑ juvenile
- ❑ juxtapose
- ❑ keen
- ❑ kinetic
- ❑ kinship
- ❑ lackadaisical
- ❑ laconic
- ❑ lament
- ❑ languid
- ❑ latent
- ❑ laud
- ❑ lavish
- ❑ lax
- ❑ legislature
- ❑ legitimate
- ❑ lenient
- ❑ lethal
- ❑ lethargic
- ❑ liaison
- ❑ liberate
- ❑ limber
- ❑ limpid
- ❑ lineage
- ❑ listless
- ❑ literal
- ❑ literate
- ❑ lithe
- ❑ litigate

- ❑ livid
- ❑ loathe
- ❑ lofty
- ❑ loiter
- ❑ loquacious
- ❑ lubricate
- ❑ lucid
- ❑ ludicrous
- ❑ lugubrious
- ❑ lull
- ❑ luminescence
- ❑ lunge
- ❑ lure
- ❑ lurk
- ❑ magistrate
- ❑ magnanimous
- ❑ magnate
- ❑ magnify
- ❑ magnitude
- ❑ malaise
- ❑ malcontent
- ❑ malfunction
- ❑ malice
- ❑ malignant
- ❑ mandate
- ❑ maneuver
- ❑ mangled
- ❑ manifest
- ❑ manipulate
- ❑ marred
- ❑ martyr
- ❑ marvel
- ❑ massive
- ❑ maven
- ❑ meager
- ❑ meander
- ❑ meddle
- ❑ mediate
- ❑ medley
- ❑ meek
- ❑ melancholy

SUMMIT
EDUCATIONAL
GROUP

- ❑ memento
- ❑ menacing
- ❑ mend
- ❑ mendacious
- ❑ mercurial
- ❑ merit
- ❑ meritorious
- ❑ mesmerize
- ❑ metamorphosis
- ❑ meticulous
- ❑ migrate
- ❑ mimic
- ❑ minister
- ❑ mirage
- ❑ misappropriate
- ❑ miscellaneous
- ❑ mitigate
- ❑ mollify
- ❑ momentum
- ❑ monotonous
- ❑ mope
- ❑ morass
- ❑ morbid
- ❑ morose
- ❑ mortal
- ❑ mortify
- ❑ motif
- ❑ motive
- ❑ mourn
- ❑ mundane
- ❑ munitions
- ❑ murky
- ❑ mutinous
- ❑ myriad
- ❑ nadir
- ❑ naïve
- ❑ natal
- ❑ nebulous
- ❑ necessitate
- ❑ nefarious
- ❑ neglect

- ❑ negligent
- ❑ negotiate
- ❑ nemesis
- ❑ nimble
- ❑ nocturnal
- ❑ nominate
- ❑ nonchalant
- ❑ nostalgic
- ❑ notorious
- ❑ nourish
- ❑ novel
- ❑ novice
- ❑ nuance
- ❑ null
- ❑ obdurate
- ❑ obedience
- ❑ obedient
- ❑ objective
- ❑ obligate
- ❑ obliterate
- ❑ obnoxious
- ❑ obscene
- ❑ obscure
- ❑ obsess
- ❑ obsolete
- ❑ obstetrics
- ❑ obstinate
- ❑ obstruct
- ❑ obtain
- ❑ obtuse
- ❑ obvious
- ❑ ode
- ❑ odious
- ❑ offensive
- ❑ ominous
- ❑ omission
- ❑ omit
- ❑ onslaught
- ❑ opinionated
- ❑ optimistic
- ❑ opulent

- ❑ oracle
- ❑ orator
- ❑ ornamental
- ❑ ornate
- ❑ ornery
- ❑ ostentatious
- ❑ ostracism
- ❑ outlandish
- ❑ outrage
- ❑ overt
- ❑ pacify
- ❑ painstaking
- ❑ palpable
- ❑ paltry
- ❑ pamper
- ❑ panacea
- ❑ pantry
- ❑ paradox
- ❑ parallel
- ❑ paralyze
- ❑ paramount
- ❑ parch
- ❑ pariah
- ❑ parity
- ❑ parody
- ❑ partake
- ❑ partial
- ❑ partition
- ❑ patent
- ❑ pathetic
- ❑ pathology
- ❑ patient
- ❑ patter
- ❑ paucity
- ❑ peculiar
- ❑ pecuniary
- ❑ pedantic
- ❑ pedestrian
- ❑ pedigree
- ❑ pejorative
- ❑ penalty

- ❑ penchant
- ❑ pensive
- ❑ perceive
- ❑ perception
- ❑ perfidy
- ❑ perforate
- ❑ perfunctory
- ❑ perilous
- ❑ perish
- ❑ permanent
- ❑ permeate
- ❑ permissible
- ❑ perpetual
- ❑ perplex
- ❑ perseverance
- ❑ persistent
- ❑ perspire
- ❑ persuade
- ❑ pertain
- ❑ pertinent
- ❑ perturbed
- ❑ peruse
- ❑ pervasive
- ❑ pettiness
- ❑ petulant
- ❑ philanthropy
- ❑ phlegmatic
- ❑ phobia
- ❑ pigment
- ❑ pious
- ❑ piquant
- ❑ placate
- ❑ placebo
- ❑ placid
- ❑ plateau
- ❑ platitude
- ❑ platoon
- ❑ plaudit
- ❑ plausible
- ❑ plead
- ❑ plebian

- plethora
- pliable
- plight
- plucky
- ply
- poignant
- polemic
- polymorphous
- pompous
- ponder
- porous
- portent
- portrayal
- posterity
- posthumous
- potency
- pragmatic
- preamble
- precarious
- precaution
- precede
- precedent
- preclude
- precocious
- precursor
- predatory
- predicament
- prediction
- prejudiced
- prelude
- premature
- premonition
- preponderance
- prerequisite
- prerogative
- presume
- presumption
- pretentious
- pretext
- prevail
- prevalent

- prey
- primary
- primeval
- principal
- principle
- prior
- pristine
- probe
- problematic
- proclivity
- procrastinate
- procure
- prodigal
- prodigious
- profanity
- proficient
- profound
- profusion
- progeny
- progression
- prohibitive
- proliferate
- prolific
- prologue
- prolong
- promenade
- prominent
- promote
- promotion
- prompt
- propagate
- propel
- propensity
- prophesy
- proportion
- propose
- propriety
- prosaic
- prosperous
- protégé
- prototype

- providential
- provoke
- prowess
- proxy
- prudent
- prudish
- pseudonym
- puerile
- pugnacious
- punctilious
- pungent
- puny
- purge
- purloin
- purport
- putrid
- quagmire
- quaint
- qualm
- quandary
- quantity
- quarrelsome
- quell
- quench
- quiver
- quixotic
- rabble
- radiate
- rampant
- rancid
- rancorous
- ransack
- ratify
- rational
- ravenous
- raze
- rebuff
- rebuke
- rebuttal
- recalcitrant
- recapitulate

- recede
- recession
- recline
- reclusive
- recognize
- recollect
- recompense
- reconcile
- recruit
- rectify
- redeem
- redress
- redundant
- reel
- refractory
- refrain
- refutation
- refute
- regal
- regale
- regress
- regretful
- rejuvenate
- relevant
- reliance
- relinquish
- reluctant
- remedy
- reminiscence
- remiss
- remorse
- remuneration
- rendezvous
- renounce
- renovate
- reparation
- repel
- replenish
- replete
- replica
- repose

- ❏ reprehensible
- ❏ repress
- ❏ reprimand
- ❏ reprove
- ❏ repudiate
- ❏ repugnant
- ❏ repulse
- ❏ reputable
- ❏ reside
- ❏ resign
- ❏ resilience
- ❏ resilient
- ❏ resolution
- ❏ respiration
- ❏ respite
- ❏ response
- ❏ responsible
- ❏ restitution
- ❏ restriction
- ❏ resuscitation
- ❏ retaliate
- ❏ reticent
- ❏ retort
- ❏ retract
- ❏ retrospect
- ❏ revel
- ❏ reverberation
- ❏ revere
- ❏ revolutionary
- ❏ rhetoric
- ❏ rickety
- ❏ ridicule
- ❏ rife
- ❏ rigor
- ❏ rile
- ❏ robust
- ❏ rotund
- ❏ rue
- ❏ ruminate
- ❏ rustic
- ❏ ruthless

- ❏ saga
- ❏ sagacious
- ❏ sage
- ❏ salient
- ❏ salvage
- ❏ salve
- ❏ sanctimonious
- ❏ sanction
- ❏ sanctuary
- ❏ sanguine
- ❏ sapient
- ❏ sarcastic
- ❏ sated
- ❏ satiate
- ❏ satirical
- ❏ satisfy
- ❏ saturated
- ❏ scandalous
- ❏ scant
- ❏ scarce
- ❏ scatter
- ❏ scold
- ❏ scorch
- ❏ scoundrel
- ❏ scrawl
- ❏ scrutinize
- ❏ seclude
- ❏ secure
- ❏ sedate
- ❏ seize
- ❏ semantics
- ❏ seminal
- ❏ sentimental
- ❏ sequence
- ❏ sequester
- ❏ serenade
- ❏ serendipity
- ❏ sever
- ❏ severe
- ❏ severity
- ❏ shameful

- ❏ sheath
- ❏ shirk
- ❏ shrewd
- ❏ signify
- ❏ simulate
- ❏ sincere
- ❏ skeptic
- ❏ skitter
- ❏ slander
- ❏ slovenly
- ❏ sluggish
- ❏ smug
- ❏ snag
- ❏ snub
- ❏ sojourn
- ❏ solemn
- ❏ solicit
- ❏ solitary
- ❏ solitude
- ❏ soluble
- ❏ somber
- ❏ soothe
- ❏ sophisticated
- ❏ sordid
- ❏ souvenir
- ❏ sovereign
- ❏ sparse
- ❏ speculate
- ❏ splice
- ❏ spontaneous
- ❏ sporadic
- ❏ spurious
- ❏ spurn
- ❏ squabble
- ❏ squalor
- ❏ squander
- ❏ stagnant
- ❏ stalwart
- ❏ stammer
- ❏ stark
- ❏ startle

- ❏ stash
- ❏ static
- ❏ stationary
- ❏ stature
- ❏ steadfast
- ❏ stifle
- ❏ stimulus
- ❏ stipend
- ❏ stipulate
- ❏ stoic
- ❏ stout
- ❏ stow
- ❏ strenuous
- ❏ strife
- ❏ strive
- ❏ stumble
- ❏ stun
- ❏ stymie
- ❏ subdue
- ❏ subjective
- ❏ subjugate
- ❏ submerge
- ❏ submission
- ❏ submit
- ❏ subside
- ❏ subsist
- ❏ substance
- ❏ substantiate
- ❏ substitute
- ❏ subtle
- ❏ subvert
- ❏ successor
- ❏ succinct
- ❏ sufficient
- ❏ suffocate
- ❏ suffuse
- ❏ summit
- ❏ sumptuous
- ❏ supercilious
- ❏ superficial
- ❏ superfluous

- ❑ superiority
- ❑ supersede
- ❑ suppress
- ❑ surly
- ❑ surmise
- ❑ surmount
- ❑ surpass
- ❑ surrender
- ❑ surreptitious
- ❑ surrogate
- ❑ susceptible
- ❑ suspicious
- ❑ sway
- ❑ sweltering
- ❑ swivel
- ❑ symmetry
- ❑ sympathy
- ❑ tacit
- ❑ taciturn
- ❑ tact
- ❑ taint
- ❑ tangential
- ❑ tangled
- ❑ tattered
- ❑ taunt
- ❑ tedious
- ❑ temperate
- ❑ temptation
- ❑ tenacious
- ❑ tenacity
- ❑ tendency
- ❑ tentative
- ❑ tenuous
- ❑ tenure
- ❑ tepid
- ❑ terminate
- ❑ terrestrial
- ❑ terse
- ❑ testify
- ❑ theorize
- ❑ therapeutic

- ❑ thesis
- ❑ threatening
- ❑ threshold
- ❑ thrifty
- ❑ thrive
- ❑ thwart
- ❑ timid
- ❑ timorous
- ❑ tirade
- ❑ tolerate
- ❑ topple
- ❑ torment
- ❑ torpid
- ❑ torrid
- ❑ totemic
- ❑ trait
- ❑ tranquil
- ❑ transaction
- ❑ transcribe
- ❑ transform
- ❑ transient
- ❑ transition
- ❑ translucent
- ❑ transparent
- ❑ transplant
- ❑ travesty
- ❑ treason
- ❑ trek
- ❑ tremor
- ❑ trenchant
- ❑ trepidation
- ❑ trespass
- ❑ tribute
- ❑ trifle
- ❑ trite
- ❑ triumph
- ❑ trivial
- ❑ truculent
- ❑ truncate
- ❑ trustworthy
- ❑ tumult

- ❑ turbulent
- ❑ turmoil
- ❑ tyrannical
- ❑ ubiquitous
- ❑ ultimatum
- ❑ unconditional
- ❑ underlying
- ❑ undulate
- ❑ unflinching
- ❑ unforeseen
- ❑ uniformity
- ❑ unique
- ❑ unorthodox
- ❑ unprecedented
- ❑ unruly
- ❑ unscrupulous
- ❑ unswerving
- ❑ unwarranted
- ❑ uproar
- ❑ urge
- ❑ utilize
- ❑ vacant
- ❑ vacillation
- ❑ vacuous
- ❑ vague
- ❑ valid
- ❑ valor
- ❑ variability
- ❑ variegated
- ❑ vehement
- ❑ velocity
- ❑ vend
- ❑ veneer
- ❑ venerate
- ❑ vengeance
- ❑ ventilate
- ❑ veracious
- ❑ verbose
- ❑ verdict
- ❑ verify
- ❑ vermin

- ❑ versatile
- ❑ veteran
- ❑ veto
- ❑ vex
- ❑ viable
- ❑ vibrate
- ❑ vicarious
- ❑ vie
- ❑ vigilance
- ❑ vigilant
- ❑ vigorous
- ❑ vile
- ❑ vindicate
- ❑ violate
- ❑ virtue
- ❑ virtuoso
- ❑ virulent
- ❑ visage
- ❑ vital
- ❑ vivacity
- ❑ volatile
- ❑ volition
- ❑ voracious
- ❑ vulnerable
- ❑ waive
- ❑ wander
- ❑ wane
- ❑ wary
- ❑ weary
- ❑ whet
- ❑ wily
- ❑ winsome
- ❑ wither
- ❑ withstand
- ❑ witty
- ❑ woeful
- ❑ wretched
- ❑ writhe
- ❑ yearn
- ❑ yield
- ❑ zealot

Learned Words

List words you have learned as you studied for the test. Include definitions, synonyms, or anything that will help you remember the meaning of the words.

Word   Definition / Synonym

_____   _____

_____   _____

_____   _____

_____   _____

_____   _____

_____   _____

_____   _____

_____   _____

_____   _____

_____   _____

_____   _____

_____   _____

_____   _____

_____   _____

_____   _____

Word

Definition / Synonym

Word   Definition / Synonym

_____   _____

_____   _____

_____   _____

_____   _____

_____   _____

_____   _____

_____   _____

_____   _____

_____   _____

_____   _____

_____   _____

_____   _____

_____   _____

_____   _____

_____   _____

_____   _____

_____   _____

_____   _____

_____   _____

_____   _____

Word

Definition / Synonym

Word   Definition / Synonym

_____   _____

_____   _____

_____   _____

_____   _____

_____   _____

_____   _____

_____   _____

_____   _____

_____   _____

_____   _____

_____   _____

_____   _____

_____   _____

_____   _____

_____   _____

_____   _____

_____   _____

_____   _____

_____   _____

_____   _____

Word

Definition / Synonym

Word

Definition / Synonym

Word

Definition / Synonym

SUMMIT
EDUCATIONAL
GROUP

Answer Key

TEST-TAKING FUNDAMENTALS

Pg. 11 – BEATING THE SSAT

1. D (E is an attractor)

Pg. 12 – MAKING YOUR BEST GUESS

(A) You might care for pitiful things, but not necessarily.
(B) Psychic and energy aren't necessarily related.
(C) Insistent and payment aren't related.
(D) Obsessive and direction aren't related.
(E) Contemptuous means having disdain.

SYNONYMS

Pg. 22 – ANTICIPATE THE ANSWER

Profanity : expletive

Try It Out

1. A
2. D
3. D

Pg. 24 – SECONDARY DEFINITIONS

Bow : curtsy

set: to set in place, to set a price, to sink (sunset), a collection, a match (tennis)

run: to go quickly, to operate (machine), to unravel (stockings), to flow (river)

stand: (to be upright, to rise, to support a policy ("stand for"), a platform or booth

trail: to drag behind, to follow, a path, a stream (smoke)

pen: a writing instrument, to write

champion: a winner, to support or defend

moral: virtuous or honest, a principle of right or wrong conduct

spring: to leap, to rise, a coiled wire, the season between winter and summer

hamper: to hold back or hinder, a basket

revolution: a radical change, a turn or rotation

Put It Together

1. A
2. A
3. B
4. E
5. C
6. B

Pg. 28 – POSITIVE OR NEGATIVE

Try It Out

1. –
2. –
3. +
4. –
5. –
6. –
7. +
8. +
9. –
10. +

Put It Together

1. C
2. E
3. E
4. E
5. D
6. A

Pg. 32 – ATTRACTORS

Try It Out

1. D
2. B
3. C

Pg. 34 – ROOTS

Try It Out

1. I
2. H
3. A
4. D
5. G
6. F
7. B
8. C
9. J
10. E

Put It Together

1. B
2. C
3. E
4. D
5. D
6. A

SYNONYMS PRACTICE – MIDDLE LEVEL

Pg. 40

1. C
2. E
3. C
4. D
5. B
6. E
7. C
8. D
9. E
10. E
11. C
12. C
13. B
14. B
15. D
16. D
17. A
18. A
19. D
20. C
21. C
22. A
23. A
24. E
25. D
26. C
27. B
28. E
29. A
30. D
31. E
32. B
33. B
34. B
35. B
36. B
37. E
38. D
39. B
40. C
41. B
42. A
43. E
44. C
45. D
46. B
47. B
48. C
49. B
50. A
51. C
52. C
53. D
54. C
55. B

56. B
57. C
58. A
59. A
60. C

SYNONYMS PRACTICE – UPPER LEVEL

Pg. 46

1. D
2. C
3. C
4. D
5. B
6. C
7. A
8. B
9. C
10. B
11. C
12. B
13. E
14. D
15. D
16. A
17. C
18. E
19. A
20. A
21. A
22. D
23. B
24. A
25. C
26. E
27. D
28. A
29. A
30. A
31. E
32. A
33. E
34. A
35. D
36. D
37. B
38. B
39. B
40. D
41. B
42. C
43. C
44. E
45. B
46. C
47. C
48. B
49. A

50. D
51. A
52. C
53. D
54. B
55. C
56. B
57. B
58. C
59. C
60. B

ANALOGIES

Pg. 56 – DEFINING THE RELATIONSHIP

Try It Out

1.   A key opens a padlock.
2.   A pyramid is a 3D triangle.
3.   A sculptor makes a statue.
4.   A playwright makes a script.
5.   Reign is what a king does, or a reign is a period in which a king rules.
6.   Cumulus is a type of cloud.
7.   A melodious sound is a nice, pleasant sound.
8.   A pancake is made from batter.
9.   A sonnet is a type of poem.
10. A neurologist is a type of physician.

Pg. 58 – APPLYING THE RELATIONSHIP

Try It Out

1.   An eye chart is used to measure vision.
     C
2.   A poem is divided into stanzas.
     C
3.   An apple is a type of fruit.
     C
4.   A person starts (startles) when surprised
     C

Put It Together

1.   E
2.   C
3.   E
4.   D
5.   B
6.   E

Pg. 62 – REFINING THE RELATIONSHIP

Try It Out

1.   A judge presides over a courthouse.
     E
2.   Goggles are used to protect welders.
     B
3.   A rhinoceros uses its sharp horn for defense.
     D

Put It Together

1.   C
2.   A
3.   E
4.   C
5.   E
6.   A
7.   B

Pg. 66 – COMMON ANALOGY RELATIONSHIPS

Try It Out

1.   Person/Tool – A carpenter uses a hammer.
2.   Characteristic – A globe is spherical.
3.   Person/Creation – A sculptor makes a statue.
4.   Part/Whole – An atlas is a collection of maps.
5.   Function – A mask covers a face.
6.   Action/Result – Stress makes one agitated.
7.   Type – A mouse is a type of rodent.
8.   Degree of Intensity – A ripple is a tiny tidal wave.
9.   Synonym or Degree – Furious means very angry.
10. Function – A scalpel is used to dissect.

Put It Together

1.   B
2.   D
3.   A
4.   B
5.   B
6.   A

Pg. 70 – FIRST AND THIRD ANALOGIES

Put It Together

1.   B
2.   A
3.   C

Pg. 72 – ATTRACTORS

Try It Out

1. Attractors: "farm," "earth," "ground," "property"
   E
2. Attractors: "swamp," "forest," "grass"
   D
3. Attractors: "blade," "target," "bullet"
   C

Pg. 74 – ELIMINATING ANSWER CHOICES

Try It Out

1. None
2. A hurricane is a type of storm.
3. None
4. None
5. Goggles are used to protect eyes.
6. None
7. Quartz is a type of rock.
8. A ticket is used to gain admission.
9. A shoe is made of leather (but not necessarily, so this is a rather weak analogy)
10. A nightmare is a bad dream.
11. None
12. None
13. Common is the opposite of rare.
14. None
15. Wheat is used to make flour.

Put It Together

1. C
2. B
3. E
4. D
5. B
6. A

Pg. 78 – SOLVING BACKWARDS

Try It Out

1. C
2. E
3. B

Put It Together

1. C
2. B
3. C
4. E
5. E
6. B

ANALOGIES PRACTICE – MIDDLE LEVEL

Pg. 84

1. B
2. E
3. C
4. B
5. B
6. A
7. E
8. D
9. C
10. A
11. C
12. B
13. C
14. E
15. A
16. E
17. C
18. E
19. A
20. D
21. B
22. D
23. A
24. C
25. D
26. B
27. D
28. D
29. B
30. E
31. B
32. A
33. A
34. B
35. D
36. A
37. C
38. E
39. B
40. E
41. E
42. C
43. D
44. C
45. C
46. C
47. B
48. E
49. D
50. D
51. E
52. C
53. D
54. C
55. C

56.	E
57.	C
58.	A
59.	A
60.	C

ANALOGIES PRACTICE – UPPER LEVEL

Pg. 90

1.	E
2.	B
3.	A
4.	A
5.	C
6.	E
7.	C
8.	B
9.	B
10.	B
11.	D
12.	B
13.	A
14.	B
15.	C
16.	A
17.	D
18.	B
19.	A
20.	D
21.	E
22.	A
23.	D
24.	E
25.	A
26.	C
27.	A
28.	B
29.	C
30.	E
31.	D
32.	A
33.	A
34.	C
35.	E
36.	B
37.	B
38.	A
39.	A
40.	B
41.	B
42.	C
43.	A
44.	B
45.	B
46.	E
47.	A
48.	D
49.	C

50.	C
51.	E
52.	E
53.	B
54.	C
55.	A
56.	E
57.	B
58.	D
59.	A
60.	E

READING COMPREHENSION

Pg. 100 – ACTIVE READING

Try It Out

1. They are symbols of "natural forces, elements, animals, or ancestors", and they also represent tradition and a source of profit.
2. The dolls have become more complex and refined. Also, they have become a source of revenue, in addition to a traditional practice.
3. Preserving tradition and making money.

Try It Out

1. He became very interested in photography.
2. Something that is difficult to describe.
3. He liked his mother's photos and the anticipation of how an image would develop.
4. New and old technologies
5. He does not like digital as much as older cameras. It goes against his interest in photography, so he still uses older types of cameras and film.

Put It Together

1. B
2. C
3. A
4. B

Pg. 104 – MAPPING THE PASSAGE

Try It Out

1. Slash-and-burn agriculture
2. Fact
3. Slash-and-burn agriculture, which is the technique of clearing sections of forest to make farm land, has been practiced for a long time.
4. In recent times, this practice has grown to become unsustainable and very destructive.
5. Slash-and-burn agriculture has been used sustainably for many years, but on a large scale it is too destructive.
6. To explain the practice of slash-and-burn agriculture and show the potential danger of how it is being used today.

Pg. 106 – CHECKPOINT REVIEW

1. The eggs produced by the maker of the nest
2. factual/informative
3. she doesn't build a nest or care for her own eggs
4. pushing other birds out of the nest, demanding food, and staying in the nest too long

1. to show how strong and present light is: "awash," "powerful," "blaze," "glow"
2. they could see the Milky Way for the first time and didn't know what it was
3. the author thinks lighting is useful but dangerous in large quantities
4. the adverse effects on health; the last sentence addresses this issue

Pg. 108 – ANTICIPATE THE ANSWER

Put It Together

1. E
2. C
3. B
4. A

Pg. 111 – PROCESS OF ELIMINATION

Try It Out

1. (A) no mention of "investing"
   (B) too broad; the passage is about waster and biodegradability
   (C) too narrow and off-topic; the passage is about the problem, not the process
   (D) too broad; the passage is about a particular problem
   (E) CORRECT
2. (A) incorrect; passage lists materials that are biodegradable (paper, food scraps, natural materials), but doesn't say which is the most biodegradable.
   (B) too broad; only focuses on one aspect of modern society
   (C) incorrect; doesn't explain why
   (D) CORRECT
   (E) incorrect; never specifies how much
3. (A) incorrect; he likely already knew this
   (B) incorrect; he likely already knew this
   (C) incorrect; he already knew this
   (D) CORRECT
   (E) incorrect; this is linked to modern consumers
4. (A) CORRECT
   (B) incorrect; no evidence of this
   (C) incorrect; changing traditions doesn't mean people are unaware
   (D) incorrect; no evidence of this
   (E) incorrect; passage is not focused on plane meals

Pg. 106 – CHECKPOINT REVIEW

1. C
2. B
3. B
4. D

1. E
2. B
3. B
4. A
5. B

Pg. 118 – MAIN IDEA QUESTIONS

Try It Out

1. Africa's impressive art serves multiple purposes.
2. E
3. B
4. C
5. A

Pg. 120 – DETAIL / SUPPORTING IDEA QUESTIONS

Try It Out

1. he believed it was a fundamental formula for peace
2. D
3. B

Pg. 122 – VOCABULARY QUESTIONS

Try It Out

1. connection / relation
2. A
3. C
4. C

Pg. 124 – TONE / ATTITUDE QUESTIONS

Try It Out

1. D
2. B
3. C

Pg. 126 – INFERENCE QUESTIONS

Try It Out

1. track (running)
   "asphalt track"
2. city
   "chain-link," "asphalt," school is "massive"
3. twenties
   Bang was twenty-five, and the rest are probably of similar age.
4. gloomy, dark, tense, harsh

Descriptions are dark, landscape is "wounded" and seems cruel and crumbling, and there is violence and danger.

5. to show that the area is going to waste
6. 11
   "my eleven years"
7. to be freed from slavery
   Margaret's will can set her free.
8. her owner who recently died
   Her will is going to be read, and if she can set Harriet free then Harriet is currently owned.
9. She loves the idea of freedom so much that the word feels physically good to her.

Put It Together

1. B
2. E
3. D

Pg. 130 – APPLICATION QUESTIONS

Try It Out

1. the current or future advancements of computer technology
2. growing more efficient and powerful
3. A
4. B

Pg. 132 – EXCEPT/LEAST/NOT and ROMAN NUMERAL QUESTIONS

Try It Out

1. D
2. D
3. C

Pg. 106 – CHECKPOINT REVIEW

1. C
2. C
3. D
4. E

1. B
2. B
3. E
4. E

READING COMPREHENSION PRACTICE – MIDDLE LEVEL

Pg. 138

1. geothermal parks have been used by humans in many ways over many years
2. vapors were thought of as the presence of a "great spirit"
3. people would not fight in this space
4. to show how hot springs have been commercialized
5. heated from the earth
6. encyclopedia, history book
7. important, essential
8. entertainment, helping the poor, art center, cultural center
9. The History of Teatro La Plaz
10. to wash the doll's clothing
11. Ruby's dolls
12. Australia, line 19
13. an omniscient narrator, not a character in the story
14. they have been washed many times
15. personification
16. flying, buzzing, moving
17. the bee flies through a field, passes a strong-smelling flower, lands on a flower with a lot of pollen, then returns to its hive
18. using sights, smell ("fragrant"), taste ("sweet"), and sound ("hum")
19. to show the bee's repetitive behavior
20. a bee is happily doing its job
21. D
22. C
23. B
24. A
25. A
26. C
27. A
28. D
29. D
30. B
31. B
32. A
33. D
34. B
35. B
36. C
37. C
38. D
39. B
40. D
41. A
42. E
43. C
44. D
45. B

46. E
47. D
48. D
49. A
50. D
51. E
52. D
53. B

READING COMPREHENSION PRACTICE – UPPER LEVEL

Pg. 150

1. a historian
2. sent
3. roads and highways were built in Japanese neighborhoods, ruining the cultural aspects of these places
4. a shift took place in how Japanese Americans were treated after WWII
5. nephew and aunt
6. not modern (written in early 1900s); the language and expressions feel older
7. the lady mistook her nephew for a shop assistant and she paid him for a hat; Adela seems to have fainted
8. she seems to be fainting from the shock of seeing her nephew lie and take money from a stranger
9. humorous
10. he believes we become dull and stale when we meet too often, because we don't have time to learn or experience new things and bring fresh conversation to our meetings
11. arguing and fighting
12. people should spend less time together so we appreciate each other more when we do meet
13. someone who only cares about gathering material goods
14. gives or plans to give
15. things the narrator remembers
16. love and memories are more important than wealth
17. true wealth
18. B
19. C
20. D
21. B
22. B
23. D
24. C
25. A
26. D
27. C
28. D
29. B
30. A
31. A

32. E
33. A
34. D
35. D
36. D
37. C
38. A
39. C
40. E
41. C
42. A
43. C
44. E
45. E
46. C
47. E
48. B
49. E
50. D
51. C
52. B
53. D
54. B
55. E
56. C
57. C
58. A
59. C
60. E
61. C
62. C
63. B
64. E
65. D
66. A
67. C
68. A
69. C
70. B
71. E
72. E
73. C
74. C
75. D
76. B
77. A
78. A
79. D
80. D
81. A
82. E
83. D
84. C
85. B
86. D
87. C
88. B

Pg. 232 – List 1

1. incoherent
2. biased
3. valid
4. esoteric
5. prosaic
6. auspicious
7. pragmatic
8. steadfast
9. static
10. intangible
11. pragmatic
12. incoherent
13. esoteric
14. valid
15. biased
16. prosaic
17. steadfast
18. intangible
19. static
20. auspicious

Pg. 234 – List 2

1. morose
2. tedious
3. prolific
4. stoic
5. hypocritical
6. sporadic
7. cryptic
8. taciturn
9. verbose
10. tentative
11. tentative
12. verbose
13. tedious
14. hypocritical
15. stoic
16. sporadic
17. cryptic
18. morose
19. taciturn
20. prolific

Pg. 236 – List 3

1. terse
2. amiable
3. virulent
4. haphazard
5. reprehensible
6. reclusive
7. gullible
8. satirical
9. marred
10. vulnerable
11. vulnerable
12. gullible
13. satirical
14. reprehensible
15. amiable
16. marred
17. reclusive
18. virulent
19. terse
20. haphazard

Pg. 238 – List 4

1. indifferent
2. relevant
3. subtle
4. vehement
5. pedestrian
6. incessant
7. futile
8. monotonous
9. stringent
10. conventional
11. vehement
12. pedestrian
13. relevant
14. conventional
15. monotonous
16. indifferent
17. subtle
18. futile
19. incessant
20. stringent

Pg. 240 – List 5

1. rhetoric
2. charlatan
3. vacillation
4. respite
5. humility
6. hindrance
7. coercion
8. virtuoso
9. guile
10. zealot
11. virtuoso
12. guile
13. humility
14. zealots
15. vacillation
16. coercion
17. rhetoric
18. charlatan
19. hindrance
20. respite

Pg. 242 – List 6

1. acclaim
2. connoisseur
3. philanthropy
4. epitome
5. animosity
6. nostalgia
7. hiatus
8. enigma
9. adversary
10. solitude
11. acclaim
12. epitome
13. solitude
14. connoisseur
15. animosity
16. philanthropy
17. hiatus
18. adversary
19. nostalgia
20. enigmas

Pg. 244 – List 7

1. compliance
2. skeptic
3. disdain
4. disparity
5. gravity
6. tirade
7. disinclination
8. remorse
9. brevity
10. candor
11. compliance
12. skeptic
13. remorse
14. candor
15. disinclination
16. disparity
17. tirade
18. brevity
19. disdain
20. gravity

Pg. 246 – List 8

1. bigot
2. strife
3. nuance
4. diligence
5. altruism
6. blasphemy
7. deterrent
8. chicanery
9. aesthetic
10. fervor
11. strife
12. diligence
13. deterrent
14. altruism
15. bigot
16. blasphemy
17. nuances
18. chicanery
19. aesthetic
20. fervor

Pg. 248 – List 9

1. abstract
2. superficial
3. superfluous
4. viable
5. capricious
6. trivial
7. objective
8. illusory
9. dubious
10. complacent
11. illusory
12. complacent
13. superfluous
14. viable
15. abstract
16. objective
17. superficial
18. trivial
19. dubious
20. capricious

Pg. 250 – List 10

1. comprehensive
2. lucid
3. adroit
4. grandiose
5. magnanimous
6. impartial
7. dogmatic
8. reticent
9. redundant
10. eccentric
11. impartial
12. adroit
13. lucid
14. grandiose
15. reticent
16. redundant
17. magnanimous
18. dogmatic
19. comprehensive
20. eccentric

Pg. 252 – List 11

1. impoverished
2. eloquent
3. obscure
4. fickle
5. frivolous
6. benign
7. furtive
8. banal
9. blithe
10. ominous
11. blithe
12. banal
13. obscure
14. ominous
15. frivolous
16. fickle
17. benign
18. impoverished
19. furtive
20. eloquent

Pg. 254 – List 12

1. benevolent
2. flagrant
3. languid
4. fastidious
5. prudent
6. ironic
7. austere
8. astute
9. concise
10. elusive
11. austere
12. benevolent
13. languid
14. elusive
15. astute
16. flagrant
17. concise
18. ironic
19. fastidious
20. prudent

Pg. 256 – List 13

1. acquiesce
2. allege
3. refute
4. disparage
5. surpass
6. retaliate
7. chastise
8. bolster
9. coalesce
10. evoke
11. retaliate
12. bolster
13. surpass
14. acquiesce
15. coalesce
16. chastise
17. disparage
18. allege
19. refute
20. evoke

Pg. 260 – List 15

1. extol
2. solicit
3. nullify
4. compromise
5. deride
6. alleviate
7. emulate
8. rejuvenate
9. digress
10. engender
11. rejuvenate
12. engendered
13. solicit
14. alleviate
15. digress
16. nullify
17. extolled
18. derided
19. emulate
20. compromise

Pg. 258 – List 14

1. exacerbate
2. mitigate
3. collaborate
4. repudiate
5. scrutinize
6. dispel
7. hamper
8. censure
9. venerate
10. corroborate
11. repudiated
12. scrutinize
13. dispel
14. collaborate
15. exacerbates
16. venerate
17. corroborate
18. censure
19. mitigate
20. hamper

Pg. 262 – List 16

1. laud
2. condescend
3. concede
4. condone
5. provoke
6. assuage
7. advocate
8. instigate
9. ameliorate
10. efface
11. advocated
12. instigate
13. conceded
14. ameliorate
15. effaced
16. assuaged
17. condescended
18. lauded
19. condone
20. provoke

Pg. 264 – List 17

1. cursory
2. prodigious
3. insipid
4. lax
5. despondent
6. pretentious
7. prodigal
8. ephemeral
9. ambiguous
10. ambivalent
11. despondent
12. ambivalent
13. prodigal
14. cursory
15. prodigious
16. lax
17. pretentious
18. ambiguous
19. insipid
20. ephemeral

Pg. 266 – List 18

1. eclectic
2. spurious
3. haughty
4. wary
5. placid
6. prudish
7. obdurate
8. affluent
9. laconic
10. mercurial
11. eclectic
12. laconic
13. obdurate
14. mercurial
15. placid
16. haughty
17. spurious
18. prudish
19. affluent
20. wary

Pg. 268 – List 19

1. indigenous
2. pedantic
3. blatant
4. tenacious
5. livid
6. opulent
7. apathetic
8. cathartic
9. stalwart
10. loquacious
11. indigenous
12. livid
13. opulent
14. apathetic
15. blatant
16. pedantic
17. stalwart
18. cathartic
19. loquacious
20. tenacious

Pg. 270 – List 20

1. inept
2. deft
3. intrepid
4. melancholy
5. latent
6. erudite
7. erratic
8. lethargic
9. cosmopolitan
10. circumspect
11. lethargic
12. cosmopolitan
13. latent
14. erudite
15. intrepid
16. inept
17. deft
18. circumspect
19. erratic
20. melancholy

Pg. 272 – List 21

1. novice
2. presumption
3. empathy
4. dissent
5. placebo
6. assessment
7. platitude
8. iconoclast
9. martyr
10. diatribe
11. diatribe
12. empathy
13. presumption
14. martyrs
15. platitudes
16. placebo
17. iconoclast
18. novice
19. assessment
20. dissent

Pg. 274 – List 22

1. despot
2. fiasco
3. impudence
4. squalor
5. prompt
6. autonomy
7. surrogate
8. archetype
9. integrity
10. amalgamation
11. integrity
12. despot
13. squalor
14. autonomy
15. surrogate
16. prompts
17. amalgamation
18. fiasco
19. archetype
20. impudence

Pg. 276 – List 23

1. pettiness
2. ingenuity
3. panacea
4. exodus
5. precursor
6. counterfeit
7. glutton
8. rigor
9. recession
10. attribute
11. counterfeits
12. recession
13. rigor
14. pettiness
15. attribute
16. gluttons
17. ingenuity
18. precursor
19. panacea
20. exodus

Pg. 278 – List 24

1. diversion
2. endorsement
3. perfidy
4. stimulus
5. indictment
6. contempt
7. malice
8. infamy
9. impediment
10. profanity
11. endorsement
12. malice
13. stimulus
14. diversion
15. perfidy
16. indictment
17. infamy
18. profanity
19. impediment
20. contempt

Pg. 280 – List 25

1. subjective
2. vacuous
3. mundane
4. lavish
5. bombastic
6. copious
7. cynical
8. tenuous
9. affable
10. meticulous
11. tenuous
12. cynical
13. affable
14. meticulous
15. subjective
16. mundane
17. lavish
18. vacuous
19. bombastic
20. copious

Pg. 284 – List 27

1. adjunct
2. belligerent
3. succinct
4. callous
5. emphatic
6. dormant
7. contingent
8. trenchant
9. somber
10. perfunctory
11. trenchant
12. perfunctory
13. succinct
14. callous
15. contingent
16. emphatic
17. adjunct
18. belligerent
19. somber
20. dormant

Pg. 282 – List 26

1. ornate
2. explicit
3. bourgeois
4. docile
5. clandestine
6. irate
7. adamant
8. eminent
9. lugubrious
10. innocuous
11. lugubrious
12. eminent
13. adamant
14. innocuous
15. ornate
16. clandestine
17. explicit
18. docile
19. bourgeois
20. irate

Pg. 286 – List 28

1. tacit
2. frugal
3. gregarious
4. quixotic
5. imminent
6. obstinate
7. arduous
8. stagnant
9. wily
10. ostentatious
11. arduous
12. frugal
13. obstinate
14. ostentatious
15. stagnant
16. gregarious
17. imminent
18. tacit
19. wily
20. quixotic

Pg. 288 – List 29

1. revere
2. infer
3. juxtapose
4. denounce
5. discern
6. wane
7. feign
8. stymie
9. conform
10. satiate
11. wanes
12. juxtaposing
13. stymied
14. feigned
15. discern
16. satiated
17. conform
18. revered
19. denounced
20. infer

Pg. 290 – List 30

1. subvert
2. harangue
3. ascertain
4. debunk
5. embellish
6. circumvent
7. innovate
8. abhor
9. placate
10. fluctuate
11. innovate
12. placate
13. abhor
14. ascertain
15. circumvent
16. debunked
17. embellished
18. subverted
19. fluctuates
20. harangued

Pg. 292 – List 31

1. aggravate
2. confound
3. discriminate
4. belie
5. beguile
6. lament
7. debase
8. curb
9. expedite
10. reconcile
11. debase
12. lamenting
13. beguiled
14. reconciled
15. confounded
16. discriminate
17. belied
18. expedite
19. curb
20. aggravated

Pg. 294 – List 32

1. assail
2. bewilder
3. foster
4. abate
5. abase
6. eradicate
7. imply
8. conjecture
9. obstruct
10. curtail
11. abate
12. curtail
13. foster
14. implied
15. bewilder
16. abased
17. obstructed
18. eradicated
19. assailed
20. conjecture

Pg. 296 – List 33

1. cantankerous
2. debilitating
3. pious
4. voracious
5. detrimental
6. replete
7. sanctimonious
8. judicious
9. prosperous
10. ineffable
11. voracious
12. pious
13. debilitating
14. judiciously
15. cantankerous
16. detrimental
17. ineffable
18. sanctimonious
19. replete
20. prosperous

Pg. 298 – List 34

1. indignant
2. quarrelsome
3. ardent
4. insolvent
5. congenial
6. aberrant
7. tangential
8. impetuous
9. sparse
10. ravenous
11. insolvent
12. aberrant
13. ardent
14. impetuous
15. congenial
16. tangential
17. sparse
18. ravenous
19. indignant
20. quarrelsome

Pg. 300 – List 35

1. precocious
2. anomalous
3. stupefying
4. insolent
5. nefarious
6. incompetent
7. negligent
8. arcane
9. prohibitive
10. rancorous
11. insolent
12. negligent
13. incompetent
14. prohibitive
15. rancorous
16. arcane
17. anomalous
18. stupefying
19. precocious
20. nefarious

Pg. 302 – List 36

1. obsolete
2. devious
3. averse
4. flamboyant
5. legitimate
6. ethereal
7. feasible
8. notorious
9. impulsive
10. antagonistic
11. legitimate
12. impulsive
13. ethereal
14. flamboyant
15. devious
16. notorious
17. averse
18. obsolete
19. feasible
20. antagonistic

Pg. 304 – List 37

1. lackadaisical
2. abrasive
3. intricate
4. authentic
5. pejorative
6. irreverent
7. idiosyncratic
8. unorthodox
9. indelible
10. assiduous
11. authentic
12. irreverent
13. indelible
14. idiosyncratic
15. abrasive
16. assiduous
17. intricate
18. unorthodox
19. lackadaisical
20. pejorative

Pg. 306 – List 38

1. adept
2. shrewd
3. polemic
4. evanescent
5. inevitable
6. ubiquitous
7. destitute
8. repugnant
9. obtuse
10. contrite
11. ubiquitous
12. repugnant
13. obtuse
14. contrite
15. adept
16. polemic
17. inevitable
18. shrewd
19. evanescent
20. destitute

Pg. 308 – List 39

1. inane
2. garrulous
3. fallacious
4. amorphous
5. immutable
6. didactic
7. innate
8. caustic
9. profound
10. novel
11. immutable
12. amorphous
13. garrulous
14. fallacious
15. caustic
16. inane
17. innate
18. novel
19. didactic
20. profound

Pg. 310 – List 40

1. renounce
2. reprove
3. barrage
4. retract
5. vex
6. ruminate
7. belittle
8. mediate
9. decree
10. squander
11. mediate
12. ruminate
13. squandered
14. belittles
15. renounced
16. vexed
17. barrage
18. reproved
19. decree
20. retracted